✓

Volcanic Hazards

Robert I. Tilling, *Editor*

Short Course Presented at the
28th International Geological Congress
Washington, D.C.

American Geophysical Union, Washington, D.C.

Maria Luisa Crawford and Elaine Padovani
Short Course Series Editors

Library of Congress Cataloging-in-Publication Data

Volcanic hazards / Robert I. Tilling, editor.
        p.   cm.
    Bibliography: p.
    ISBN 0-87590-705-9
    1. Volcanoes.   I. Tilling, Robert I.   II. American Geophysical Union.
QE522.V88   1989   89-14890
363.3′495–dc20   CIP

CONTENTS

FOREWORD AND ACKNOWLEDGMENTS

The catastrophic eruption of Mount St. Helens on May 18, 1980, inaugurated the worst decade of volcanic disasters and crises since 1902, the year when three eruptions in a 6-month period (Mont Pelée, Martinique; Soufrière, St. Vincent; and Santa María, Guatemala) claimed more then 36,000 human lives (Tilling, 1989, in press). The volcanic disasters and crises in the 1980's greatly enhanced scientific and public awareness of volcanic eruptions and associated hazards, spurred advances in volcanology and the establishment of new volcano observatories, and launched numerous international conferences, symposia, and workshops on volcanic-hazards topics. Thus, it was fitting that the organizers of the 28th International Geological Congress [IGC] (Washington, D.C., July 9-19, 1989) and the General Assembly on Continental Magmatism of the International Association of Volcanology and Chemistry of the Earth's Interior [IAVCEI] (Santa Fe, New Mexico, June 25-July 1, 1989) decided to offer a jointly sponsored "Short Course on Volcanic Hazards."

The chapters herein provide the framework for the two-day short course, to be convened July 2-3, 1989, at the College of Santa Fe, New Mexico. This short course, also co-sponsored by the Division of Earth Sciences of the United Nations Educational, Scientific and Cultural Organization [UNESCO] (Paris), will be open to registrants of either the IGC or the IAVCEI meeting. Obviously, the vast topic of volcanic hazards cannot be treated comprehensively in only two days. The primary aim of the short course is to review some basic principles and methods of the mitigation of volcanic hazards, with special focus on the developing countries, which contain most of the world's dangerous volcanoes. In addition to lectures and classroom discussion, the short course also includes a half-day field excursion to examine volcanic deposits and features and to demonstrate some volcano-monitoring measurements.

These short-course notes pertain only to the classroom activities and may be supplemented by unpublished hand-outs given to the participants. [The interested reader may obtain a set of these handouts at no cost by contacting any of the authors.] Because of space and time limitations, the notes are necessarily brief and general; they are not intended to constitute complete coverage of the topics, but instead to provide a context for discussion and to point to directions for more specialized and detailed studies (given in REFERENCES). In some respects, the Santa Fe short course follows the coverage and format of the volcanic hazards component of the successful "Geologic and Hydrologic Hazards Training Program"

conducted by the U.S. Geological Survey in March 1984 (Williams and Kitzmiller, 1984).

This short course could not have been offered and conducted without the participation of many groups and individuals. The organizing committees of the 28th IGC and the IAVCEI General Assembly on Continental Magmatism and the Division of Earth Sciences (UNESCO, Paris) provided encouragement and logistical support. My deep appreciation goes to my Co-Convenor, Raymundo S. Punongbayan, and to the lecturers Norman G. Banks, John Ewert, David Harlow, and William E. Scott for taking time from their busy schedules to serve on the short-course team. One or more draft chapters of these short-course notes were reviewed by Steven Brantley, John J. Dvorak, C. Dan Miller, L.J. Patrick Muffler, Christopher G. Newhall, Donald W. Peterson, Patrick Pringle, and Donald A. Swanson--all of the U.S. Geological Survey (USGS). Their critical comments and helpful suggestions materially improved the content and presentation of the chapters. Special thanks go to Manuel Nathenson (USGS, Menlo Park) for technical advice and assistance in the preparation of camera-ready copy, and to Pamela Hanback (American Geophysical Union, Washington, D.C.) for the careful paste-up of this volume.

The governments of Canada, Iceland, France, Italy, Japan, United States and several other countries helped to provide and/or coordinate logistical support in connection with scientific responses to some volcanic disasters and crises in the 1980's. In this regard, the following international organizations played especially prominent roles: Nordic Volcanological Institute, Reykjavik; Division of Earth Sciences, UNESCO, Paris; Office of the United Nations Disaster Relief Co-ordinator, UNDRO, Geneva; and World Organization of Volcano Observatories (WOVO), a commission of the IAVCEI.

Finally, on behalf of all the members of the short-course team, I wish to express our appreciation for the studies and observations of eruptive phenomena made by our colleagues working at active or potentially active volcanoes around the world. Significant advances in volcano monitoring and eruption prediction will come only from an improved understanding of the workings of many individual volcanoes, rather than of only a select few.

Robert I. Tilling, Editor
Menlo Park, California

iv

CHAPTER 1. INTRODUCTION AND OVERVIEW

Robert I. Tilling

U.S. Geological Survey, Menlo Park, California 94025

Introduction

Volcanism has played a major role in the geologic past of our planet, as evidenced by the volcanic origin of much of the Earth's crust, above and below the sea. On a geologic time scale, volcanic activity has benefited mankind by creating scenic and fertile terranes that foster and sustain the growth of civilization. On a human time scale, however, volcanic eruptions adversely affect society if they occur in populated and/or cultivated regions.

More than 1,300 volcanoes are known to have erupted during the past 10,000 years; about half of these have been active within recorded history. Two thirds of the active volcanoes are located along or near the tectonic-plate boundaries in the circum-Pacific region. Typically, about 50 volcanoes are active each year, and this average eruption frequency has not changed appreciably in historic time (Simkin et al., 1981). Peterson (1986, Table 15.1) has estimated that about 360 million people--about 10 per cent of the world's population--live on or near potentially dangerous volcanoes. With the rapidly expanding world population, mostly in the already densely populated developing countries, and a continuation of the present eruption frequency, many more millions of people will be threatened by future volcanic activity. Because the "total abandonment of all volcanic areas...is not realistic" (Walker, 1982, p. 156), the scientific community and the civil authorities face a chronic and increasingly acute problem in coping with potential hazards from future eruptions.

Volcanology: Study of Eruptive Phenomena

The science of volcanology, in the broadest sense, encompasses all studies of magmatic and volcanic phenomena in the mantle and crust. For the purposes of the short course, volcanology is more narrowly viewed as the study of the transport and eruption of magma (Sigurdsson, 1987), with emphasis on active or potentially active volcanoes (Tilling,

Published in 1989 by the American Geophysical Union.

1987). Table 1.1 summarizes the general qualitative relationships between volcano type, lava composition, and eruption style; for more specific information about volcanoes and their products and behavior, the reader is referred to volcanology textbooks (e.g., Macdonald, 1972; Bullard, 1984; Williams and McBirney, 1979; Fisher and Schmincke, 1984). Many geoscientists map in ancient volcanic terranes or conduct research on volcanic and associated magmatic phenomena that occurred in the geologic past, but only a few work in volcanology (as defined above), and fewer still are directly involved in the assessment and/or monitoring of volcanic hazards.

The science of volcanology has been associated with, and catalyzed by, volcanic hazards and disasters. For example, the first accurate description of an eruption was contained in two letters from Pliny the Younger to the Roman historian Tacitus, describing the death of his uncle, the famous scholar Pliny the Elder, by asphyxiation while observing the A.D. 79 eruption of Vesuvius (Sigurdsson et al., 1985b). Yet, the 1815 eruption of Tambora (Sumbawa, Indonesia)--the largest and deadliest eruption in recorded history--had little scientific impact because because of the volcano's remote location, poor global communications, and the immature status of the natural sciences at the time (Simkin and Fiske, 1983). No scientific expedition was dispatched to Tambora until 1847, and another eight years passed before the expedition report was published (Zollinger, 1855)! In contrast, the 1883 eruption of Krakatau (Sunda Straits, Indonesia) attracted tremendous scientific and public interest. It prompted the first well-organized investigations of a volcanic disaster and its aftermath, because, by the end of the 19th century, global transportation and communications had improved substantially during an era of rapid scientific and technological advances (Francis and Self, 1983; Simkin and Fiske, 1983). Several comprehensive scientific studies were published within five years of the disaster (e.g., Verbeek, 1885; Judd, 1888; Symons, 1888). Volcanology truly began to emerge as a modern, multidisciplinary science with the establishment of volcano observatories in Japan and Hawaii in 1911, in part spurred by

TABLE 1.1. General relationships between volcano types, predominant lava, eruption styles, and common eruptive characteristics (after Tilling, 1987, Table 2).

Volcano type	Predominant lava		Eruption style	Common eruptive characteristics
	Composition	Relative viscosity		
Shield[1]	Basaltic	Fluidal	Generally non-explosive to weakly explosive	Lava fountains, lava flows (long), lava lakes and pools
Composite[2]	Andesitic	Less fluidal	Generally explosive but sometimes non-explosive	Lava flows (medium), explosive ejecta, tephra falls, pyroclastic flows and surges
	Dacitic to Rhyolitic	Viscous to Very viscous	Typically highly explosive but can be non-explosive, especially after a large explosion	Explosive ejecta, tephra falls, pyroclastic flows and surges, lava flows (short) and lava domes

[1]Generally located in the interior of tectonic plates ("intraplate") and presumed to overlie "hot spots," but also may occur in other tectonic settings (e.g., Galapagos, Iceland, Kamchatka).
[2]Generally located along or near the boundaries of convergent tectonic plates (subduction zones); also called stratovolcanoes.

the three volcanic disasters in 1902 in the Caribbean-Central American region (Apple, 1987; Tilling, 1989, in press).

Volcanic and Related Hazards

Let us first make clear the distinction between hazards and risks. The following definitions are adapted from Fournier d'Albe (1979):

Hazard   the probability of a given area being affected by potentially destructive volcanic processes or products within a given period of time.

Risk   the possibility of a loss--such as life, property, productive capacity, etc.--within the area subject to the hazard(s). Assessment of risk involves the consideration of the relation: risk = (value) x (vulnerability) x (hazard), where value may include the number of lives, property and civil works, and productive capacity threatened, and vulnerability is a measure of the proportion (0 to 100 %) of the value likely to be lost in a given hazardous event.

Compared with other natural or man-made "disasters," those caused by volcanic and related hazards, if considered on a global basis, occur infrequently, "affect" far fewer people,

and cause correspondingly fewer human casualties and smaller economic loss (Figures 1.1 and 1.2). However, the perceptions and definitions of what constitutes a "disaster" (Figure 1.1) differ widely among government officials, journalists, and the people affected themselves. Also, there is no general agreement on what is meant by "people affected" (Figure 1.2) by a disaster (killed, injured, displaced, lost family member, lost livelihood, inconvenienced, etc.?). Thus, the statistical validity of the data shown in Figures 1.1 ands 1.2 must be considered in light of these inherent vagaries in accounts of disasters. Nonetheless, the general patterns shown in these two figures probably would hold, regardless of the definitions and data sets used.

The deadliest eruption in history (Tambora, Indonesia, 1815) killed 92,000 people, compared with 500,000 killed in the worst hurricane (Ganges delta, Bangladesh, 1970). Perhaps the worst natural disaster in history was the Huahsien earthquake (Shensi, China) in 1556, which killed more than 820,000 people (DeNevi, 1977). More recently, some outside observers speculate that as many as 800,000 people perished in the 7.8-magnitude Tangshan (China) earthquake in July 1976, even though official Chinese figures place the number of deaths at about 240,000 (Shi Diguang, 1987).

For the United States, the annual economic loss from volcanic eruptions probably is an order of magnitude smaller

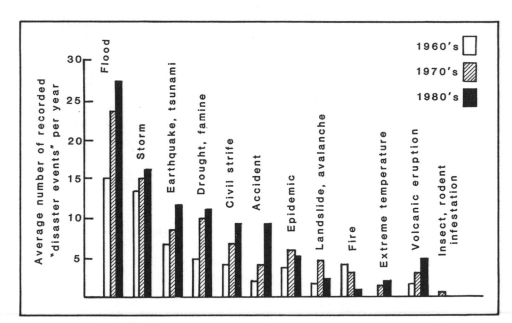

Fig. 1.1. Average number of recorded "disaster events" per year in the world (see text); other than for volcanic eruptions the data for the 1980's cover only the period 1980-81. (Modified from Wijkman and Timberlake, 1984, Fig. 1). In this figure, a "disaster event" refers to a "manifestation of an interaction between extreme physical or natural phenomena and a vulnerable human group" that results in "general disruption and destruction, loss of life and livelihood and injury." (O'Keefe and Westgate, 1976).

than that from earthquakes, which in turn is nearly an order of magnitude less than the loss from either floods or ground failures (Hays and Shearer, 1981). White and Haas (1975) suggest that the average person living in the U.S. is much more likely to die from a heart attack while shovelling snow or a lightning strike than from either an earthquake or a volcanic eruption. For more densely populated countries (e.g., Indonesia, Philippines, and Japan), however, volcanic and

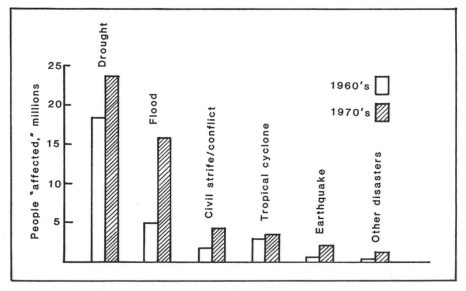

Fig. 1.2. Number of people "affected" per year by disasters, natural and man-made (see text); volcanic disasters are included in the category "Other disasters." Between the 1960's and 1970's, the number of people affected each year nearly doubled. (From Wijkman and Timberlake, 1984, Fig. 4).

TABLE 1.2. Some notable volcanic disasters since the year A.D. 1000 involving fatalities (figures rounded off to nearest ten). (Modified from Yokoyama et al., 1984, Table 1; UNDRO/UNESCO, 1985, Table 1).

Volcano	Country	Year	Primary cause of death				
			Pyroclastic flow	Debris flow	Lava flow	Post-eruption starvation	Tsunami
Merapi	Indonesia	1006	*1,000				
Kelut	Indonesia	1586		10,000			
Vesuvius	Italy	1631			**18,000		
Etna	Italy	1669			**10,000		
Merapi	Indonesia	1672	*300				
Awu	Indonesia	1711		3,200			
Oshima	Japan	1741					1,480
Cotopaxi	Ecuador	1741		1,000			
Makian	Indonesia	1760					
Papadajan	Indonesia	1772	2,960				
Lakagigar	Iceland	1783				9,340	
Asama	Japan	1783	1,150				
Unzen	Japan	1792					15,190
Mayon	Philippines	1814	1,200				
Tambora	Indonesia	1815	12,000			80,000	
Galunggung	Indonesia	1822		4,000			
Nevado del Ruíz	Colombia	1845		1,000			
Awu	Indonesia	1856		3,000			
Cotopaxi	Ecuador	1877		1,000			
Krakatau	Indonesia	1883					36,420
Awu	Indonesia	1892		1,530			
Soufrière	St. Vincent	1902	1,560				
Mont Pelée	Martinique	1902	29,000				
Santa María	Guatemala	1902	6,000				
Taal	Philippines	1911	1,330				
Kelut	Indonesia	1919		5,110			
Merapi	Indonesia	1951	1,300				
Lamington	Papua New Guinea	1951	2,940				
Hibok-Hibok	Philippines	1951	500				
Agung	Indonesia	1963	1,900				
Mount St. Helens	U.S.A.	1980	***60				
El Chichón	Mexico	1982	> 2,000				
Nevado del Ruíz	Colombia	1985		> 22,000			
TOTALS			65,140	53,900	28,000	89,340	53,090

*   Includes deaths from associated mudflows; however, the validity of the 1006 eruption has been questioned (Djumarma et al., 1986).

**   Includes deaths from associated explosions and/or mudflow activity; estimates are unreliable and probably too high.

*** Principal causes of deaths were a laterally directed blast and asphyxiation.

TABLE 1.3. Human fatalities from volcanic activity, 1600-1986, grouped according according to primary causes of death. (Modified from Blong, 1984, Table 3.2).

Primary cause	1600 - 1899		1900 - 1986	
Pyroclastic flows and debris avalanches	18,200	(9.8 %)	36,800	(48.4 %)
Mudflows (lahars) and floods	8,300	(4.5 %)	28,400	(37.4 %)
Tephra falls and ballistic projectiles	8,000	(4.3 %)	3,000	(4.0 %)
Tsunami	43,600	(23.4 %)	400	(0.5 %)
Post-eruption starvation, disease, etc.	92,100	(49.4 %)	3,200	(4.2 %)
Lava flows	900	(0.5 %)	100	(0.1 %)
Gases and acid rains	--------	--------	*1,900	(2.5 %)
Other or unknown	15,100	(8.1 %)	2,200	(2.5 %)
TOTALS	186,200	(100 %)	76,000	(100.%)
Fatalities per year (average)	620		880	

*Includes the deaths caused by lethal gas bursts at two volcanic-crater lakes in Cameroon, 37, Lake Monoun, August 1984 (Sigurdsson et al., 1987b); and >1,700, Lake Nyos, August 1986 (Kling et al., 1987). The lethal gas (carbon dioxide) in both these cases is of volcanic origin, but the causative mechanisms of gas release are not well understood.

related hazards have much greater potential for causing catastrophic economic loss and human deaths.

The main types, nature, and selected examples of volcanic and related hazards are discussed in CHAPTER 2.

Historical Review of Volcanic Hazards and Disasters

The incidence of human fatalities from eruptions (Table 1.2) provides the only relatively complete basis to evaluate the frequency and magnitude of volcanic disasters; comparable information on the economic losses incurred and attendant adverse environmental impacts is fragmentary or unavailable. It should be emphasized, however, that the figures in Table 1.2 largely reflect a few low-frequency, but highly destructive events. For example, the three volcanic catastrophes in 1902 in the Caribbean-Central America region and the November 1985 eruption at Nevado del Ruíz (Colombia) account for about 75 percent of the deaths from volcanic activity in the 20th century.

Since the year A.D. 1000, more than 300,000 people have been killed directly or indirectly by volcanic activity. Table 1.2 clearly shows that the circum-Pacific volcanic zone ("Ring of Fire") has sustained the greatest human losses; indeed, about two thirds of all eruption-related deaths occurred in only three countries (Colombia, Indonesia, and Japan). Blong (1984, Table 3.2) analyzed the human fatalities from volcanic activity for the period 1600-1982 in terms of the causative volcanic hazards. A modified tabulation of his analysis, updated through 1986 (Table 1.3), permits the following observations:
1) The average number of fatalities per year for the 1900-1986 period (880) is higher than that for the preceding three centuries (620), despite the emergence of modern volcanology in the 20th century.
2) In the 20th century, the incidence of deaths caused by indirect hazards (e.g., post-eruption starvation, tsunami; see CHAPTER 2) has been significantly reduced. This reduction in part reflects the development of rapid global

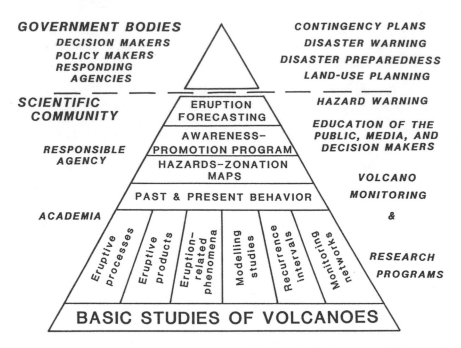

Fig. 1.3. Diagram illustrating that an effective program to mitigate volcanic hazards and risk must be built on a strong foundation of long-term basic studies. The apex is separated from rest of triangle to indicate the division of primary responsibility between the scientists and civil authorities. Modified from Tilling and Bailey (1985, Fig. 1).

communications, quick-response relief-delivery systems, and an effective international tsunami warning network. Equally if not more important, no large, near-source destructive tsunami have been generated by eruptions in this century.

3) Deaths caused by some direct hazards involving flowage processes (e.g., pyroclastic flows, debris avalanches, mudflows; see CHAPTER 2) have increased dramatically in the 20th century, largely reflecting the disastrous impact of only two catastrophes (Mont Pelée, 1902; and Nevado del Ruíz, 1985).

Some possible explanations for the above observations are discussed later.

Mitigation of Hazards and Reducing Volcanic Risk

Volcanic-hazards studies must be built on a strong foundation of fundamental research on volcanoes (Figure 1.3), including the well-integrated geologic and geophysical mapping, petrologic and geochemical characterization of eruptive products, and the dating of stratigraphically well-controlled samples. Such studies must be carried out systematically in a long-term program--ideally before the volcanoes exhibit any signs of unrest; they cannot be done under rushed circumstances in the high-anxiety environment that prevails during a volcanic emergency. The results of these long-term basic studies provide the basis for deciphering past eruptive behavior, better understanding present behavior, and, by extrapolation, predicting possible future behavior of the volcano. Specifically, a comprehensive understanding of eruptive phenomena and eruption frequency is the starting point for mitigation of volcanic hazards and risk.

An effective program to mitigate the risk from volcanic and related hazards must include the following components: 1) identification of high-risk volcanoes; 2) hazards assessment and zonation; 3) volcano monitoring and eruption forecasting; and 4) volcanic emergency management. These topics are the prime focus of subsequent chapters, but some introductory remarks, largely drawn from Tilling (1989, in press), are given below.

Identification of High-risk Volcanoes

Of the some 600 active or potentially active volcanoes known in the world, only a small fraction of them have been, or are being, studied in any detail. The problem is simply a matter of too many volcanoes, too few scientists and equipment, and too little money to study and monitor them. While this problem plagues even the developed countries (e.g., France, Iceland, Italy, Japan, and the United States), it is especially serious for the developing countries (e.g., Indonesia, Philippines, those in Latin America). Thus, by necessity, identification of high-risk volcanoes is required to determine which ones should receive the most and, perhaps, immediate attention by scientists and government officials.

Compilations of "dangerous" or high-risk volcanoes have been made in the past (e.g., Shimozuru, 1975; Lowenstein, 1982; Lowenstein and Talai, 1984; Yokoyama et al., 1984), based on various rating criteria involving eruptive history and behavior, composition and distribution of eruptive products, known ground-deformation or seismic events, and demographic considerations. However, all such compilations are deficient, because the needed geological and geophysical data are inadequate, incomplete, or lacking for many volcanoes. For example, Nevado del Ruíz was not included in the list of high-risk volcanoes compiled in 1983 (Yokoyama et al., 1984); its eruption two years later produced the worst volcanic disaster since the 1902 eruption of Mont Pelée. Also, Yokoyama et al. (1984) point out that had El Chichón Volcano been rated, using the same criteria, before its 1982 eruption (Alcayde, 1983; Duffield et al., 1984; Luhr and Varekamp, 1984), it too would not have been identified as being high risk.

Hazards Assessment and Zonation

As summarized by Crandell et al. (1984), the essential data needed for an adequate hazards assessment should include the following: 1) complete records of historical eruptions; 2) prehistoric eruptive activity deduced from the geologic record; 3) geologic (especially stratigraphic), petrologic, and geochemical data on the nature, distribution, and volume of the eruptive products, and 4) dating of the volcanic products and events interpreted from them. Collectively, these data allow the reconstruction of a volcano's past eruptive behavior, which provides the basis for assessing potential hazards from future eruptions.

Hazards assessments are usually premised on the assumption that the same general areas on the volcano are likely to be affected by future eruptive events of the same kinds, at about the same average frequency as in the past. The longer the period of time spanned by the database to reconstruct past eruptive behavior, the more useful and reliable is the resulting hazards assessment. Hazards-zonation maps at appropriate scales should be an integral part of the hazards assessment, because they portray the pertinent information in a summary manner most readily understood by scientists as well as civil authorities. Such maps serve two important purposes: 1) provide guidelines for long-range land-use planning around volcanoes that take into account potential hazards from future eruptions; and 2) determine which areas should be evacuated and avoided during eruptions. However, volcanoes may not always or closely follow past eruptive behavior, and catastrophic events can exceed any known precedent at the same volcano (Crandell et al., 1984). Thus, even the best hazards assessments and hazards-zonation maps, based on good knowledge of past eruptive behavior, are not perfect. For example, the hazards-zonation map of Crandell and Mullineaux (1978, Plate 2), while remarkably accurate, did not fully anticipate the force of the lateral blast that occurred during the climactic eruption of Mount St. Helens. The blast on May 18, 1980 extended about three times farther from the volcano than the largest known previous blast at Mount St. Helens, and it affected an area about 10-15 times larger (Miller et al., 1981).

Ideally, hazards assessments should be made for all high-risk volcanoes before any of them become restless. Perhaps the most successful example of a timely hazards assessment was that for Mount St. Helens published two years before its reawakening in 1980 (Crandell and Mullineaux, 1978). Volcanic-hazards assessments and/or hazards-zonation maps are now available for a number of the world's high-risk volcanoes, but many of these are preliminary and lack adequate detail. Unfortunately, hazards assessments of any quality are still not available for many potentially dangerous volcanoes in densely populated areas.

Volcano Monitoring and Eruption Forecasting

Experience gained at well-monitored volcanoes clearly indicates that most, perhaps all, eruptions are preceded and accompanied by measurable geophysical and/or geochemical changes in the state of the volcano. To date, measurements of variation in seismicity and ground deformation have provided the most widely used and reliable volcano-monitoring data. Several other geophysical monitoring techniques (e.g., microgravity, geomagnetic, geoelectrical, radar, and thermal radiation), though beginning to show promise, must still be considered experimental. Similarly, geochemical monitoring methods, based on the temporal variation in the amount and/or rate of emission of certain volcanic gases (e.g., sulfur dioxide, carbon dioxide, hydrogen, radon, helium, and mercury), also are being tested at a number of volcanoes. Optimum volcano monitoring is best achieved by employing a combination of approaches, rather than relying on any single method or precursory indicator. Only seismic and ground-deformation monitoring techniques are covered in this short course (see CHAPTER 4).

Progress in volcano monitoring has involved the development of increasingly sophisticated and complex electronic instruments and the intensive computer processing and modelling of data. These "high-tech" techniques are expensive and require considerable monetary and scientific resources, neither of which are readily available, especially in developing countries. It is not always possible or easy to apply or utilize high-tech resources successfully. Therefore, an urgent need exists to develop reliable but widely applicable "low-tech" methods, more affordable and easier to use. For example, regular measurement of distances between benchmarks using a steel tape provides a simple, low-cost but effective, means to monitor large horizontal displacements. Such measurements of the movements of small thrust faults around the base of the growing lava dome have provided excellent results in predicting dome-building eruptions at Mount St. Helens (Swanson et al., 1983).

Volcano-monitoring provides the primary data for short-term forecasts (hours to months) of eruptions; the eruptive record of the volcano generally provides the principal data for longer term forecasts (one year or longer). In recent years, the state-of-the-art in short-term eruption forecasts has advanced significantly at some well-monitored volcanoes. For example, the scientists at the Cascades Volcano Observatory of the USGS have successfully predicted nearly all of the dome-building events at Mount St. Helens since June 1980 (Swanson et al., 1983, 1985). A routine predictive capability for large explosive eruptions or for long-term eruption forecasts still has not yet been achieved. However, with wider and more intensive application of current monitoring technology, precursory signals of larger explosive eruptions should be recognizable and possibly useful in predicting such events.

Volcanic Emergency Management.

Of all the elements in an effective program of volcanic-risk mitigation, the management of volcanic emergencies (UNDRO/UNESCO, 1985) is the most critical, because it is the vital link in translating the scientific information from hazards assessment and volcano monitoring into life- and property-saving plans and actions during a volcanic disaster or crisis. For example, better volcanic-emergency management almost certainly could have reduced greatly the high death toll of the 1985 volcanic tragedy at Nevado del Ruíz (Herd et al., 1986; Tomblin, 1988; Tilling, 1989, in press). Yet, this most important element in reducing volcanic risk has drawn, and continues to draw, little attention from scientists and decision makers alike, even in the developed countries with active or potentially active volcanoes. This situation is unfortunate but perhaps understandable, given the fact that volcanic hazards occur infrequently relative to the human lifespan and compared to other types of hazards, natural or man-made.

Because of its broad socio-economic ramifications, prime responsibility for volcanic-emergency management properly rests with the civil authorities (see Figure 1.3). Although the topic of volcanic-emergency management is beyond the purview of this short course focused on the scientific aspects of volcanic hazards, some actions that geoscientists could and should take to improve volcanic-emergency management are discussed in CHAPTER 6.

CHAPTER 2. VOLCANIC AND RELATED HAZARDS

William E. Scott

U.S. Geological Survey, Vancouver, Washington 98661

Introduction

Volcanic events both directly and indirectly affect peoples' lives and health, their activities, and their property. The purpose of this chapter is to discuss the character of volcanic events, the hazards posed by them, and some short-term measures that have been used to mitigate such hazards. Two publications, "Volcanic Hazards" by Blong (1984) and "Source-Book for Volcanic-Hazards Zonation" by Crandell et al. (1984) are excellent sources of information about hazardous volcanic events and the book by Blong contains an extensive list of references. An earlier version of this chapter was prepared for a U.S. Geological Survey short course in geologic and hydrologic hazards (Scott, 1984).

Types of Hazardous Volcanic Events

Many geologic processes that originate on volcanoes are potentially hazardous (Table 2.1). Lava flows, pyroclastic density currents (including laterally directed blasts and pyroclastic flows and surges), debris avalanches, volcanic debris flows (lahars), and floods are gravity-driven flows that typically impact areas in valleys that head on volcanoes. However, such events of large magnitude can overwhelm large regions around volcanoes and can extend exceptional distances down valleys. Tephra ejected into the atmosphere by volcanic explosions is dispersed by winds and can blanket large areas. Volcanic gases are released during and between eruptions and, under certain circumstances, can affect significant areas. Several other hazards associated with volcanic activity include earthquakes, tsunamis, and atmospheric shock waves; of these, tsunamis probably pose the greatest hazard. A brief description of these hazardous events follows. Also included is discussion of some of the mitigative measures that are presently employed to reduce the impacts of these events. Longer-term mitigative measures, such as long-term land-use planning that incorporates volcanic-hazard zonation, are topics of CHAPTER 3.

Published in 1989 by the American Geophysical Union.

TABLE 2.1. Types of hazardous volcanic events.

Lava flows and domes
Pyroclastic density currents

Pyroclastic flows
    Hot pyroclastic surges
    Cold, or base, surges
    Directed blasts

Lahars, lahar-runout flows, and floods
Structural collapse
Debris avalanches   Gradual or jerky sector collapse
Tephra falls and ballistic projectiles
Volcanic gases
Volcanic earthquakes
Atmospheric shock waves
Tsunamis

Lava Flows and Lava Domes

The rate of effusion of lava, the slope of the surface onto which it is erupted, and the viscosity of the lava determine the morphology of extrusions (Williams and McBirney, 1979). Of these, the effusion rate is the most important (Walker, 1973). At low effusion rates (<10 m^3/sec), basaltic lava tends to produce many small flows that pile up near the vent and do not extend long distances. Basaltic lava discharged at rates of tens

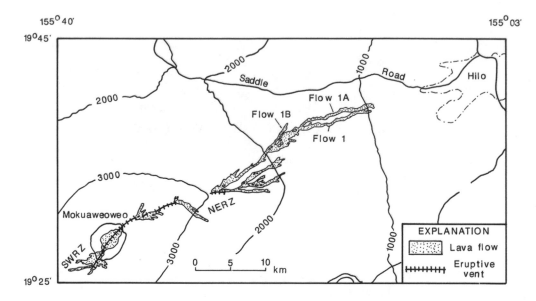

Fig. 2.1. Map showing vents and lava flows of 25 March-15 April 1984 eruption of Mauna Loa volcano, Hawaii (modified from Lockwood and others, 1985; Lipman and Banks, 1987). Eruptions occurred initially in the summit area (Mokuaweoweo) and then migrated down the southwest (SWRZ) and northeast (NERZ) rift zones. Sustained eruptions occurred at vents just east of Pu'u Ula'Ula. These first formed several small flows that moved to the east before activity was focussed on flow 1, which advanced rapidly toward Hilo. Blockage and overflow of the channel at about the 1800-m level diverted lava away from flow 1 and fed a parallel flow (1A) that advanced slightly farther downslope than did flow 1. Subsequent blockages and overflows diverted lava to flow 1B, which moved rapidly toward the northeast until declining lava production brought the eruption to an end.

of cubic meters per second has covered areas of tens of square kilometers as during the 1975-1976 Great Tolbachik Fissure Eruption in Kamchatka (Fedotov and Markhinin, 1983). An effusion rate of 5,000 m^3/sec during the Laki fissure eruption in Iceland in 1783 generated lava flows that covered more than 500 km^2 (Thorarinsson, 1969). Exceptionally in the geologic past, single flood basalt flows discharged at estimated rates of 1 x 10^6 m^3/sec have covered tens of thousands of square kilometers (Swanson et al., 1975). In contrast to the sheetlike flows formed of basaltic and other mafic lavas, viscous lavas such as dacite and rhyolite, which are typically erupted at low rates, form short, stubby lava flows or steep-sided domes that cover only a few square kilometers.

Rates of movement of lava flows vary considerably, from a few to hundreds of meters per hour for silicic lava flows to several kilometers per hour for basaltic lava flows. Because of their slow rates of movement, lava flows seldom threaten human life. However, in exceptional circumstances rates may be much higher as in the case of the rapid draining of very fluid lava from a lava lake on Mt. Nyiragongo, Zaire, in which as many as 300 people were killed by thin lava flows advancing at rates of 30-100 km/hr (Tazieff, 1977).

The major hazard from lava flows is damage or total destruction by burying, crushing, or burning everything in their paths. In addition, fires started by lava flows can affect areas

far beyond their borders. Lava flows also melt snow and ice that can produce floods and debris flows. However, because they do not erode and mix turbulently with snow and ice as do pyroclastic flows and surges, lava-flow eruptions in ice- and snow-covered areas typically do not produce large floods and debris flows unless meltwater can be stored and released in large quantities, as during Icelandic jokulhlaups. Because lava flows follow valleys, they can dam tributaries and form lakes. The lakes can backflood large areas as well as be a potential source of floods and debris flows if dams fail, although the failure of lava-flow dams is not as significant a hazard as failure of other types of natural dams (Costa and Schuster, 1988). Many lava-flow dams are so permeable that the lakes behind them do not fill and overflow and the dams remain stable.

Once potential or actual vents of lava flows are identified, their likely paths can be predicted based on the surrounding topography and evacuations can be planned. A more difficult problem is predicting the ultimate extent of lava flows. The 1984 eruption of Mauna Loa produced a lava flow that moved 25 km toward the city of Hilo during the first 5 days of the eruption (Figure 2.1; Lockwood et al., 1985). Subsequent decreases in the effusion rate and increase in the viscosity of the lava due to degassing and crystal growth caused blockages in the midsection of the flow that led to a series of overflows (Lipman and Banks, 1987). These overflows diverted lava from the main stream and caused the flow front to stagnate. Monitoring of the effusion rate and physical properties of lava flows during eruptions could therefore provide important information for predicting their behavior.

Several methods for controlling the paths of lava flows have been attempted including barriers and diversion channels, disruption of lava channels and tubes to promote diversions, and cooling of lava flows with water in hopes of causing the flow to thicken and stop advancing (Blong, 1984; Mullineaux et al., 1987; Tilling, 1989, in press). Substantial, engineered barriers and associated diversion channels have been considered in Hawaii (Macdonald, 1962), but have not been constructed because of their great cost, unknown effectiveness, and complex legal implications (Decker, 1986). A modest V-shaped barrier was constructed upslope from the Mauna Loa Observatory in Hawaii (Lockwood et al., 1987), but it remains untested. Notable successes in lava-flow protection include the halting of an advancing lava-flow front at Heimaey, Iceland, in 1973 by spraying seawater on the flow and erecting barriers that averted destruction of a valuable harbor (Williams and Moore, 1973; 1983), and diversions of Etna lava flows in Italy in 1983 by using explosives and barriers (Lockwood and Romano, 1985).

Pyroclastic Density Currents

Among the most hazardous of volcanic events are pyroclastic density currents, which vary widely but share many characteristics. All are gravity-driven, rapidly moving, ground-hugging mixtures of rock fragments and gases. Recent books by Fisher and Schmincke (1984) and Cas and Wright (1987) provide good summaries of our understanding of the origin, flow characteristics, and deposits of pyroclastic density currents. These books also include numerous references. Pyroclastic density currents having a relatively high concentration of solids and a density that is similar to that of the resulting deposit are called pyroclastic flows. Low-concentration currents whose density is much less than that of the resulting deposit are called pyroclastic surges. Catastrophic, laterally directed blasts are treated here as a third category, although they differ from flows and surges more in magnitude and reputation than in any fundamental physical sense. Blasts are complex density currents that display characteristics of both flows and surges. Each of these types is treated separately below, but a continuum probably exists among them.

Pyroclastic flows. Pyroclastic flows are masses of hot (300->800 degrees C), dry, pyroclastic debris and gases that move rapidly along the ground surface at velocities ranging from 10 to several hundred meters per second. A flow is composed typically of two parts: (1) a ground-hugging, dense basal flow that is the pyroclastic flow proper, and (2) a preceding or overriding turbulent ash-cloud surge of ash elutriated from the flow. Convecting clouds of ash also are associated with pyroclastic flows and form one type of tephra-fall deposit.

Pyroclastic flows have been observed to form in several ways (Figure 2.2), including from the gravitational collapse of parts of high vertical eruption columns (Hay, 1959; Smith, 1960; Sparks and Wilson, 1976; Davies et al., 1978a; Nairn and Self, 1978; Sparks et al., 1978; Wilson et al., 1980), from low fountains of pyroclasts that appear to "boil-over" from the vent and precede development of a high vertical column (Anderson and Flett, 1903; Taylor, 1958; Rowley et al., 1981; Hoblitt, 1986), and from gravitational or explosive disruption of hot lava domes or lava flows (Perret, 1937; Macdonald and Alcaraz, 1956; Rose et al., 1977).

Once initiated, flow is sustained by several processes--the most important of which appears to be partial fluidization of the flow by escaping gases (McTaggart, 1960; Sparks, 1976, 1978; Wilson, 1980, 1984). Gases that fluidize the flow come from (1) degassing of pyroclasts in the flow, (2) air and magmatic gases trapped during flow formation, (3) air engulfed by the advancing front of the flow which is then heated and expands, (4) burning of vegetation incorporated in the flow, and (5) vaporization of surface water, snow, or ice.

Pyroclastic flows are common at many andesitic and dacitic composite volcanoes and at silicic calderas. They vary widely in composition, temperature, volume, and eruption rate, which is reflected in their great range in extent. Block-and-ash flows composed mostly of dense to slightly vesicular lithic fragments in an ash matrix are of lower volume, are less mobile, and are typically restricted to within a few tens of kilometers of vents. In contrast, large pumiceous pyroclastic flows composed mostly of lapilli and ash can extend up to 200 km from vents and cover thousands to tens of thousands of square kilometers. The momentum imparted to voluminous pumiceous pyroclastic flows by their mass and speed allows the flows to surmount topographic barriers hundreds of meters high (Miller and Smith, 1977; Barberi et al., 1978) and thereby affect areas that lie outside of the drainage basins that head on the source volcano.

Owing to their mass, high temperature, high velocity, and potentially great mobility, pyroclastic flows and related pyroclastic surges (see next section) pose grave hazards from asphyxiation, burial, incineration, and impact. In addition to these direct effects, pyroclastic flows can mix with surface water or water melted from snow and ice to form lahars and floods that can affect valleys farther downstream. A review of more than 100 historical eruptions of snow-clad volcanoes by Major and Newhall (1987; in press) indicates that pyroclastic flows, surges, directed blasts, and avalanches of hot rocks are very effective processes for generating large amounts of meltwater. Fires started by pyroclastic flows can also extend far beyond the limits of a flow.

Pyroclastic surges. Pyroclastic surges are turbulent, low-particle-concentration, gas-solid dispersions that flow above the ground surface at high velocities (Wright et al., 1980). Pyroclastic surges are typically treated in two categories, hot and cold. Hot pyroclastic surges are generated by many of the same processes that form pyroclastic flows (Figure 2.2); cold

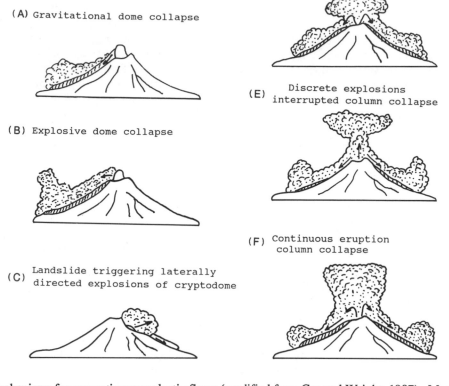

Fig. 2.2. Mechanisms for generating pyroclastic flows (modified from Cas and Wright, 1987). Mechanisms B and C represent formation of laterally directed blasts; catastrophic blasts would have an origin as in C. D, E, and F represent three of many origins based on collapse of eruption columns.

pyroclastic surges are generated by hydromagmatic or hydrothermal explosions.

Hot pyroclastic surges are intimately associated with pyroclastic flows, and may be formed ahead of a pyroclastic flow (ground surge of Sparks et al. [1973]), by collapse of an eruption column that may or may not also be spawning pyroclastic flows (Fisher, 1979), or by the overriding ash cloud that is formed by a pyroclastic flow (Crandell and Mullineaux, 1973; Fisher, 1979; Fisher and Heiken, 1982). Observations of pyroclastic flows at Mount St. Helens in 1980 indicate that they undergo marked changes in solid/gas ratio along their paths in response to segregation and inflation processes and that there is a clear genetic relationship between pyroclastic flows and surges (Figure 2.3; Hoblitt, 1986). Although pyroclastic flows may be controlled by topography, surges derived from them are much more mobile and may affect areas well beyond the limits of the pyroclastic flow. Therefore, whereas pyroclastic flows are likely to be restricted to valley floors, accompanying pyroclastic surges could affect areas high on valley walls and even in adjacent valleys. Surge clouds separated from pyroclastic flows may in turn undergo segregation processes to form secondary pyroclastic flows

(Fisher and Heiken, 1982; Fisher, 1983). Hot pyroclastic surges can affect areas many tens of kilometers from vents (Figure 2.4).

Cold pyroclastic surges, or base surges, originate from hydrovolcanic explosions in which shallow groundwater or surface water interacts with magma (Moore, 1967; Nairn, 1979; Sheridan and Wohletz, 1983). They typically contain water and(or) steam and are at temperatures below the boiling point of water. Base surges are typically restricted to within 10 km of their source vent. Explosions and accompanying surges can also be generated by heating of water trapped beneath lava flows or pyroclastic flows, especially along streams, lakes, oceans, or ice and snow fields (Fisher, 1968; Moyer and Swanson, 1987). Such surges are typically small, but very large explosions have resulted from voluminous pyroclastic flows entering the sea (Walker, 1979).

Pyroclastic surges pose a variety of hazards including destruction by high-velocity ash-laden clouds, impact by rock fragments, and burial by surge deposits. Hot pyroclastic surges present several additional hazards, including incineration, noxious gases, and asphyxiation. Notable volcanic catastrophes have been caused by hot pyroclastic

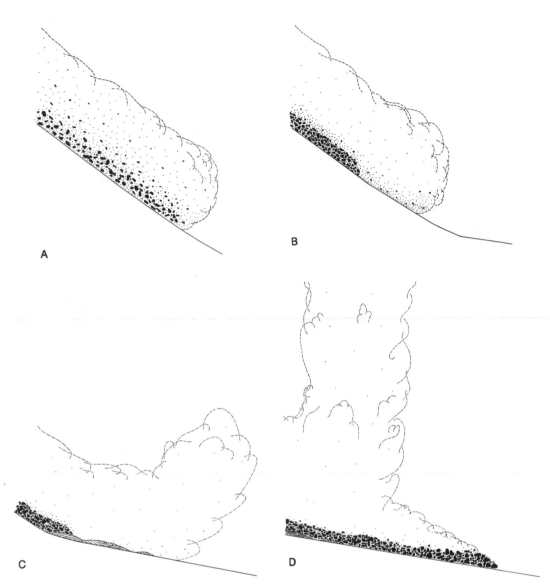

Fig. 2.3. Mechanisms of formation and interrelations of pyroclastic flow and surge as observed at Mount St. Helens on 7 August 1980 (Hoblitt, 1986). A, Highly inflated suspension generated by collapse of pyroclastic fountain or by passage of flow over steep, irregular terrain. B, Segregation of suspension into basal high-concentration phase (flow; dense pattern) and upper low-concentration phase (surge; sparse stipple). C, Surge separates from flow, deposits bedded sediments, decreases in density, rises, and decelerates. D, Flow overtakes surge. If the flow were to accelerate over steep terrain, this sequence could be repeated.

surges including Vesuvius in 79 A.D., >2000 deaths (Sheridan et al., 1981; Sigurdsson et al., 1985b), Mt. Pelée in 1902, 30,000 deaths (Lacroix, 1904; Fisher and Heiken, 1982), Mt. Lamington in 1951, 3000 deaths (Taylor, 1958), and El Chichón in 1982, 2000 deaths (Figure 2.4; Sigurdsson et al., 1987a).

Owing to their high velocities (several tens of meters per second) and great mobility, escape is impossible once pyroclastic density currents are generated. Evacuation prior to eruptions from areas likely to be affected by pyroclastic density currents is the only effective method of mitigation available. Blong (1984) summarizes the effects of several historical

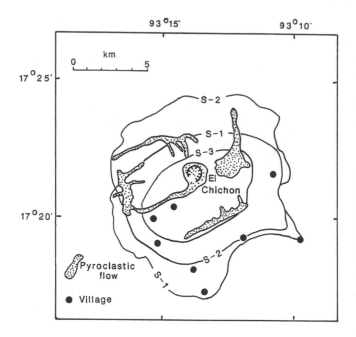

Fig. 2.4. Distribution of the deposits of three hot pyroclastic surges (S-1, S-2, and S-3) and related pyroclastic flows (stipple pattern) from the 29 March to 4 April 1985 eruptions of El Chichón volcano, Mexico (from Sigurdsson and others, 1987a). 2000 people were killed in the devastated villages indicated by dots. Vent area outlined by ticked line.

pyroclastic flows and surges. People have survived surges in underground and even in some above-ground shelters, especially in distal areas. Construction of shelters to protect inhabitants from pyroclastic density currents might be feasible in certain situations, although few data are available on which to base their design. Regardless, providing shelter from pyroclastic flows and surges for a large number of people is probably too costly to ever be undertaken.

Laterally directed blasts. Large laterally directed blasts are complex phenomena that share characteristics of pyroclastic flows and surges, but they are treated separately here because they have a significant, initial, low-angle component and can affect broad sectors of a volcano up to 180 degrees and outward for tens of kilometers. Large directed blasts result from the sudden depressurization of a magmatic and(or) hydrothermal system within a volcano by landsliding or some other cause (Figure 2.2C; Christiansen and Peterson, 1981; Kieffer, 1981; Eichelberger and Hayes, 1982). Explosions thus formed generate a density current that moves at exceptionally high speeds (more than 100 m/s) and is highly mobile, being little-affected by topographic features.

Notable catastrophic directed blasts occurred at Bezymianny, Kamchatka, in 1956 (Gorshkov, 1959, 1963; Bogoyavlenskaya et al., 1985; Belousov and Bogoyavlenskaya, 1988) and in 1980 at Mount St. Helens.

Evidence of several prehistorical examples has been described recently (see review by Siebert et al., 1987). The processes active within the St. Helens directed blast have been the subject of considerable debate (Hoblitt et al., 1981; Hoblitt and Miller, 1984; Moore and Sisson, 1981; Moore and Rice, 1984; Sparks et al., 1986; Waitt, 1981, 1984; Walker and McBroome, 1983; Walker and Morgan, 1984; Walker, 1984; Fisher et al., 1987), but observations of the blast and investigations of its deposits show that flow, surge, and fall were all involved.

Within the 500-600-km^2 areas affected by the Bezymianny and St. Helens blasts, virtually all above ground life was killed and all structures were destroyed by the force of the blast cloud, impact by debris, abrasion, burial, asphyxiation, and heat. Temperatures within the St. Helens' blast cloud varied from less than 100 degrees C to more than 300 degrees C (Banks and Hoblitt, 1981; Moore and Sisson, 1981). Survivors near the outer limit of the cloud reported that the blast was initially cold for a few seconds but then was hot for a period of several minutes (Rosenbaum and Waitt, 1981).

Structural Collapse

Structural collapses are common on volcanoes owing to steep slopes, faults, weak materials, internal deformation caused by intrusions, and other factors. Sudden failures such as rockfalls, rockslides, and debris avalanches constitute a great hazard because they can be triggered suddenly and move very rapidly. Gradual collapse of large sectors of volcanoes is a less catastrophic process, but has numerous associated hazards.

Debris avalanches. Debris falls, slides, and avalanches on volcanoes range from relatively small events to some of the most voluminous mass movements of Quaternary age. Debris avalanches have occurred at numerous composite volcanoes in historical time (Schuster and Crandell, 1984; Siebert, 1984; Ui et al., 1986; Siebert et al., 1987). Some have followed days to months of precursory seismic, deformational, or explosive activity; others have occurred with apparently little warning. Intrusions, hydrothermal alteration, erosion, and other processes aid in the progressive weakening of an edifice by developing shear surfaces that can act as bounding surfaces for detachments (Voight et al., 1983). This progressive weakening can lead to failure, but, more likely, a failure will be triggered by an earthquake or an explosion.

Volcanic debris avalanches are more mobile than their non-volcanic counterparts; that is, for a given volume and vertical drop, volcanic debris avalanches travel farther (Figure 2.5; Ui et al., 1986; Siebert et al., 1987). Ui (1983) and Voight et al. (1983) have attributed this to the high degree of fracturing of rocks within volcanoes and to the presence of hydrothermal and(or) magmatic fluids and gases. Known debris avalanches extend up to 85 km from their sources and cover tens to more than 1000 km^2. The momentum of debris avalanches allows them to run up slopes and to cross divides up to several hundred meters high. In addition, very large debris avalanches,

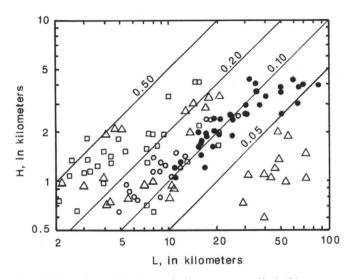

Fig. 2.5. Plot of horizontal distance travelled (L) versus vertical drop (H) for volcanic-debris avalanches (open circles, volume < 1 km³; solid circles, volume >1 km³), large nonvolcanic landslides (squares), and pyroclastic flows (triangles). (Modified from Siebert, 1984; Siebert et al.,1987).

those with volumes > 10 km³, appear to be more mobile than smaller ones (Siebert et al., 1987).

Debris avalanches bury and destroy everything in their paths and greatly alter pre-existing topography. In addition, lahars

and floods can be generated directly from the dewatering of debris avalanches (Janda et al., 1981). Debris avalanches can also dam streams and form lakes that can drain catastrophically and generate lahars and floods (Costa and Schuster, 1988; Scott, 1988). Furthermore as at Mount St. Helens and Bezymianny, large avalanches can abruptly decrease the lithostatic pressure on magmatic and hydrothermal systems, which can generate explosions ranging from small phreatic explosions to large directed blasts. Finally, debris avalanches that enter a body of water and suddenly displace large volumes of water can form waves. Debris avalanches that enter restricted bays and lakes can form very high waves (Slingerland and Voight, 1979); those that enter the sea can form tsunamis (Kienle et al., 1987). Large slope failures on the submarine flanks of volcanoes can also generate tsunamis. Evidence from Hawaii indicates that such events have formed waves that have run up hundreds of meters on nearby islands (Moore and Moore, 1984).

Gradual or jerky sector collapse. Many island volcanoes display evidence of gradual or jerky subsidence of large sectors. On Kilauea, Hawaii, the sudden displacement of large blocks has generated damaging earthquakes and tsunamis (Tilling et al., 1976). At Piton de la Fournaise on La Reunion (Figure 2.6) and at Kilauea, forceful injection of magma into rift zones is causing seaward displacement of entire, unbuttressed flanks of large shield volcanoes at the rate of meters per century and forming high fault scarps (Swanson et al., 1976; Duffield et al., 1982). Presumably these large displacements are aided by thick sequences of hyaloclastite,

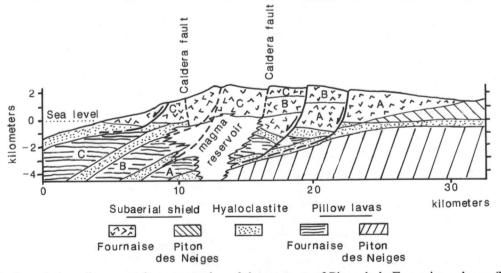

Fig. 2.6. Speculative, diagrammatic cross section of the structure of Piton de la Fournaise volcano (La Reunion), which is a basaltic shield volcano built on the east flank of another shield, Piton des Neiges (from Duffield et al., 1982). No vertical exaggeration. Units A, B, and C represent sequences of subaerial lava flows and submarine pillow lavas and hyaloclastite that date from successively younger stages in the growth of Fournaise. Location of faults are interpreted to be controlled by formerly active rift zones. Sites of possible future faults are shown below Dolomieu Crater, where fracture systems of the currently active rift zones cross the volcano. Position and size of magma reservoir are highly speculative.

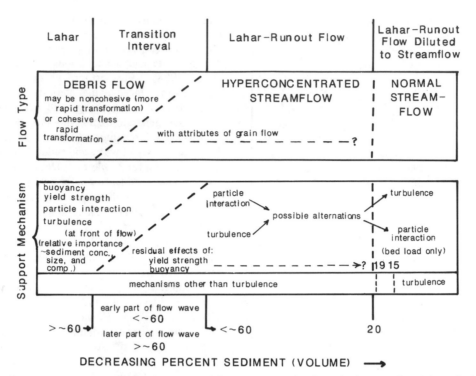

Fig. 2.7. Sequential changes in flow type and particle-support mechanisms in the transformation of a lahar to lahar-runout flow, and then to normal streamflow (Scott, 1988; Table 9). Flow direction and decreasing sediment concentration are left to right.

perhaps altered to clay, that underlie the subaerial parts of the volcanoes. On Tenerife, sector collapse has displaced areas as large as 100 km^2 downward through vertical distances of hundreds of meters over short periods of time (Booth, 1979).

Lahars and Floods

Lahars and floods are end members of a continuum of processes ranging from dense lahars dominated by laminar flow to turbulent water floods. Lahars are rapidly flowing mixtures of rock debris mobilized by water that originate on the slopes of volcanoes (Crandell, 1971). The physical properties of lahars are controlled by grain-size and water content (Fisher, 1971), but typically include high yield strength, high bulk density (as great as 2000 kg/m^3), and high apparent viscosities (Neall, 1976; Costa, 1984). Flow transformations occur between floods and lahars (Figure 2.7; Fisher, 1983; Pierson and Scott, 1985; Scott, 1988): (1) water floods incorporate progressively more sediment and become lahars, a process called bulking; (2) lahars are diluted by the addition of water or the removal of sediment and can transform to hyperconcentrated flood flows called lahar-runout flows (approximately 20-60 percent by volume sediment) and water floods.

The velocities of historic lahars have varied greatly owing to differences in channel dimensions, volume, and grain-size distribution. Lahars at Mount St. Helens in 1980 had velocities as low as 1.3 m/s along low-gradient reaches and as great as 40 m/s on steep slopes near the volcano (Janda et al., 1981). Other historical lahars have had similar velocities, with mean values on the order of 10-20 m/s (Macdonald, 1972; Blong, 1984).

Areas of inundation and lahar length are greatly influenced by lahar volume, grain-size characteristics, flow transformations, and topography. Large volume, high clay content, and confinement to a narrow valley promote long travel distance; some such historical lahars have travelled hundreds of kilometers down valleys. In contrast, the peak discharges of lahars having low clay contents attenuate rapidly downstream, as do lahars that spread out over broad, low-relief areas. Lahars moving at high velocities can rise on the outside of bends and can surmount topographic barriers.

Lahars are generated in many ways that result in the mixing of rock debris and water on a volcano (Crandell, 1971; Macdonald, 1972; Neall, 1976). Volcanic explosions can catastrophically release water contained in crater lakes (Zen and Hadikusumo, 1965). Avalanches of water-saturated debris can transform into lahars, and debris avalanches that come to rest can generate lahars as they release water and small mass failures (Janda et al., 1981). Pyroclastic flows can overrun and incorporate streamflow and form lahars. Meltwater produced by the interaction of pyroclastic flows and surges with snow and ice (Major and Newhall, 1987; in press) can mix with sediment as during the 1985 eruptions of Nevado del Ruíz (Lowe et al., 1986). Some have argued that lahars were generated directly from the directed-blast cloud at Mount St. Helens in 1980 with water supplied from groundwater in the volcano (Janda et al., 1981; Scott, 1988) or meltwater incorporated into the deflating cloud (Pierson, 1985); others do not find support for these hypotheses (Brantley and Waitt, 1988).

Several other mechanisms that generate lahars and floods are indirectly related to eruptive activity. Dams formed by lava flows, lahars, debris avalanches, pyroclastic flows, or crater rims can fail by overtopping or mass failure (Houghton et al., 1987; Lockwood et al., 1988; Costa and Schuster, 1988). Torrential rainfall on recently deposited tephra or other unconsolidated material can also form lahars (Waldron, 1967). These types of lahars can also be generated during eruptions by rainstorms related to convecting eruption columns (Moore and Melson, 1969).

Lahars threaten lives and property both on volcanoes and in the valleys that drain them. Because of their high bulk density and velocity lahars can destroy vegetation and even substantial structures in their paths, such as bridges. The deposits of lahars can deeply bury crops and developments. They can also fill stream channels, thus decreasing the channels' capacity to carry flood flows (Janda et al., 1981; Lombard et al., 1981; U.S. Army Corps of Engineers, 1984). In addition, increased sedimentation in streams impacted by lahars can affect capacity and navigation of channels (Schuster, 1983).

Flood-control structures provide protection from floods and can also mitigate the effects of lahars (Blong, 1984). Japan (Disaster Prevention Bureau, 1988a, 1988b; Japan Sabo Association, 1988) and Indonesia (Sudradjat and Tilling, 1984; Suryo and Clarke, 1985) have undertaken the building of levees, diversion and check dams, and sediment-retention structures to divert, trap, or at least to decrease the peak flow of lahars and related floods. Voluminous lahars are less subject to control; however, the lowering of large reservoirs can provide storage for substantial amounts of water and sediment as at Mount St. Helens (Crandell and Mullineaux, 1978; Miller et al., 1981). Reservoirs not lowered are susceptible to overtopping if a large amount of water were displaced by a lahar, debris avalanche, or other type of flow. Subsequent dam failure could obviously greatly increase damage downstream.

Detection of a lahar close to its source can provide timely warnings to people in downstream areas if proper communication systems exist. In contrast to pyroclastic flows and surges, lahars and floods have sharply defined upper limits along valleys and in many cases people can quickly climb to safety if safe areas are identified beforehand. Tragically, most of the 21,000 residents of Armero, Columbia, who were killed in 1985, could have saved themselves by walking a short distance (typically much less than 2 km), had they received warning and known where to seek safety (Figure 2.8; Voight, 1988).

Tephra Falls and Ballistic Projectiles

Tephra consists of fragments of rock and lava that are ejected into the atmosphere and fall back to the Earth's surface. The particles are carried upward by eruption columns that consist of a lower gas-thrust region and an upper convective region (Sparks and Wilson, 1976). A column will continue to rise convectively until its density is equal to that of the surrounding atmosphere. It will then expand laterally but will also continue upward due to its momentum to form a broad umbrella cloud (Sparks, 1986; Sparks et al., 1986) that plays an important role in the transport of pyroclasts (Carey and Sparks, 1986). Temperature of the erupted material and mass eruption rate determine the height of an eruption column, which, along with wind strength and direction, exert the principal controls on the long-distance transport of tephra. In contrast, large ballistic projectiles leave the vent at speeds of tens to hundreds of meters per second on trajectories that are little affected by column dynamics or the wind. Consequently, they are typically restricted to within 5 km of vents (Blong, 1984).

Tephra ranges in size from ash (<2 mm), to lapilli (2-64 mm), to blocks and bombs (>64 mm) that may reach several meters in diameter (Fisher, 1961). Densities vary from low-density, vesicular pumice and scoria to dense crystals and lithic fragments. Materials may be juvenile (formed of magma involved in the eruption) or accidental (derived from pre-existing rocks).

Tephra fall poses the widest-ranging direct hazard from volcanic eruptions. For instance, areas of 10^3 to 10^4 km^2 may be covered with >10 cm of tephra during some large eruptions, and fine ash can be carried over areas of continental size or larger. Tephra typically becomes finer-grained and forms thinner deposits as distance from the vent increases (Figure 2.9; however, in some historical eruptions, isolated areas of increased thickness are present in distal portions of tephra plumes (for example, Sarna-Wojcicki et al., 1981a). Carey and Sigurdsson (1982) proposed that aggregation of fine ash into larger particles during the 18 May 1980 eruption of Mount St. Helens caused rapid deposition from the tephra cloud in downwind areas of increased thickness.

Tephra fall and ballistic projectiles endanger life and property by (1) the force of impact of falling fragments, (2) burial; (3) producing a suspension of fine-grained particles in air and water, and (4) carrying noxious gases, acids, salts, and, close to the vent, heat.

The hazard from the impact of large fragments is greatest close to the vent and decreases with increasing distance. Walker's (1980) plots of maximum lithic and pumice clast sizes with distance from vents show that small (64-100 mm) bombs of pumice were carried horizontal distances as great as 20-80 km, depending on erupion size, whereas lithic bombs were carried as far as 10-30 km. People can survive falls of small bombs with minimal shelter; however, falls of larger bombs can harm people even in substantial shelters. In the 1938

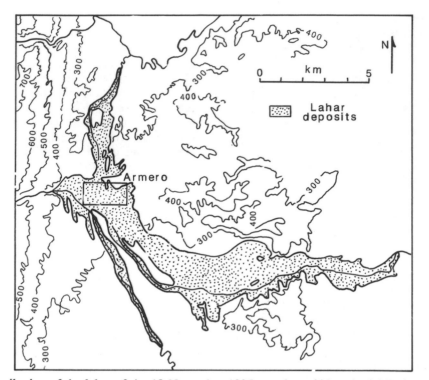

Fig. 2.8. Distribution of the lahar of the 13 November 1985 eruption of Nevado del Ruíz near Armero, Columbia, where more than 20,000 people were killed (from Lowe et al., 1986). Armero is situated on a gently sloping surface at the mouth of the canyon of Río Lagunillas, 50 km east of Ruíz.

explosions of Asama, 1-m-diameter bombs were thrown as far as 4.5 km (Minakami, 1942). Blong (1981, 1984) presents the limited data available on the effects of bomb impacts on some common building materials.

Burial by tephra can collapse roofs of buildings, break power and communication lines, and damage or kill vegetation. Dry, uncompacted tephra has densities ranging from 0.4-0.7 g/cm^3, whereas wet, compacted tephra has a density of about 1 g/cm^3 (Blong, 1981, 1984). Sarna-Wojcicki et al. (1981a) report bulk densities as high as 1.25 g/cm^3 for moist tephra. Thus, the load imparted by a 10-cm-thick tephra-fall deposit could range from 40-70 kg/m^2 for dry tephra to 100-125 kg/m^2 for moist tephra. Moisture also increases the cohesiveness of tephra. The effects of tephra loads on buildings vary greatly with their design and construction; flat roofs are more prone to failure than steeply pitched ones. Wind-drifting of tephra on roofs can locally produce tephra loads that greatly exceed loads on nearby flat ground. The effects on vegetation of burial are also highly variable. Falls of >1 m will kill most types; even thin falls can be severely damaging depending on species, time of year, and stage of growth (Rees, 1979; Blong, 1982).

The suspension of fine-grained particles in air affects visibility and health (especially for people with respiratory problems), and can damage unprotected machinery (especially internal-combustion engines). Air, rail, and highway traffic are especially vulnerable. The relatively thin tephra fall in eastern Washington, northern Idaho, and western Montana from the 18 May 1980 eruption of Mount St. Helens disrupted transportation and several types of community services rapidly and uniformly regardless of the thickness of tephra; however, recovery was more rapid in communities that had thinner deposits (Figure 2.10; Warrick, 1981). The resuspension of fine-grained tephra by wind, especially in dry climates, can prolong many problems. Even thin (< 2 cm) falls of ash can damage such critical facilities as hospitals, electric-generating plants, pumping plants, storm sewers and surface-drainage systems, and water- and sewage-treatment facilities (Schuster, 1981, 1983). Fine ash can also cause short circuits in electric-transmission facilities. In addition, communications can be affected greatly by damage to telephone lines and radio and television transmitters, and by electrical disturbances due to lightning. Darkness caused by tephra falls during daylight hours can persist from a few hours to several days (Blong, 1982), cause panic, and compound other problems.

In contrast to the hazards posed by other volcanic events, many of the hazardous effects of tephra falls can be quite practically mitigated with proper planning and preparation. Blong (1981, 1984) reviews several methods used during past tephra falls including clearing tephra from roofs or other structures as it accumulates, designing roof orientation and pitch to discourage thick buildups, strengthening roofs and walls to withstand loading and projectile impacts, removing or

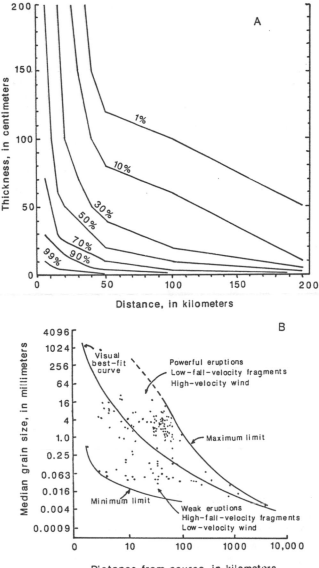

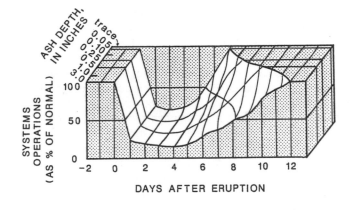

Fig. 2.10. A generalized "disruption surface" for communities in eastern Washington and western Montana from the 18 May 1980 eruption of Mount St. Helens (modified slightly from Warrick, 1981, Fig. VI-4).

Fig. 2.9. Variations in thickness and median grain size of tephra-fall deposits. A, Percentage of tephra deposits with thickness greater than or equal to indicated value plotted against distance (measured along axis of plume) from vent (data from Newhall, 1982). Based on a sample of 36 eruptions with tephra-fall volumes equal to or greater than 0.1 km³. Newhall (1982) corrected the data set to balance a reporting bias toward larger eruptions. Thus, in only 10 percent of the eruptions did tephra thickness at 100 km exceed 60 cm. B, Plot of median grain size of numerous tephra-fall deposits at various distances from vents (modified slightly from Fisher and Schmincke, 1984, Fig. 6-36). Note that median grain size decreases with increasing distance from vent, but that data scatter widely due to variations in eruption intensity, particle density, and wind strength.

stabilizing tephra on the ground after a fall to prohibit reworking, designing filters for machinery, and wearing respirators or wet cloths over mouth and nose to reduce inhalation of tephra and gases.

Tephra can contain harmful gases adsorbed on particles, as acid aerosols, and as salt particles (Thorarinsson, 1979). The effects of these are discussed in the section on volcanic gases.

Tephra falls have caused fires both by lightning generated in eruption clouds and by hot fragments. Fragments large enough to retain sufficient heat to start fires typically fall within a few kilometers of vents; although fires were started 10 km from Fuji during the 1707 eruption by pumice fragments 20-30 cm in diameter (Tsuya, 1955). In certain cases, tephra fall deposits can be so hot that welding occurs several kilometers from the vent (Wright, 1980; Mahood and Hildreth, 1983). The effects of this type of event would be catastrophic.

Once dispersed over a drainage basin, tephra can greatly change rainfall/runoff relationships. Low permeability of fine ash deposits leads to increased runoff, accelerated erosion, and stream-channel adjustments (Segerstrom, 1950; Waldron, 1967; Davies et al., 1978b; Collins et al., 1983; Lehre et al., 1983). In contrast, thick, coarse-grained deposits can increase infiltration capacity and essentially eliminate surface runoff.

Volcanic Gases

Magma contains dissolved gases that are released to the atmosphere both during eruptions and while the magma lies close to the surface. Gases are also released from hydrothermal systems. By far the most abundant volcanic gas is water vapor; other important gases include carbon dioxide, carbon monoxide, sulfur oxides, hydrogen sulfide, chlorine, and fluorine (Williams and McBirney, 1979). These gases are transported away from vents as acid aerosols, as compounds adsorbed on tephra, and as microscopic salt particles (Rose, 1977; Thorarinsson, 1979).

Sulfur compounds and chlorine and fluorine react with water to form acids that are poisonous and, even in low concentrations, are damaging to eyes, skin, and respiratory systems of animals. These acids can also damage or kill vegetation depending on their concentration and the type of vegetation; they can also damage fabrics and metals (see summaries in Wilcox, 1959; Bolt et al., 1977; and Thorarinsson, 1979).

Carbon monoxide and carbon dioxide are odorless and, unlike the noxious gases, cannot be detected by people. Carbon monoxide is poisonous and carbon dioxide, which is denser than air, can collect in low-lying areas and asphyxiate any animals that enter the area. Several recent events have underscored the hazards from large quantities of carbon dioxide being emitted from phreatic eruptions (Dieng Plateau, Indonesia in 1979 [Le Guern et al., 1982]) and from the sudden overturn of stratified tropical maar lakes that probably accumulate carbon dioxide through volcanic exhalations (Lake Monoun in 1984 [Sigurdsson et al., 1987b] and Lake Nyos in 1986 [Kling et al., 1987], both in Cameroon).

The effects of a volcanic gas are directly related to its concentration, which generally decreases downwind from its source vent as the gas becomes diluted by air. Harmful effects are usually restricted to within 10 km of vents except under exceptional circumstances. However, stratospheric veils of dust and, more importantly, acid aerosols caused by explosive, large-volume eruptions or by even modest eruptions of sulfur-rich magmas can have effects on regional or global climate (Rampino and Self, 1982, 1984; Stothers, 1984; Rampino and Stothers, 1988).

Volcanic Earthquakes

Earthquakes in volcanic areas can be generated by (1) the movement of magma and associated crack formation, (2) volcanic explosions, (3) large-scale mass movements, and (4) tectonic forces (Blong, 1984). Earthquakes of the first two categories are typically shallow, of small to moderate magnitude ($M \leq 5$), and seldom cause damage far from the source volcano; however, there are some notable exceptions (Machado et al., 1962; Rittmann, 1962; Shimozuru, 1972; Okada et al., 1981; Latter, 1981). Newhall and Dzurisin (1988) note that there is often no clear distinction between purely tectonic and purely volcanic earthquakes, especially in volcanic systems that are showing signs of unrest, and that both processes contribute to earthquake generation. During this decade, swarms of small to moderate earthquakes have occurred at three, large, restless calderas, Rabaul (Papua New Guinea), Phlegraean Fields (Italy), and Long Valley (California). The swarms were preceded and(or) accompanied by strong extracaldera earthquakes, persisted for periods of years, and in some instances caused damage to structures located within the

calderas. All were accompanied by rapid rates of uplift of broad areas.

Shocks generated by large mass movements or tectonic forces are typically much stronger than those generated by volcanic explosions or movement of magma. Strong, damaging earthquakes ($M \geq 7$) have occurred in response to sudden seaward displacements of Kilauea volcano, Hawaii (see section on structural collapse; Tilling et al., 1976). Numerous strong ($M \geq 7$) tectonic earthquakes, including some of the largest events on record, have occurred at convergent plate boundaries that are the sites of volcanic arcs. Eruptions have been associated with some of these earthquakes. For example, the great Chilean earthquake of 1960 (M=9.5) was followed 48 hours later by a fissure eruption near Puyehue volcano, 300 km from the epicenter (Katsui and Katz, 1967). Assessments of the hazards associated with the great plate-margin earthquakes are not discussed here.

The damaging effects of volcanic earthquakes are typically restricted to proximal areas, and are the result of ground shaking, and perhaps ground breakage. Earthquakes can also trigger mass movements that can lead to a host of other hazardous events such as debris avalanches.

Atmospheric Shock Waves

Atmospheric shock waves have been created by rapidly moving volcanic ejecta during some explosive historical eruptions. Although the energy of a shock wave decreases with increasing distance from source, such waves can be sufficiently energetic to damage structures long distances away. Blong (1984) gives several examples of the effects of shock waves reported hundreds of kilometers from source. The 1815 eruption of Tambora, Indonesia, generated a shock wave that broke windows at a distance of 400 km (Stewart, 1820), and Simkin and Howard (1970) reported damage to buildings 100 km from Fernandina in 1968. Banister (1984) assembled barograph records and calculated the response of the atmosphere within 500 km of Mount St. Helens to the directed blast of 18 May 1980. He determined minimum overpressures of 1600 Pa at 10 km and 400 Pa at 50 km and noted that actual values may have been twice these. Such pressures would not be capable of damaging structures; however, ejecta velocities several times larger than those at Mount St. Helens are plausible for larger eruptions and pressures approaching the threshold for damage to buildings (about 10,000 Pa) are conceivable at distances of tens of kilometers from source.

Tsunamis

Tsunamis are long-period sea waves or wave trains that are generated by the sudden displacement of water; they travel at high speeds through deep water as low broad waves and build to great heights as they approach shores. Most are caused by fault displacements on the sea floor; however, tens of historic

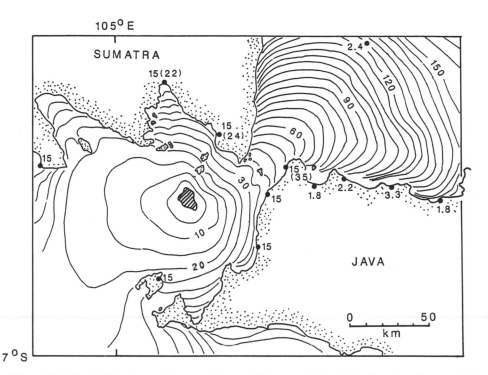

Fig. 2.11. Map of the Sunda Straits area between Java and Sumatra, Indonesia, showing the travel time (in minutes) of the tsunami generated by the 1883 eruption of Krakatau (densely ruled area). This figure is a combination of Figures 7 and 8 of Yokoyama (1981), which were reproduced as Figures 119 and 120 in Simkin and Fiske (1983). Numerals by filled circles along coasts are maximum heights of tsunami in meters as given by Yokoyama (1981); values in parentheses are those given by Wharton (1888; *in* Simkin and Fiske, 1983).

tsunamis of volcanic origin have caused many deaths and much destruction of property on ocean and lake shores, even at great distances from eruptions. Latter (1981) discusses numerous mechanisms for generating tsunamis of volcanic origin including volcanic or volcano-tectonic earthquakes; explosions; collapse or subsidence; landslides, lahars, or pyroclastic flows entering bodies of water; and atmospheric shock waves that couple with the sea (Press and Harkrider, 1966). The 1883 eruption of Krakatau produced tsunamis that ran up coasts to heights of 35 m, killed more than 30,000 people, and totally or partly devastated almost 300 villages (Figure 2.11; see numerous sources in Simkin and Fiske, 1983). The causes of the larger tsunamis have long been debated, but they likely had multiple origins related to collapse, explosions, and pyroclastic flows; the smaller waves were most likely due to air-sea coupling of pressure waves (Latter, 1981; Simkin and Fiske, 1983; Francis, 1985).

A warning system in the Pacific basin provides timely alarms of approaching tsunamis to areas hundreds to thousands of kilometers from sources; however, owing to the high velocity of tsunamis, people in areas close to sources would have little time to act. In addition, waves in proximal areas can be very high and can affect extensive areas along low-lying coasts--areas that might not normally be affected by tsunamis induced by distant earthquakes. In such cases, evacuation prior to a tsunami-generating event is probably the only reliable means of mitigation. Before authorities can justify the evacuation of large, populous, proximal areas, however, the character of a tsunami-generating event would need to be forecast. For example, deformation precursory to a debris avalanche might allow an estimate to be made of the direction of movement and potential size. Numerical modelling could then predict the time of travel and heights of waves produced by such events (e.g., Kienle et al., 1987), which could be considered in evacuation plans. For areas not evacuated prior to an event, mitigation requires that observers or some monitoring system detect the tsunami-generating event or the tsunami itself and communicate warnings to people in hazardous areas, and that people know where to seek shelter. On steep coasts, people might have to move only a short distance inland, whereas on low-lying coasts they might be far from safety.

Discussion

A wide range of hazardous events are directly or indirectly associated with volcanic activity, and all have caused losses of

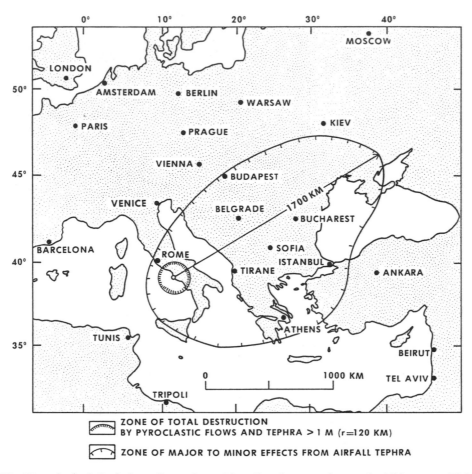

Fig. 2.12. Hypothetical depiction of a major caldera-forming eruption at the Phlegraean Fields, Italy, showing the potential for local devastation and regional disruption. The zones shown are those expectable from an eruption similar to one that produced the Bishop tephra fall and ignimbrite (740 ka) from Long Valley, California (Miller et al., 1982). Total volume of the Bishop is about 600 km^3. Preserved tephra-fall thicknesses along the axis are 100 cm at 120 km, 40 cm at 200 km, 15 cm at 500 km, and 8 cm at 800 km. This scenario is not meant as a forecast of future activity at the Phlegraean Fields, but merely as an illustration of the magnitude of the societal impacts that might result from a catastrophic eruption in a densely developed area.

human life, property, and resources during historical time. Twin catastrophes during the 1980's in Cameroon caused by releases of carbon dioxide from tropical lakes (Sigurdsson et al., 1987b; Kling et al., 1987) serve as a reminder that poorly known or unknown types of volcanic hazards may yet surprise us; however, most volcanic hazards are reasonably well understood as a result of observations of historical eruptions and studies of the geologic record of prehistorical eruptions. Perhaps the greatest uncertainty regards the effects of a large caldera-forming eruption that would be one to two orders of magnitude larger than the largest eruptions of historical time (Figure 2.12). The problems of monitoring, warning, and evacuation that are present in most volcanic crises would be greatly increased because of the size of the area that could be impacted by voluminous pyroclastic flows and thick tephra fall. In many areas of the world, populations at risk would number in the millions and significant portions of countries could be destroyed. Needless to say, plans for dealing with such situations have not been made, and many would argue that the probability of such an eruption is so low that long-term planning is not warranted.

The hazards of small- to moderate-size eruptions are reasonably well understood; however, much can probably be accomplished in the promotion of engineering measures to mitigate the effects of eruptions. Building designs to cope with tephra fall and ballistic projectiles and channel works to provide protection from lahars and floods have been developed in many areas. Hopefully such methods can be improved and put into wider use in the future. Protection from lava flows and especially pyroclastic flows and surges is much more problematic and may not be feasible.

As was dramatically demonstrated in 1985 during the Ruíz eruption, a critical need for mitigating the effects of most hazardous volcanic events is the development of systems for detecting events, providing warnings, and developing workable mitigation plans (Tilling, 1989, in press). These issues will be addressed in CHAPTERS 4-6.

Other important aspects of volcanic-hazard studies are identifying hazardous areas, providing estimates of the long-term probabilities of these areas being impacted by various volcanic events or at least assessing the relative degrees of hazard in these areas, and producing hazard-zonation maps that portray the results of these analyses. Such information can be used for long-term, land-use planning, in which volcanic hazards are taken into account in making decisions about future developments and plans for dealing with future volcanic crises. These topics are addressed in CHAPTER 3.

CHAPTER 3. VOLCANIC-HAZARDS ZONATION AND LONG-TERM FORECASTS

William E. Scott

U.S. Geological Survey, Vancouver, Washington 98661

Introduction

Mitigating the effects of future volcanic eruptions and related events includes several steps, such as (1) assessing the potential hazards from future eruptions, (2) developing long-term land-use plans based on the assessment, (3) evaluating volcanic risk and planning for managing a crisis if premonitory activity or an eruption occurs, (4) monitoring the state of a volcano to detect the onset and progress of an eruption, and (5) devising protective measures for people, their property, and critical facilities. The past two decades of volcano studies have witnessed significant progress in most of these topics, spurred by the numerous volcanic crises that occurred during this time period (Tilling, 1989, in press). Two broad levels of volcanic hazards are reflected in these topics, short-term, or immediate, and long-term, or potential (Crandell et al., 1984). Other chapters in this report deal with assessments of short-term hazards, volcano monitoring, eruption prediction, and volcanic-emergency management. Such activities are focused on volcanoes that have erupted frequently or recently such as Etna in Italy, Mount St. Helens in the United States, Cotopaxi in Ecuador, Taal in the Philippines, Sakurajima in Japan, and Merapi in Indonesia.

This chapter addresses the assessment of long-term volcanic hazards, or those that have such a low frequency of occurrence that people are unlikely to experience them in their lifetimes. The hazards at volcanoes that erupt infrequently can be evaluated by preparing a long-term hazards assessment; some such volcanoes may pose sufficient risks to warrant being monitored closely. Conversely, many volcanoes that are currently active and monitored should also be the subject of assessments of long-term hazards, because of the possibility that past behavior may have differed greatly from recent behavior, and such activity may recur in the future.

Several aspects of assessing long-term volcanic hazards are treated in this chapter: (1) identifying volcanoes that pose a hazard, (2) documenting the past activity of those volcanoes in order to evaluate the types and scales of hazardous activity

Published in 1989 by the American Geophysical Union.

expectable in the future, and (3) identifying areas that are likely to be impacted during future eruptions. The latter topic also includes the preparation of hazard-zonation maps that delimit hazardous areas and provide information about the relative degree of hazard in volcanic regions. Much of this chapter is modelled after Crandell et al. (1984).

Identification of High-Risk Volcanoes

Simkin et al. (1981) have cataloged at least 1343 volcanoes that have erupted during the past 10,000 years; more than 500 have erupted in historical time. Of these, most are located along convergent or divergent plate margins (Figure 3.1). About two-thirds lie in the Pacific rim; the remainder are concentrated in the Caribbean and Mediterranean basins, in East Africa, and along the mid-Atlantic ridge. Future eruptions will occur at most of these 1343 volcanoes, at volcanoes that have not been identified as having been active during the past 10,000 years, and at as yet unborn volcanoes. Volcanoes of the latter two categories will almost all be located in regions represented by volcanoes of the first category.

To mitigate effectively the hazards posed by future volcanic eruptions, scientists and public officials must have a hazard assessment in hand before premonitory activity or an eruption begins, because a thorough volcanic-hazard assessment typically requires months to years to complete. Such time commitments, and constraints of budgets, personnel, and competing needs, often mean that a country cannot prepare adequate hazard assessments for all of its potentially active volcanoes in a timely manner. This is especially true in countries with limited resources and(or) many volcanoes. Even highly developed countries with relatively few volcanoes may neither muster the resolve nor commit the necessary resources to complete a hazard-assessment program. Therefore, priorities must be established with high-risk volcanoes studied first.

The most recent global attempt at identifying high-risk volcanoes employed a rating system composed of hazard and

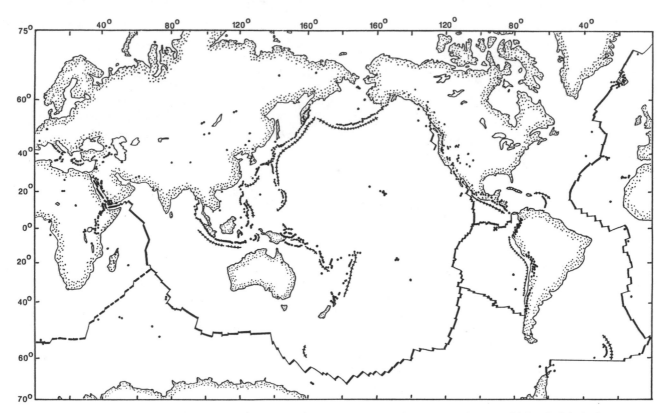

Fig. 3.1. Volcanoes of the world (Peterson, 1986; adapted from Simkin and Siebert, 1984). Solid circles are volcanoes that have erupted during the past 10,000 years. Heavy lines are divergent plate boundaries; cross-hatched lines are convergent plate boundaries. Most submarine eruptions along divergent boundaries go undetected; hence few submarine volcanoes are shown.

risk factors such as type of past activity, age of last major explosive activity, size of areas affected during past eruptions, occurrence of seismicity or deformation, size of the population at risk, and past fatalities (Table 3.1; Yokoyama et al., 1984; Tilling, 1989, in press). Eighty of the more than 500 volcanoes active in historical time were identified as high-risk volcanoes; however, the authors cautioned that the list was incomplete. Indeed, during the following year, one volcano not listed, Nevado del Ruíz in Colombia, caused the second worst volcanic disaster of this century. The shortcomings of establishing a list of high-risk volcanoes include: (1) the prehistoric activity of many volcanoes is poorly known, (2) the historical record at many volcanoes is short and(or) incomplete, (3) events of a type or magnitude unprecedented in historical or prehistorical time can occur, (4) owing to a non-characteristic morphology, some volcanoes in poorly explored areas may not yet have even been identified, (5) repose intervals between large explosive eruptions may be long (hundreds to thousands of years; Simkin and Siebert, 1984), and (6) many volcanoes that are not given a high priority may be ignored and thereby become even more dangerous if the effects of future eruptions are unanticipated.

Despite these shortcomings, priorities need to be established, and the 80 volcanoes with scores equal to or greater than ten identified by Yokoyama et al. (1984) certainly deserve high-risk status (Table 3.2). Periodic updates of this list of high-risk volcanoes would no doubt create additions, but few, if any, deletions. Certainly many volcanoes judged not to be high-risk should also be afforded some level of attention. This can be assured by expending some level of effort in reconnaissance studies of entire volcanic regions. Indeed regional investigations aimed at geothermal or mineral exploration, geologic mapping, geophysical studies, and soil investigations all can provide new information about the age and character of prehistoric activity that is critical for establishing and revising priorities.

Documentation of Past Eruptive Behavior

The historical and prehistorical records of a volcano's activity and its current state have provided the basis for most volcanic-hazard assessments (Crandell et al., 1984). The current state of a volcano is determined by techniques discussed in CHAPTER 4; the methods of documenting past eruptive behavior are discussed below.

TABLE 3.1 Proposed criteria for identification of high-risk volcanoes (from Yokoyama et al., 1984). A score of 1 is assigned for each rating criterion that applies; 0 if the criterion does not apply.

HAZARD RATING	SCORE
1) High silica content of eruptive products (andesite/dacite/rhyolite)	
2) Major explosive activity within last 500 yr	
3) Major explosive activity within last 5,000 yr	
4) Pyroclastic flows within last 500 yr	
5) Mudflows within last 500 yr	
6) Destructive tsunami within last 500 yr	
7) Area of destruction within last 5,000 yr is $> 10 \text{ km}^2$	
8) Area of destruction within last 5,000 yr is $> 100 \text{ km}^2$	
9) Occurrence of frequent volcano-seismic swarms	
10) Occurrence of significant ground deformation within last 50 yr	

RISK RATING	
1) Population at risk > 100	
2) Population at risk $> 1,000$	
3) Population at risk $> 10,000$	
4) Population at risk $> 100,000$	
5) Population at risk > 1 million	
6) Historical fatalities	
7) Evacuation as a result of historical eruption(s)	

TOTAL SCORE

Historical records of eruptions

At many volcanoes, observations of historical eruptions provide an important source of information about the character of past eruptions, their age, the areas impacted, and the effects of eruptions on people and their surroundings. Some volcanoes have historical records that cover more than 1000 years, but many others have had no observed eruptions or have records that span a century or less. Even long historical records are of limited use because the descriptions of past eruptions, many of which have been conveyed through oral traditions, were not made by experienced volcanologists and are difficult to interpret (Blong, 1982). However, detailed studies of the deposits of historical eruptions, in combination with interpretation of observations and photographs, have provided valuable information about the character of the eruptions and have added much to our understanding of

volcanic processes (e.g., Taylor, 1958; Nakamura, 1964; Simkin and Fiske, 1983; Sigurdsson et al., 1985b). Extensive observations of eruptions by volcanologists (Perret, 1950; Thorarinsson, 1954; Swanson, 1973; Sparks et al., 1976; Davies et al., 1978a; Hoblitt, 1986) have been especially fruitful. The study of the geologic record of historical eruptions employs most of the techniques used in investigations of prehistoric eruptive products.

Geologic record of past eruptions

Detailed investigations of the geologic record of past eruptions is essential for assessing the long-term hazards at all volcanoes. The perspective gained by the study of a volcano's behavior for a long time increases the probability that its range of eruption types, scales, and frequencies are known. Also, a long record might document patterns of episodic or cyclic behavior, or evidence of a distinct evolutionary pattern, that would be valuable for estimating probabilities of the timing and character of renewed activity at a dormant volcano.

The requirements for constructing a geologic record of past eruptions and related activity include the following:

(1) Establishing a stratigraphic sequence of the products of past eruptions.

(2) Tracing the extent of individual deposits or groups of deposits and estimating the magnitude of the eruptions that produced them.

(3) Determining the origin of the deposits.

(4) Dating the deposits by various techniques in order to develop a chronology of events and to estimate their frequency.

Stratigraphic sequence and extent of products of past eruptions. Standard stratigraphic principles, such as superposition and correlation, are used to establish the sequence of deposits of past eruptions. Fragmental deposits and lava flows are rarely exposed on the surface. More typically they are seen in stream banks, landslide scars, road cuts, and other excavations; where exposures are few, trenching or coring may be necessary. Numerous localities around a volcano must be investigated, because some events leave thin or discontinuous deposits, and because erosion caused by subsequent eruptions or subaerial processes during periods of quiescence can remove part of the record. Even with detailed work, the evidence of some past events or the full extent of the deposits of some recognized events will probably be missed--a factor that dictates added conservatism in judgments based on the reconstructed history.

From past experience, the best places to begin stratigraphic studies are the lower flanks of a volcano and the ridges downwind from the volcano where most of the fragmental deposits of an eruption are preserved. Unconsolidated deposits are easily eroded from the steep upper parts of a cone, and many lahars and pyroclastic flows and surges move so rapidly over steep slopes that they may leave only thin deposits. Flowage deposits are concentrated in fans and valley floors,

TABLE 3.2. High-risk volcanoes and their scores (see TABLE 3.1) identified by Yokoyama et al. (1984). For those volcanoes given a range of scores, the highest score is shown here. Names in **bold print** denote volcanoes for which a hazard assessment is referenced in TABLE 3.5.

SCORE	15	14	13	12	11	10
Italy	**Phlegraean Fields** **Vesuvius** (16)					**Etna**
France/Reunion Island			Piton de Fournaise			
New Zealand			Tarawera			**Ruapehu** Taupo
Papua New Guinea	**Rabaul**		Lamington		**Karkar** **Manam**	**Uluwan**
Indonesia	Api Siau Gamalama **Kelut** **Merapi** **Semeru**		Agung Awu Lamongan Slamet Tangkuban Parahu	Ili Boleng Ili Werung **Lokon** Paluweh Sundoro	Guntur Ijen	Ciremai Marapi Raung
Philippines	Hibok-Hibok	**Mayon**		Canlaon Taal		Bulusan
Japan		Sakurajima	**Asama** Usu	**Fuji**	Komagatake Unzen	Bandai Tokachi
United States	**Mount St. Helens**		**Kilauea**			**Lassen Peak** **Mauna Loa** **Mono-Inyo Craters**
Mexico	Colima El Chichón				Ceboruco	
Guatemala	Santa María/ **Santiaguito**	Fuego	Agua/ **Pacaya** Amtitlán	**Tacaná** Tajumulco		
El Salvador				San Miguel	Izalco San Salvador	Ilopango
Nicaragua		Coseguina			Santiago	San Crístobal
Costa Rica		Arenal		Irazú		Poás
Colombia				Galeras		Puracé
Ecuador		**Cotopaxi**	Guagua Pichincha		Tungurahua	
Lesser Antilles		Dominica **Pelée** Soufrière de St. Vincent	**Soufrière de Guadeloupe**			

whereas tephra-fall deposits are typically best preserved on broad ridges. For volcanoes that produce a significant number of identifiable tephra layers, many workers have benefited from first establishing the stratigraphic sequence of tephra-fall deposits and then using the tephras as stratigraphic markers in subdividing sequences of flowage deposits in the valleys (Table 3.3).

The extent of the products of past eruptions and related events is needed in order to estimate the magnitude of past events and thereby to identify areas that are likely to be affected by future eruptions. Geologic-mapping techniques are used in tracing the extent of flowage deposits. For deposits of lahars and floods, special attention should be paid to determining the inundation levels and peak flows of events (for example, Scott,

TABLE 3.3. Eruptive history of Mount St. Helens Volcano, Washington. Compiled from Mullineaux (1986), Crandell (1988), Major and Scott (1988), and Scott (in press). Symbols denoting nature of activity: d, dome; lf, lava flow; t, tephra; pf, pyroclastic flow and(or) surge; db, laterally directed blast; da, debris avalanche; l,lahar; lr, lahar-runout flow. Most eruptive stages and periods were accompanied by multiple events of the types.

Eruptive stage or period *(dormant interval)	Approximate ^{14}C age in years before A.D. 1950	Major tephra units	Nature of activity
Spirit Lake eruptive stage			
Present eruptive period *(Dormant interval of 123 yr)	A.D. 1980-1986	1980	da,db,t,pf,l,lr,d
Goat Rocks eruptive period *(Dormant interval of less than 200 yr)	123-180[1]	T	t,lf,d,l
Kalama eruptive period *(Dormant interval of about 650 yr)	350-500[2]	X,W	t,pf,d,lf,l
Sugar Bowl eruptive period *(Dormant interval of about 600 yr)	1,150	unnamed	d,db,pf,t,l
Castle Creek eruptive period *(Apparent dormant interval of about 300 yr)	1,700-2,200	B	lf,t,pf,l
Pine Creek eruptive period *(Apparent dormant interval of about 300 yr)	2,500-3,000	P	t,d,pf,l,lr
Smith Creek eruptive period (probably included dormant intervals of a few centuries)	3,300-4,000	Y	t,d,pf,l,lr
*Apparent dormant interval of about 5,000(?) yr			
Swift Creek eruptive stage (probably included dormant intervals of at least a few centuries)	10,000-13,000	J,S	t,d,pf,l,lr
*(Apparent dormant interval of perhaps 5,000(?) yr)			
Cougar eruptive stage (probably included dormant intervals of at least several centuries)	18,000?-21,000?	K,M	t,d,lf,pf,da,l,lr
*(Apparent dormant interval of about 15,000(?) yr)			
Ape Canyon eruptive stage	36,000?-<50,000	C	t,pf,l,lr

[1]Years before 1980, based on tree-ring dates and historical records.
[2]Years before 1980, based on radiocarbon ages and tree-ring dates.

in press). Care should be taken in correlating individual units, using tephrostratigraphy, similarity of physical characteristics, various dating methods, and other techniques. For some deposits, especially tephra falls, information about thickness and grain-size is also important, because they relate closely to the severity of an event.

Initial studies at a volcano can be of a reconnaissance nature and aimed at developing general information about a volcano's past behavior. Then a decision can be made as to the time interval for which a detailed record should be constructed. This interval will vary among volcanoes, but the record should consist of at least several eruptive episodes in order to obtain a broad view of the type and frequency of past events. In general, the required effort and the incompleteness of the record increase as one attempts to extend the record back in time.

Origin of deposits of past eruptions. Determination of the genesis of some volcanic deposits is one of the most difficult aspects of a study, because similar-appearing deposits can be formed by different processes. Grain-size, lithology, sorting, bedding, evidence of heat, topographic expression, and areal distribution are some of the key characteristics necessary for determining the mode of origin of fragmental deposits. Multiple lines of evidence should always be used.

Recognition of lava flows and domes is typically much less ambiguous than the identification of the origin of many fragmental deposits. However, in some cases, fragmental deposits can retain sufficient heat to compact and weld. The resulting rocks may be difficult to distinguish from lava flows. Thickly ponded pyroclastic-flow deposits are commonly welded, but vertical and lateral variations in welding, presence of gas-escape structures, and locally preserved clastic textures have long been used to identify their fragmental origin (Smith, 1960; Ross and Smith, 1961). Under circumstances of extreme welding, however, units can acquire many features of and be mistaken for lava flows (Ekren et al., 1984). Some tephra-fall deposits, especially those near vents, can also be strongly welded, but their mantle bedding and internal stratification, and the character of their non-welded distal equivalents aid in distinguishing them from welded pyroclastic-flow deposits and lava flows (Cas and Wright, 1987).

The events that generate fragmental deposits are discussed in CHAPTER 2; the character of these deposits and ways in which they can be distinguished are discussed below. Much of the information is taken from recent books by Fisher and Schmincke (1984) and Cas and Wright (1987) that provide good summaries of our understanding of volcanic deposits and also include extensive reference lists.

Tephra-fall deposits: Tephra-fall deposits typically have mantle bedding, that is, they drape the preexisting ground surface with a layer that has nearly uniform thickness in a given area of low-to-moderate relief. In steep terrain, reworking during and immediately following deposition can lead to pronounced thickness changes (for example, Duffield et al., 1979). Fall deposits are moderately to well sorted compared with other types of pyroclastic deposits (Figure 3.2) and are commonly stratified; individual beds can be of uniform grain size or be normally or reversely graded. Coarse-grained beds are typically clast supported with little, if any, matrix. Changes in the vigor of the erupting column, composition of the erupted material, and direction and speed of the wind cause variations in successive beds. Clasts are either juvenile (derived from new magma) or accidental (older rock torn from the vent

walls). Juvenile clasts can range widely in type, from free crystals to dense glassy or poorly vesicular fragments to frothy scoria or pumice. Clasts are typically angular, reflecting breakage by explosions. Sequences of some fall deposits are interrupted by interbedded pyroclastic-flow or pyroclastic-surge deposits.

Volcanic deposits formed by other processes share some of the characteristics of tephra-fall deposits. For instance, Walker (1983) enumerates several ways in which fines-depleted, relatively well sorted deposits can be formed by pyroclastic flows and surges. He concludes that grain-size characteristics alone are not good criteria of origin (Figure 3.2). Lateral tracing of units is especially important, because many of the well-sorted deposits formed by processes other than fall are of restricted distribution. For example, many such deposits in pyroclastic flows are lenses deposited in the lee of obstacles, or vertical pipes formed by gas flow.

Detailed reconstruction of a tephra-fall deposit, including thickness, grain-size, sorting, and maximum-size distribution of pumice and lithic fragments provides information about eruption dynamics, including column height, mass-discharge rate, and wind patterns (Carey and Sparks, 1986).

Deposits of pyroclastic density currents: Pyroclastic density currents include a wide range of phenomena that form (1) pyroclastic-flow deposits, (2) pyroclastic-surge deposits, and (3) deposits of laterally directed blasts.

(1) Pyroclastic-flow deposits form from high-concentration dispersions of solids and gas that typically follow topographically low areas and therefore are generally preserved along valley floors and in depressions. The deposits are mostly massive and nonsorted (Figure 3.2), although some better-sorted and bedded zones occur as discussed above. Some deposits display normal grading of lithic clasts and inverse grading of pumice clasts. Pumice clasts are typically rounded by abrasion. The dominant clast composition of pyroclastic-flow deposits varies from pumice to juvenile lithic clasts; accidental fragments torn from vent walls and picked up along the path of the flow are also present. Many pumice-rich pyroclastic flows form from collapse of eruption columns that also produce tephra-fall deposits. Gravitational collapse of or explosions at growing lava domes typically generate pyroclastic-flow deposits that contain mostly dense lithic clasts.

(2) Pyroclastic-surge deposits form from low-concentration dispersions that are highly inflated and are therefore less topographically controlled than pyroclastic flows. Deposits of a single surge are also typically much thinner than those of a pyroclastic flow. The deposits of both hot pyroclastic surges and cold, or base, surges are typically well-bedded, display unidirectional bedforms, and tend to mantle the surface as well as to pond in low areas. Individual laminae or beds of surge deposits can be relatively well sorted (Figure 3.2), but grain size typically varies markedly throughout an entire bed set, and surge deposits are overall poorly sorted. Deposits of base surges typically show evidence that the surges were wet, including plastering on steeply sloping surfaces, accretionary

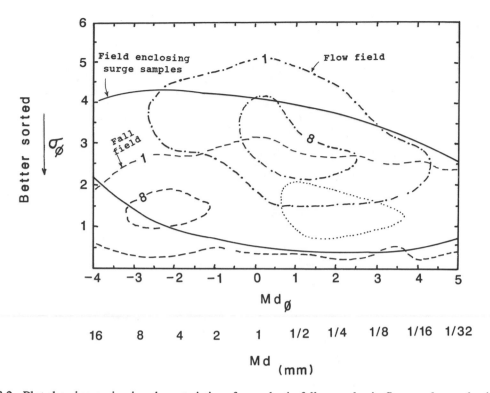

Fig. 3.2. Plot showing grain-size characteristics of pyroclastic-fall, pyroclastic-flow, and pyroclastic-surge deposits. Mdø is median grain diameter in phi units and $\sigma_\emptyset$ is graphical standard deviation in phi units after Inman (1952). Fields of pyroclastic-flow and pyroclastic-fall deposits enclosed by contours that include 99% (1) and 92% (8) of samples. Large field of surge deposits includes both hot and cold (base) surges; inner surge field (dotted line) includes selected crossbedded base-surge deposits and ash-cloud deposits. Figure modified from Fisher and Schmincke (1984; Fig. 5-30).

lapilli, and syn- and post-depositional deformation indicative of wet or moist conditions.

Plots of sorting versus median grain size help to distinguish between the bulk of flow and surge deposits (Figure 3.2); however, the data sets overlap and other criteria, such as bedding, are needed to identify the origin of a deposit with confidence.

(3) Deposits of large laterally directed blasts have characteristics of both pyroclastic surges and flows (Hoblitt et al., 1981; Waitt, 1981; Fisher et al., 1987). The deposit of 18 May 1980 at Mount St. Helens, the only one that has been studied in detail, is normally graded overall and consists of several separate units with gradational to locally sharp contacts (Figure 3.3). A basal unit (layer A1 and A0) is massive to normally graded and consists of grain-supported blocks, lapilli, and ash as well as a large amount of charred and uncharred wood and soil. A mostly coarse- to fine-grained ash unit (layer A2) overlies the basal unit, locally displays dunes and exhibits sand-wave bedding. Pyroclastic-flow deposits occur within layer A2 along some valley floors and are thought to represent the remobilization of the lower two units on steep slopes and their flowing into topographically low areas. The sequence is

capped by a fine-grained tephra-fall deposit (layer A3) that locally contains accretionary lapilli. The deposit generally thins and fines away from source, and mantles an area of more than 500 km^2; the lower units tend to thicken in depressions and thin on ridge tops.

Currently a controversy exists as to whether the St. Helens' event is best classified as a pyroclastic surge or pyroclastic flow (Walker, 1983, 1984; Walker and McBroome, 1983; Walker and Morgan, 1984; Hoblitt and Miller, 1984; Waitt, 1984; Fisher et al., 1987). Of special significance for hazard studies is the relative thinness of the St. Helens deposit, as well as that of other deposits formed by other highly energetic wide-ranging pyroclastic density currents. Such deposits, although representing catastrophic events, could be eroded, overlooked, or misinterpreted in eruptive-history studies (Walker, 1983).

Evidence of the emplacement temperature of a deposit is an important factor that can aid in determining its origin, because several types of nonbedded, poorly sorted, lithic-rich deposits are formed in volcanic terranes by volcanic (lithic pyroclastic flow and lahar) and nonvolcanic (debris flow, debris avalanche, glacier) processes. Evidence for a high emplacement temperature includes welding, prismatically

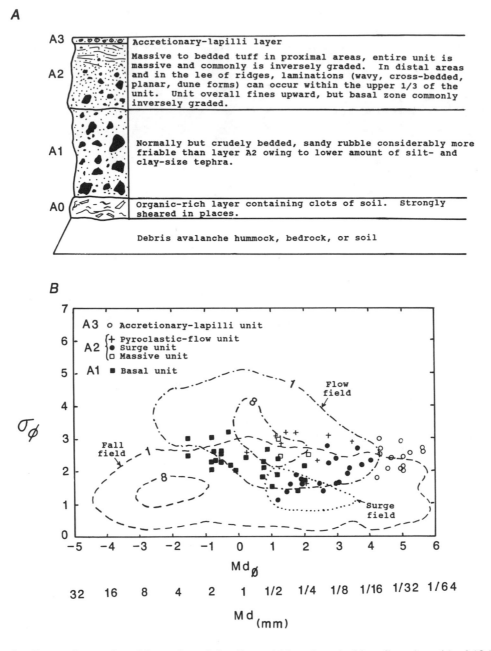

Fig. 3.3. **A.** Composite stratigraphic section of the directed-blast deposit (blast-flow deposit) of 18 May 1980 at Mount St. Helens from Fisher et al. (1987; Fig. 4). **B.** Grain-size characteristics of units within blast deposit plotted on fields of Figure 2 (data from Hoblitt et al., 1981; Fisher et al., 1987).

jointed or breadcrusted blocks, carbonized wood, reddened oxidized zones near tops of deposits, fumarolic alteration, and gas-escape pipes. Studies of thermoremanent magnetization (TRM) can also provide evidence of emplacement of clasts at temperatures above or below their Curie temperature (Aramaki and Akimoto, 1957; Mullineaux and Crandell, 1962). Small portable fluxgate magnetometers can be used in the field to

determine the TRM direction of clasts, which should be the same in a given deposit for all clasts emplaced above their Curie temperatures. More sophisticated paleomagnetic studies can provide an estimate of the emplacement temperature itself (Hoblitt and Kellogg, 1979; Kent et al., 1981).

<u>Deposits of lahars</u>: Lahars are typically coarse-grained and poorly sorted mixtures of sediment ranging in size from clay to

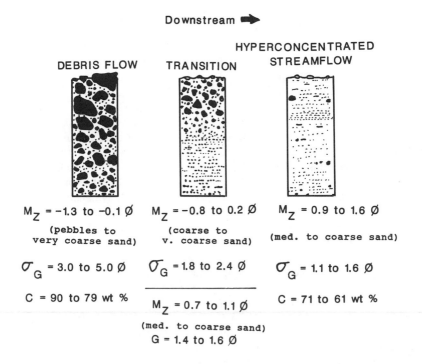

Fig. 3.4. Schematic diagrams showing downstream transition from lahar to hyperconcentrated streamflow and resulting deposits, 19 March 1982 at Mount St. Helens (from Pierson and Scott, 1985; Fig. 8). M_G, graphic mean grain size in phi units; σ_G, graphic standard deviation (measure of sorting; smaller the number, the better the sorting); C, sediment concentration of flow by weight. Change in size of large particles represents grading of deposit.

boulders with the coarser clasts supported in a fine-grained matrix (Figure 3.4; Crandell, 1971; Costa, 1984; Scott, 1988). Lahars share many features with other volcanic and nonvolcanic diamicts (a nongenetic term for a deposit that is poorly sorted, nonbedded, and contains a wide range of clast sizes). Several features can be quite diagnostic; however, it is sometimes impossible to differentiate lahars from other diamicts, especially lithic pyroclastic-flow deposits, with certainty. Some lahars are normally graded, especially in their upper parts, others are nongraded or reversely graded. Some have a sole layer of crudely stratified sand or fine gravel from which coarser clasts have been excluded, possibly by intense shearing. Vesicles are commonly present in the matrix of lahars and were probably formed by trapped air bubbles. Lahars are remarkably nonerosive on moderate and shallow gradients as evidenced by the presence of undisturbed easily erodible materials such as ash, sand, or organic matter below many lahars. Lahars form flat-topped fills in valleys but only thin, discontinuous veneers on steeper slopes. A combination of several such features provides strong evidence that a diamict is a lahar. In addition, evidence of emplacement temperature can provide useful clues to the origin of a deposit. For example, uncharred wood and lack of a preferred direction of TRM would be consistent with a laharic origin. However, charred wood and large blocks with preferred TRM direction would not rule out a laharic origin. Lithic pyroclastic flows can transform into hot lahars that inherit charcoal and large blocks capable of maintaining high temperatures. A combination of magnetically oriented and unoriented blocks and wood that is carbonized only where in contact with large blocks is consistent with a hot lahar.

Deposits of lahar-runout flows: Observations of lahars and lahar-runout flows at Mount St. Helens (Pierson and Scott, 1985), and investigations of Tertiary arc-derived basin-fill deposits (Smith, 1986), have stressed the significance of deposits of hyperconcentrated flows. Sediment concentrations in the range of 40-80 weight percent are typical of such flows (Beverage and Culbertson, 1964). A lahar transforms into a hyperconcentrated flow as sediment is lost (a lahar-runout flow; Figure 3.4); a flood flow transforms into a hyperconcentrated flow by incorporation of sediment. Deposits of hyperconcentrated flows have characteristics that suggest very rapid grain-by-grain deposition from suspension and traction, rather than deposition en masse as in lahars. Coarse-grained hyperconcentrated-flow deposits are poorly sorted but may be clast-supported and commonly are normally graded. Sandy deposits are dominated by horizontal bedding that is defined by alternations in sorting and grain size.

Hyperconcentrated-flow deposits are distinguished from normal flood deposits by the absence of cross-bedding and other evidence of turbulent flow.

Deposits of floods: Erosional and depositional evidence of floods generated by volcanic processes are similar to those of meteorologically-induced events. A recently published book on flood geomorphology by Baker et al. (1988) contains several excellent review papers on these topics. For a flood to leave behind erosional evidence of its passing, the resistance threshold of bed and bank materials must be exceeded by the power generated during the flood flow (Baker, 1988). Thus, erosional evidence can be extremely irregular in its distribution and degree of development. Scour of vegetation, bank erosion, and development of chutes that cut across bends are typical effects on alluvial channels. The effects on steep, rocky channels may be less pronounced, but include abrasion and plucking of bedrock, development of narrow inner channels, and small-scale features such as fluting and polishing of canyon walls.

Depositional evidence is more likely to be preserved in a stratigraphic context that will be useful for determining the age and magnitude of a flood event. Gravel bars and large current ripples are conspicuous deposits of many floods, but fine-grained slackwater deposits preserved in alcoves and in the lower reaches of tributary streams provide valuable information about the sizes of flood flows (Baker and Kochel, 1988; Kochel and Baker, 1988). Such deposits are also good candidates for preserving datable materials. Floodplains also contain important depositional records for understanding flood history (Brakenridge, 1988).

Deposits of volcanic debris avalanches: Debris-avalanche deposits are composed of fractured clasts of widely varying sizes from the source volcano. Good descriptions of debris-avalanche deposits are in Voight et al. (1981, 1983), Ui (1983), Ui et al. (1986), Siebert (1984), Crandell et al. (1984), Crandell (in press), and Schuster and Crandell (1984). Most large debris avalanches begin as slides of large segments of an edifice that break up and transform into fragmental flows of megaclasts. Therefore, most debris-avalanche deposits are characterized by hummocky surfaces, commonly with very large blocks at proximal sites and smaller hummocks at distal sites. However, a debris-avalanche deposit at Lastarria volcano, Chile, that was derived mostly from unconsolidated tephra deposits has only a slightly hummocky, corrugated relief (Naranjo and Francis, 1987). Many debris-avalanche deposits are characterized by levees, transverse and longitudinal ridges, and steep lobate margins. Debris avalanches commonly contain saturated parts of a volcano or incorporate water or saturated sediments as they move; hence some debris-avalanche deposits contain a lahar-like matrix facies between blocks and injected into fractures in blocks. If sufficient water is present, portions of an avalanche can transform directly into lahars or generate lahars by dewatering after they come to rest. Such lahars are capable of transporting blocks of debris avalanche material, which can be preserved as clasts within the lahar or as

large mounds projecting above the surface (Crandell, 1971; Scott, 1988; in press).

Movement related to an initiating rockfall or slide, to transport of the avalanche, and to lateral spreading of the deposit causes numerous cracks to open, but lack of turbulence inhibits mixing. Therefore, debris commonly displays jigsaw fractures, in which fragments can be visually refitted across fractures. Movement also causes abrasion and crushing of fragments that generate a matrix of similar composition.

A debris avalanche initiated by collapse of a large sector of a volcano typically leaves a horseshoe-shaped avalanche caldera up to several kilometers in diameter with a wide breach open in the direction of avalanche movement (Siebert, 1984). Mass movements of smaller volume create shallow depressions or reentrants on flanks or steep walls. Glaciers and other agents of erosion and volcanic explosions can also form horseshoe-shaped depressions on volcanoes that could be mistaken for debris-avalanche scars. Furthermore, post-avalanche cone- or dome-building activity can fill depressions and heal scars.

Dating volcanic deposits. To estimate the frequency of past eruptions, the stratigraphic record of eruptive and related activity needs to be dated accurately. A variety of methods are available, and their uses and limitations have been reviewed in several recent publications (Goudie, 1981; Grootes, 1983; Mahaney, 1984; Bradley, 1985; Pierce, 1986; Easterbrook, 1988) from which information has been taken for this summary.

The following discussion is limited to dating techniques used in volcanic terranes (Table 3.4). Some of the techniques in Table 3.4 have been used widely, et al. are largely experimental but show promise. Dating techniques fall into several categories (Pierce, 1986). Numerical-age methods are based on processes that do not require calibration and yield quantitative age estimates. Relative-age methods provide information on the magnitude of age differences between deposits. Some relative-age methods can be calibrated using numerical-age methods and in turn be used to estimate numerical ages. Correlation methods rely on recognition that a feature correlates with a feature or event of known age.

Numerical-age methods: Several numerical-age methods provide the most accurate dating available; brief discussion of the most commonly used methods is given below.

Historical records, as discussed previously, are valuable but not everywhere available, long, accurate, or complete.

Dendrochronology (Fritts, 1976) is useful where trees develop annual growth rings and can provide accurate ($\pm$ 1 year) ages for volcanic events (Brantley et al., 1986). Tephra falls (Yamaguchi, 1983, 1985), lahars (Cameron and Pringle, 1987), and climatically induced debris flows on volcanoes (Ostercamp and Hupp, 1987) have been dated by counting the number of growth rings that post-date damage inflicted on a tree by an event. The most accurate dating employs cross-dating techniques, in which a series of ring-width variations from an affected tree is compared to a control series derived from nearby unaffected trees (Yamaguchi, 1985; Figure 3.5).

TABLE 3.4. Techniques used or of potential use in dating volcanic events younger than 25,000 yr. Modified from Pierce (1986). Methods indicated by asterisk (*) are widely applicable.

Numerical Methods		Relative-Dating Methods		Correlation Methods
Annual	Radiometric and radiologic	Simple process	Complex process	
Historical records*	Carbon-14*	Obsidian hydration	Soil development*	Stratigraphy*
Dendrochronology*	Thermoluminescence and electron-spin resonance	Lichenometry	Rock and mineral weathering*	Tephrostratigraphy*
Varves	Uranium-series	Amino-acid racemization	Progressive landform modification*	Paleomagnetism
	Potassium-argon			Fossils and artifacts
	Argon-argon		Rate of deposition	
	Fission track			
	Cosmogenic isotopes other than C-14			

Matching of the series avoids errors caused by missing rings in the damaged trees. Cross-dating can also be used to date the time of death of standing dead trees or logs (even if carbonized) contained in volcanic deposits if a sufficiently long control record exists from living trees. A control record can also be extended beyond the age of living trees by using cross-dating techniques on trees contained in progressively older deposits; these records can then be used to date deposits thousands of years old.

Minimum tree-ring ages come from determining the age of the oldest tree growing on a deposit. The time necessary for trees to begin growing on a deposit depends on distance from a seed source and growing conditions. Other uncertainties of this minimum-age method include finding the oldest tree and acquiring the skill to core to the center of large trees. The useful range of the method is limited by the life expectancy of the local types of trees.

Varves, or annually laminated lacustrine sediments, have not been used widely to date volcanic events but could be useful in glacierized areas that contain lakes and in areas that produce biologic or geochemical varves. The rate of pollen influx in lake sediments has been used to determine the duration and time of year of tephra falls and also the time interval between successive tephra falls (Mehringer et al., 1977; Blinman et al., 1979; Mehringer, 1985).

Radiocarbon dating is an especially useful technique for dating volcanic deposits in the age range of interest for most volcanic-hazard assessments--the past 10,000 yr--and has been used more widely than other techniques. Lava flows (Lockwood and Lipman, 1980) and many types of fragmental volcanic deposits are hot enough to convert wood and other organic material to charcoal and other forms of carbon that can be preserved for a long time. Lahar, flood, and tephra deposits may also contain or bury organic material appropriate for dating. Generally ten or more grams of sample are needed for traditional radiocarbon analysis; however, newly developed techniques that use accelerator mass spectrometry (AMS) are capable of dating milligram-size samples (Grootes, 1983). The scant organic material in desert varnish on exposed clasts has also been radiocarbon-dated by AMS (Dorn et al., 1986) and provides a new technique for use on volcanic deposits in arid regions.

Several factors influence the usefulness of radiocarbon dating. The stratigraphic context of a sample is especially important. Samples that underlie or overlie a deposit can provide only maximum or minimum limiting ages, respectively. Even organic matter collected from a deposit may be tens to hundreds of years older than the deposit; this is especially true of wood from the centers of centuries-old trees. Material that provides the most unambiguous ages include

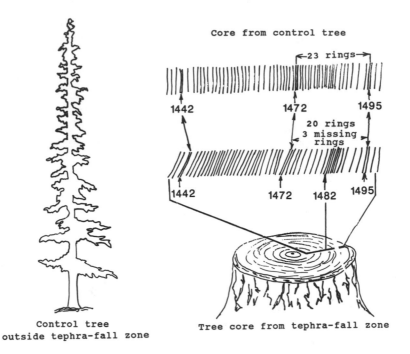

Fig. 3.5. Diagram illustrating the principle of cross-dating and identification of missing rings in tree affected by eruption (from Brantley et al., 1986). The control tree has 23 annual rings formed between 1472 (all dates are A.D.) and 1495, which are years that in this region are known to be represented by anomalously thin rings due to severe climatic conditions. The tree in the tephra-fall zone has only 20 rings from this interval. The series of missing and narrow rings in the damaged tree starting with the 1482 ring were caused by the tephra fall of 1482. Because of the missing rings, a date for this event determined solely by counting back to the earliest ring of a series of narrow rings in the damaged tree would be 3 years too young. In many cases, sophisticated statistical techniques must be used to develop and compare time series of ring-width variations.

small twigs, leaves, needles, cones, or seeds. Second, material can yield misleading ages if samples are contaminated by carbon that has a different radiocarbon content (Figure 3.6). This can occur either while a sample is in place or during or after collection. Regardless of a sample's age, contamination by carbon that contains no radiocarbon increases an age by 80 yr for each percent of contamination. A greater potential problem is contamination by carbon that has more radiocarbon than the sample, thus making an age too young. This is especially true for samples more than a few tens of thousands of years old, in which contamination with the equivalent of one percent or less of modern carbon can affect ages by thousands to tens of thousands of years.

Natural variations in the radiocarbon content of the atmosphere create an additional uncertainty in the interpretation of some radiocarbon ages. Figure 3.7A shows the general relationship between radiocarbon years and sidereal, or calendar, years for the past 12,000 years. Note that for the past 3000 years no more than a few centuries separate radiocarbon and calendar years, whereas prior to that time radiocarbon ages underestimate the calendar age by as much as

1000 yr. Figure 3.7B shows the detailed relationship between radiocarbon years and calendar years for the past 1000 yr. A special issue of the journal Radiocarbon (Stuiver and Kra, 1986) contains reports that show how to calibrate radiocarbon ages for various time intervals during the past 13,300 radiocarbon yr. The corrections for ages older than 13,300 years have not yet been determined.

Potassium-argon and $^{40}argon/^{39}argon$ dating is applied widely to volcanic deposits but generally does not provide reliable ages for material of interest to volcanic-hazard studies (typically less than a few tens of thousands of years old). Exceptions are some potassium-rich phases, such as sanidine, but at best the analytical uncertainties of the ages range from 10-75 percent. Likewise, *fission-track dating* is of limited use with young volcanic deposits.

Uranium-series dating has been applied widely to carbonate materials of Quaternary age; the dating of volcanic rocks has been much more problematic and subject to considerable debate (Condomines, 1978; Capaldi and Pece, 1981; Ivanovich and Harmon, 1982; Hemond and Condomines, 1985; Capaldi et al., 1985). Some ages agree well with those obtained by other

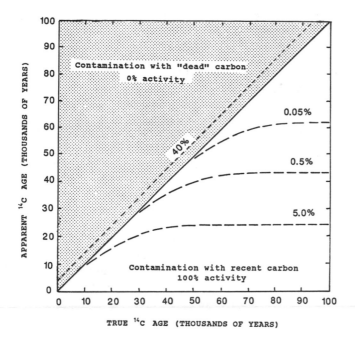

Fig. 3.6. Unequal effects of contamination of samples for radiocarbon dating with various amounts of recent and "dead" (no ^{14}C) carbon (from Grootes, 1983, and Pierce, 1986). For contamination with dead carbon (shaded area), effect is a simple ratio as shown by the line for 40% contamination. However, for contamination with recent carbon, the effect is nonlinear and older ages are affected more than younger ages.

methods, but others do not. The lack of closed-system behavior of U and Th in magmatic and postmagmatic processes is thought to cause the inconsistencies.

Thermoluminescence (TL) and *electron-spin-resonance (ESR)* dating methods rely on measuring the radiation dose that a sample has received since an event such as transport, crystallization, exposure to sunlight, heating, or faulting. TL is an established technique for use in fine-grained sediments, especially loess, (Wintle and Huntley, 1982). However, it has not been as successful in dating tephra because of problems in the stability of the TL signal in high-temperature feldspars and the deleterious effects of hydration on the TL signal of glass (Berger, 1985, 1988). The technique holds promise, especially where volcanic deposits are interbedded with loess or other fine-grained deposits that can be dated (Berger, 1987). TL has also been used with uneven results to date lava flows in Italy (Hwang, 1971) and Hawaii (May, 1979). More reliable results are possible by dating both the lava flow and enclosing deposits, such as baked sediments below the flow (Gillot et al., 1979).

ESR dating is rapidly developing but has been used only sparingly for young volcanic material (for example, Imai et al., 1985).

Several *cosmogenic isotopes* that accumulate through time in soils and sediments occur in low abundances but can be measured by accelerator mass spectroscopy. They are being investigated for use as dating methods and may be useful in the future.

Relative-age methods. Relative-age-dating methods are based on physical, biological, or chemical processes whose rates are controlled by conditions such as climate, chemical composition, and species effects. They determine the relative-age differences among deposits and, when calibrated by some numerical technique, an estimate of numerical ages.

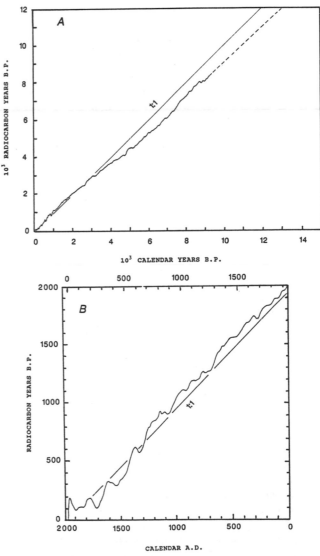

Fig. 3.7. Relationship between radiocarbon years and calendar, or sidereal, years. **A.** Generalized curve for the past 12,000 yr constructed from data in several papers in Stuiver and Kra (1986). **B.** Detailed calibration curve for A.D. part of time scale (from Stuiver and Pearson, 1986).

Obsidian-hydration dating is based on the rate of hydration of obsidian along cracks and surfaces, which is a function of chemical composition and temperature (Friedman and Obradovich, 1981). The method can be used for obsidian lava flows and domes and obsidian fragments in tephra-fall and pyroclastic-flow deposits, lahars, alluvium, and till. A major source of uncertainty for determining calibrated numerical ages is the temperature history of a sample; however this problem is less important for samples of Holocene age that have not been subjected to major climatic changes since deposition.

Lichenometry is based on the rate of growth of certain species of lichens on boulders or barren rock substrates in alpine and Arctic terrains (Locke et al., 1979). Growth curves must be developed for each region and species of interest by measuring diameters of individuals living on a substrate of known age. The age of senescence of various lichens limits the usefulness of the technique to the past few thousand years or less. Uncertainties in evaluating factors that govern lichen survival and growth are significant. Despite its shortcomings and limited use to date, lichenometry could be useful in some volcanic-hazard studies.

Several *weathering techniques* are used widely as relative-age methods, including degree of soil development and degree of etching of mineral grains in soils (Birkeland, 1984), thickness of weathering rinds on volcanic clasts in soil B horizons (Colman and Pierce, 1981; Colman, 1981), and ratios of cations in desert varnish on surface stones (Dorn, 1983). Such weathering techniques provide estimates of the time represented by weathering profiles within a sequence of volcanic deposits. The latter two are amenable to calibration; however, numerous environmental factors affect rates of weathering and lead to large uncertainties.

Other relative-age methods are based on *degree of landform modification* caused by erosional processes. Wood (1980) studied the progressive degradation of scoria cones. Significant advances have been made in understanding the rates and controlling factors of the modification of scarps produced by faulting, shoreline processes, and streams in unconsolidated deposits (Nash, 1986; Keller, 1986); in some instances calibrated models provide numerical-age estimates.

Correlation methods. Correlation of an event or feature with one of known age can provide reliable and precise age control. Tracing or other forms of physical stratigraphic correlation are used in nearly all studies of eruptive history. Several other techniques are invaluable in local and regional correlations.

Tephrochronology is widely used in volcanic stratigraphy, as tephra layers can be used to demonstrate time equivalence of strata over short or long distances (Thorarinsson, 1981). Recognition of specific tephra layers typically requires petrochemical information (Sarna-Wojcicki et al., 1983), but around a given volcanic center having diverse products, reliable identification can often be made with relatively inexpensive petrographic techniques (Mullineaux, 1986).

Paleomagnetism provides several types of dating control for volcanic and related sedimentary deposits, but the one of greatest significance for volcanic-hazard studies is based on *secular variations of the Earth's magnetic field*. Magnetic mineral grains in lava flows (Champion, 1980) and in clasts in pyroclastic-flow deposits (Hoblitt et al., 1985) record the direction of the magnetic field as they cool below their Curie temperatures after coming to rest. Secular variations in field direction and intensity have occurred throughout latest Pleistocene and Holocene time as recorded in lake sediments (Banerjee, 1983; Verosub, 1988). However, because these variations occur with periodicities on the order of hundreds to thousands of years, the field may have had the same direction several times during the past 10,000-20,000 yr. Therefore, a deposit can not be dated solely on its paleomagnetic-field direction. Even though secular-variation techniques can not usually provide reliable ages, field directions can be an important characteristic for correlating units. For example, units with different field directions cannot be of the same age, successive units with the same direction are likely all close in age, two sequences of units that have the same succession of directions are likely correlative, and so forth.

Fossils and artifacts have had limited use in dating young volcanic deposits. Pollen has been used in studies of tephra falls. Climatically-induced vegetation changes during the past 10,000-20,000 years have altered the types and amount of pollen accumulating in a given area and thus provide a basis for dating volcanic deposits intercalated with pollen-bearing sediments. Such a method has not been used widely but is currently being developed and used in the Colombian Andes (Salomons, 1986). Artifacts associated with volcanic deposits can also provide age information.

Volcanic-hazards Assessments Based on Eruptive History

A major goal of long-term volcanic-hazards assessments is to provide information that can be incorporated into decisions about future land use, because, once established, land-use patterns are difficult to change (Crandell and Mullineaux, 1975; Crandell et al., 1979, 1984). With an assessment available, locations and designs of transportation systems, critical facilities, and major engineering works can be selected with a realistic understanding of potential volcanic hazards, and high-risk areas can be avoided. In many places, especially in volcanic areas in low latitudes, large populations and important installations are already located in volcanically hazardous areas; however, assessments are still important for land-use planning.

Another significant role for long-term hazard assessments is in developing measures to mitigate the effects of future eruptions. Information about types of events, probable magnitudes, and areas affected is needed to properly and economically design protective structures. This same information is needed to develop emergency-response plans for future or immediate volcanic crises. For example, selecting safe and effective evacuation routes and temporary shelters requires a complete understanding of the potential types of eruptions and the areas that are likely to be affected by them.

Once an eruption begins, information obtained through studies of past eruptions, especially their course and duration, is crucial for appraising longer-term needs, such as relocation of people, flood protection from eruption-impacted stream channels, water quality, and food production.

Reasonably detailed records of eruptive and related activity, reconstructed using the techniques outlined in the preceding sections, are available for many volcanoes and provide the basis for hazards assessments and zonation (Table 3.5). In identifying potential hazards from such a record, most investigators have assumed that the future behavior of a volcano will be similar to its past behavior in terms of the type, frequency, and magnitude of events. Thus, an assessment of hazards on Etna volcano, which during the past few centuries has produced many lava flows accompanied by small explosive eruptions, focuses on such eruptions as the most likely to occur in the future (Guest and Murray, 1979). Decisions are more complex on volcanoes with a wider variety of eruption types and scales, such as Mount St. Helens, which has experienced large explosive Plinian eruptions as well as small eruptions of domes and mafic tephra and lava flows (Table 3.3; Crandell and Mullineaux, 1978). In either case, several shortcomings of this method need to be understood both by the people producing a hazard assessment and the people using it. These shortcomings can be illustrated by using the eruptive record of Mount St. Helens (Table 3.3), which is one of the most complete eruptive records over a 10^4-yr interval available.

1) The farther back in time a record is extended, the less complete it is likely to be. Thus, eruptions may have occurred during the apparent 15,000-yr dormant interval between Mount St. Helens' first two recognized eruptive periods, but the record of these events has not been preserved or found. Times of landscape instability during major climatic changes of the late Pleistocene may partly explain the absence of evidence of eruptions during this time.
2) Eruptive behavior of a volcano may change over time, so that past behavior is not necessarily a reliable predictor of future behavior. An apparently abrupt change occurred at Mount St. Helens about 2000 yr ago during the Castle Creek eruptive period. Basalt lava flows and related tephras of limited extent began to be erupted in addition to the more explosive dacitic eruptions. Such a change would not have been expected at that time based on previous activity.
3) Events may occur of a magnitude unprecedented in the eruptive history of a volcano, such as the debris avalanche and directed blast of 18 May 1980 at Mount St. Helens.
4) A volcano can grow and change shape, and consequently alter the likelihood of areas being affected by various events. For example, the growth of a volcano can fill valleys and engulf drainage divides, thereby directing pyroclastic flows and lahars down previously unaffected valleys. Major topographic changes such as those caused

by the 1980 sector collapse of Mount St. Helens modified the expectable routes of future flowage events enough that the existing hazard assessment was revised (Miller et al., 1981).

Some shortcomings of using past behavior as a guide to future activity can be eliminated by modifying forecasts to include events that have occurred at other volcanoes of similar composition and structure. Thus, directed blasts at Bezymianny in 1956 and Mount St. Helens in 1980 and large sector collapses at those and other volcanoes (Siebert et al., 1987) have profoundly influenced views of potential hazards at andesitic and dacitic composite volcanoes. Such low-probability, large-magnitude events can be incorporated into a hazard assessment even though unprecedented at a particular volcano (Crandell and Hoblitt, 1986). Moreover an understanding of the more frequently observed types of eruptive behavior at many different volcanoes is also beneficial in gaining a fuller appreciation of potential hazards.

Many volcanic-hazards assessments develop scenarios (Warrick, 1979) of likely types of future eruptions based on the eruptive record. Often several past eruptions of different type or magnitude are chosen to illustrate the range of activity possible (Miller et al., 1982; Rosi and Santacroce, 1984). Such scenarios describe possible precursory activity and the succession of events during an eruption or a sequence of eruptions. They also show the areas that would be affected by eruptive products. Their greatest value is in providing officials with a more concrete idea of the possible consequences of an eruption and thereby aiding them in planning proper response measures.

Volcanic-Hazards-Zonation Maps

Information about long-term volcanic hazards gained from detailed studies of the eruptive history of a volcano and the behavior of similar volcanoes can be presented in several formats. A volcanic-hazard-zonation map is perhaps the most useful. Such a map should delimit the zone of hazard related to each type of event and should also show relative degree of hazard. With sufficient details, more quantitative expressions of the degree of hazard are possible, such as the probability of future impact. A map prepared on an appropriate base can be readily used for land-use planning. It can also be used by scientists and governmental authorities to identify critical facilities, transportation routes, population centers, and other key features with regard to hazard zones, and to develop volcanic-risk maps. Citizens can use a hazard-zonation map to judge for themselves the relation between hazardous areas and their daily activities, and to identify places that could offer refuge during an eruption. Maps of varying degrees of detail have been prepared for numerous volcanoes (Table 3.5).

The extent of a lava flow, pyroclastic density current, or lahar is dependent on several variables, including volume, mobility, velocity, and flow transformations, which are all

TABLE 3.5. List of volcanic-hazards assessments and zonation maps. o, preliminary or map without detailed topographic base (many are sketch maps in reports); x, map is on detailed topographic base.

Country or region	Volcano or area	Hazard-zonation map	References
Italy	Phlegraean Fields	o	Rosi and Santacroce (1984)
	Vesuvius	o	Barberi et al. (1983)
	Etna	o	Guest and Murray (1979)
New Zealand	Mount Egmont	x	Neall (1982)
	Ruapehu	o	Houghton et al. (1987)
	Auckland field	o	Searle (1964)
			Cassidy et al. (1986)
	North Island		Dibble et al. (1985)
Papua New Guinea	Rabaul caldera	o	McKee et al. (1985)
	Karkar	o	Lowenstein (1982)
	Uluwan	x	McKee (1983)
	Langila	x	Talai (1987)
	Manam	x	de Saint Ours (1982)
	Papua New Guinea (entire country)	o	Lowenstein (1982); Lowenstein and Talai (1984)
Indonesia	Merapi	x	Pardyanto et al. (1978); Kusumadinata (1984)
	Kelut	x	Alzwar (1985); Hamidi et al. (1985)
	Lokon-Empung	x	Matahelumual (1986)
	Semeru	o	Suryo (1986)
	Banda-Api	x	Matahelumual (1988)
Philippines	Mayon	o	Peña and Newhall (1984)
Japan	Fuji	o	Shimozuru (1983)
	Asama	o	Aramaki (1984)
Soviet Union	Kamchatka	o	Markhinin et al. (1962)
United States	Mount Baker	x	Hyde and Crandell (1978)
	Glacier Peak	o	Beget (1983)
	Mount Rainier	x	Crandell and Mullineaux (1967); Crandell (1973)
	Mount Adams	o	Vallance (in press)
	Mount St. Helens	x	Crandell and Mullineaux (1978); Miller et al. (1981)
	Mount Hood	x	Crandell (1980)
	Mount Shasta	x	Miller (1980)
	Lassen Peak	o	Crandell and Mullineaux (1970)
	Mono-Inyo Craters	o	Miller et al. (1982)
	Mount St. Augustine	x	Kienle and Swanson (1980)
	Island of Maui	x	Crandell (1983)
	State of Hawaii	o	Mullineaux et al. (1987)
	State of Washington	x	Crandell (1976)

TABLE 3.5 (continued).

Country or region	Volcano or area	Hazard-zonation map	References
	State of California	x	Miller (in press)
	Western U.S.	x	Mullineaux (1976)
	Pacific Northwest	x	Hoblitt et al. (1987)
Mexico/Guatemala	Tacaná	x	Rose and Mercado (1986)
Guatemala	Santiaguito	o	Rose et al. (1988)
	Pacaya	o	Banks (1987b)
Colombia	Nevado del Ruíz	x	Parra et al. (1986)
	Nevado del Huila	x	Cepeda et al. (1986)
Ecuador	Cotopaxi	x	Miller et al. (1978); Hall and von Hillebrandt (1988a,b)
	Tungurahua	o	Hall and Vera (1985)
Lesser Antilles	Mont Pelée	x	Westercamp and Traineau (1983) Westercamp (1983, 1984)
	Soufrière de Guadeloupe	x	Westercamp (1980, 1981a,b, 1983, 1984)
Azores	São Miguel	x	Booth (1979); Booth et al. (1983); Forjaz (1985)

difficult to forecast. Therefore, the boundaries between hazard zones shown on hazard maps are only approximately located and gradational. Both of these points must be emphasized by those who make hazard maps and understood by those who use them. For example, the degree of hazard for flowage phenomena decreases gradually in a downstream direction and more rapidly with height above valley floors (Figure 3.8). Although not yet widely used for volcanic-hazards maps, numerous cartographic techniques are available for showing gradational boundaries and uncertainties, such as varying color intensity or screening patterns.

Hazard Zonation for Various Types of Events

Some of the techniques that have been used to delimit hazard zones are briefly reviewed below.

Tephra falls. Hazard zonation for tephra falls is based on the frequency and magnitude (expressed as total volume of tephra or more often as thickness versus distance away from a vent) of past tephra falls and regional wind patterns. Figure 3.9 shows the tephra-hazard zonation for Mount St. Helens, a volcano that produced numerous tephra falls of varied sizes during late Quaternary time (Crandell and Mullineaux, 1978). The zones reflect the thickness-distance relations of three past

falls of representative sizes and the wind patterns in the Pacific Northwest. The boundaries of the zones are placed arbitrarily at distances of 30, 100, and 200 km from the volcano and aid users in locating areas with respect to potential tephra thicknesses. The shape of the hazard zones takes into account the dominant wind directions and speeds. Other workers have defined circular zones at varying distances and have identified the sectors toward which the wind blows most frequently (for example, Beget, 1983). In either case, authors need to inform users that a future tephra fall will probably cover only a relatively narrow sector of a hazard zone. Considering the area of downwind (>200 km) thickening (Sarna-Wojcicki et al., 1981a) and the effects of even thin tephra accumulations during the 18 May 1980 eruption of Mount St. Helens (Warrick, 1981; Schuster, 1981, 1983), zonation maps should probably be extended to cover distal areas as well.

Detailed studies of volcanoes that have produced many tephra falls in the recent geologic past can provide a large enough statistical sample to estimate numerical probabilities of tephra accumulations (Booth, 1979; Booth et al., 1983).

Numerical models are being developed for use in estimating the extent and thickness of potential tephra falls (Armienti et al., 1988) and may aid in delimiting tephra-hazard zones. The input to the models includes wind data, eruption rate and

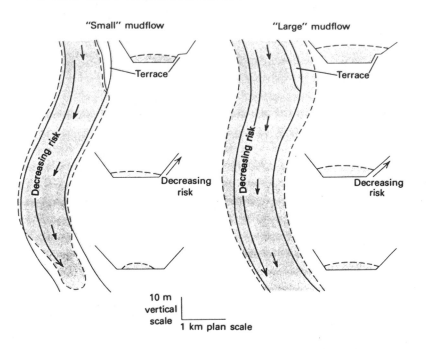

Fig. 3.8. Diagrammatic maps and cross sections of hypothetical small and large lahars (mudflows), showing changing relative risk (long arrows) with distance downvalley (short arrows) and height above valley floors. The shaded areas show maximum extent and height reached by lahars. Diagram from Crandell (1980; Fig. 19).

duration, column height, grain-size distribution and settling velocities of the tephra, and various coefficients. The uncertainties related to selection of inputs seriously limit the method. The value of the tephra-dispersal models, including those that focus on maximum-size parameters (Carey and Sigurdsson, 1986; Carey and Sparks, 1986), is probably more significant for understanding eruption processes and dynamics than for hazard zonation.

Short-term forecasting of tephra hazards employs the same techniques as do long-term forecasts but may consider a narrower range of eruption sizes based on the current state of the volcano and an up-to-date forecast of wind directions and strengths. Miller et al. (1981) and Crandell et al. (1984) describe the method used to produce daily forecasts at Mount St. Helens in 1980.

Lava flows. Hazard zones for lava flows are based on the frequency with which areas have been covered by lava flows in the recent geologic past, likely vent areas for future lava flows, lengths and areas of lava flows typical for a volcano or type of volcano, and topographic considerations that make an area more or less likely to be inundated by lava flows. Hazard-zonation maps have been completed for several volcanoes whose dominant eruptive products are lava flows including Etna volcano, (Guest and Murray, 1979), and Haleakala volcano (Crandell, 1983), as well as for fields of monogenetic volcanoes, such as Auckland, New Zealand (Searle, 1964).

The hazard zonation for lava flows on the island of Hawaii (Figure 3.10; Mullineaux et al., 1987) relied on a large amount of geologic (Holcomb, 1987; Lockwood and Lipman, 1987; Moore et al., 1987) and age (Rubin et al., 1987) information. Such data bases could be used to determine numerical probabilities of an area being covered by a lava flow. Models of the magma supply to a volcanic system that are constrained by geologic, petrologic, age, and geophysical data can also aid in long-term forecasts, especially if they elucidate cyclic behavior (for example, Kuntz et al., 1986).

Zonation techniques for lava-flow hazards at composite volcanoes, on which lava flows pose just one of many types of flowage hazards, rely on data similar to that outlined above. However, the statistical sample of young lava flows on such volcanoes is typically much smaller than for large shield volcanoes. Therefore, meaningful numerical probabilities can not be calculated, although some distinction of the relative degree of hazard is usually possible. For many composite volcanoes, lava flows represent a much less extensive hazard than pyroclastic flows and surges, which are much more mobile. Therefore hazard zones for pyroclastic flows on many hazard maps incorporate hazard zones for lava flows. Such an approach may be useful for a long-term land-use decisions, but has shortcomings for response to a volcanic emergency. For example, if a lava-flow eruption were forecast or began, map users would want to have more specific information about

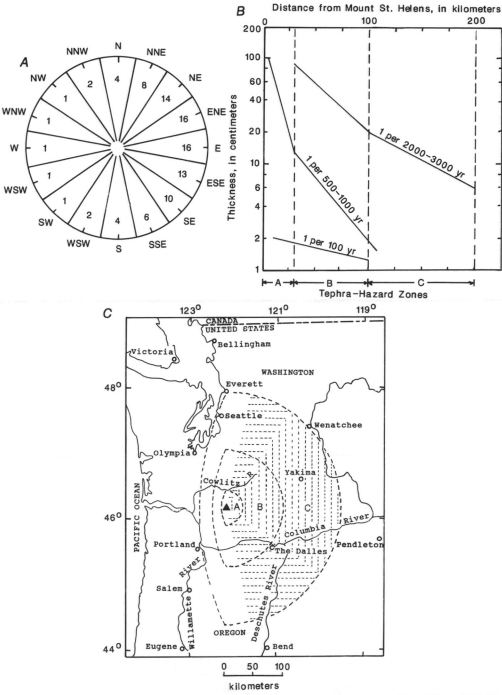

Fig. 3.9. Preparation of map of tephra-hazard zones for Mount St. Helens (from Crandell and Mullineaux, 1978; Figs. 8, 9, and 10). **A.** Wind data for altitudes between 3 and 16 km. Approximate percentage of time, annually, that the wind blows toward various sectors in western Washington. **B.** Expectable tephra-fall thicknesses in hazard zones 30, 100, and 200 km downwind from the volcano. Thicknesses are based on tephra falls of about 1, 0.1, and 0.01 km^3 that have occurred at Mount St. Helens during past 4500 yr with the estimated indicated frequencies. **C.** Tephra-hazard zones. Extension of zones farther to east than west reflects prevailing winds that blow dominantly toward the east; also, winds that blow toward west are weaker than those toward east. Winds blow toward sectors with patterns 80% of time and toward vertically lined sector 50% of time.

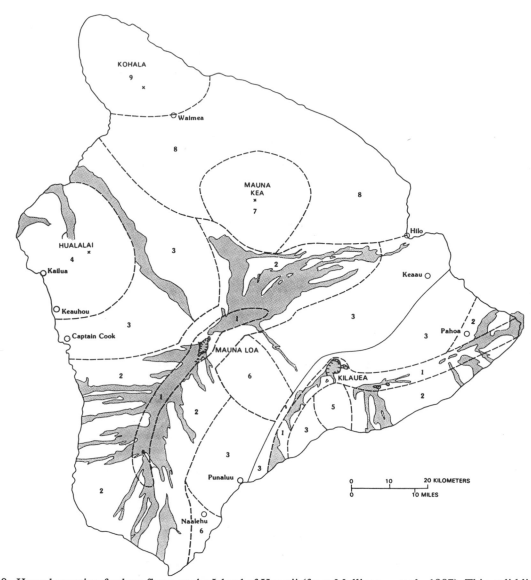

Fig. 3.10. Hazard zonation for lava flows on the Island of Hawaii (from Mullineaux et al., 1987). Thin solid line marks boundary between Mauna Loa and Kilauea volcanoes. Stipple pattern indicates areas covered by pre-1975 historical lava flows. Explanation of zones of decreasing hazard follows: **1.** Summit areas and active rift zones of Mauna Loa and Kilauea in which more than 25% of the land surface has been covered by lava flows during historical time--the 19th and 20th centuries. A large majority of future lava flows will originate in zone 1. **2.** Areas adjacent to and downslope from area 1 that are subject to burial by lava flows of even small volume erupted from vents in zone 1. In the area south of the east rift zone of Kilauea as much as 25% of the surface has been covered by lava flows during historical time and 10-15% has been covered since 1950. On Mauna Loa, about 20% of this zone has been covered by lava flows. **3.** Less than 5% of this zone on Kilauea and 1-3% of this zone on Mauna Loa has been covered by lava flows during historical time. However, more than 75% on Kilauea and 15-20% on Mauna Loa has been covered during the past 750 yr. **4.** Hualalai volcano has been less active than Kilauea and Mauna Loa during historical time, and less than 15% of this zone was covered during the past 750 yr. **5.** More than half of this area on the lower south flank of Kilauea has been covered by lava flows during the past 750 yr, but it is presently protected from lava flows by the geometry of Kilauea caldera and several upslope-facing fault scarps. **6.** These two areas on Mauna Loa contain the oldest lava flows exposed on the surface of the volcano and are not expected to be affected in the near future. However, the hazard could increase greatly if the summit caldera were to fill with lava. **7.** About 20% of the summit and upper flanks of Mauna Kea were covered by lava flows between 3500 and 5000 yr ago, but none have occurred since. **8.** The lower flanks of Mauna Kea have not been affected by lava flows during the past 10,000 yr, but an unusually long lava flow from the summit region could reach this zone. **9.** No eruption has occurred on Kohala volcano for about 60,000 yr, but even though the hazard there is extremely low, the volcano should not be regarded as extinct.

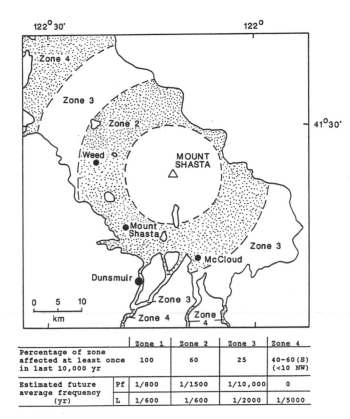

Fig. 3.11. Hazard zones for pyroclastic flows and lahars at Mount Shasta, California (from Crandell et al., 1984; after Miller, 1980). The boundaries lie 10, 20, and 30 km from the summit. Unshaded areas within the zones and beyond the irregular boundaries of the zones are topographically high and judged to be too high to be affected by future pyroclastic flows and lahars.

		Zone 1	Zone 2	Zone 3	Zone 4
Percentage of zone affected at least once in last 10,000 yr		100	60	25	40-60(S) (<10 NW)
Estimated future average frequency (yr)	Pf	1/800	1/1500	1/10,000	0
	L	1/600	1/600	1/2000	1/5000

likely locations of vents and expected paths and lengths of lava flows. Such information would be lacking if the hazard-zonation for lava flows were combined with that for more extensive and mobile pyroclastic flows and surges.

Pyroclastic flows and surges. Hazard zones for pyroclastic flows and surges vary greatly among volcanoes, owing to the great range in energy of such events. Some previous workers have defined one or more hazard zones on the basis of the extent of pyroclastic flows and surges of historical age (Merapi volcano, Indonesia, Pardyanto et al., 1978; Mayon volcano, Philippines, Peña and Newhall, 1984) or of some other appropriate time interval. For example, Crandell and Mullineaux (1978) chose the past 4500 yr at Mount St. Helens, a time of relatively frequent eruptive activity after a dormant interval of thousands of years. Other workers defined two or three zones of different degrees of hazard on the basis of either possible shifts in vent location (Mount Hood, Oregon; Crandell, 1980) or several model events for past pyroclastic

flows or surges of different sizes and frequencies (Figure 3.11; for example, Mount Shasta, California; Miller, 1980; Soufrière de Guadeloupe, French West Indies; Westercamp, 1980, 1981a, 1981b, 1983, 1984; Asama volcano, Japan; Aramaki, 1984; Rabaul caldera, Papua New Guinea; McKee et al., 1985; Phlegraean Fields, Italy; Rosi and Santacroce, 1984; Nevado del Ruíz volcano, Colombia; Parra et al., 1986).

Model events developed for one volcano can be applied to hazard zonation at other comparable volcanoes, taking into account differences in vent location, topography, and other factors. Zonation at volcanoes with poorly preserved deposits, or at those that are little studied but require rapid zonation during an emergency, can take advantage of this method. The height-to-length ratios of various types of pyroclastic flows can be used to estimate potential runout distances and therefore the dimensions of hazard zones for pyroclastic flows and surges (for example, Miller, 1980).

More sophisticated computer-assisted models that use height-to-length ratios (energy-line or energy-cone methods) can generate maps of the potential extent of various types of events, which can serve as hazard-zonation maps (Malin and Sheridan, 1982). Such maps have been prepared for pyroclastic surges at several volcanoes in Italy (Sheridan and Malin, 1983; Armienti and Pareschi, 1987). Selection of the height above a vent at which surges might be generated and of an appropriate slope of the energy line or cone create uncertainties in this method. However, the method can be used to check the soundness of field reconstructions and the boundaries of hazard zones that were based on the extent of past pyroclastic flows and surges. For example, significant changes in the height of an edifice would greatly affect the potential extent of pyroclastic flows and surges, but the edifice height at the time of a given eruption is not always known. A check by either a computer model or simple height-to-length ratios could indicate if boundaries were reasonable in light of the current topography.

Laterally directed blasts. Hazard zones for laterally directed blasts are difficult to define on the basis of past activity because (1) they are rare and may not have occurred at a given volcano, (2) their deposits are typically thin and easily eroded or difficult to interpret, and (3) they range widely in magnitude. Crandell (1980), Crandell et al. (1984), and Crandell and Hoblitt (1986) discuss the techniques and rationale for establishing hazard zones for directed blasts using historical events as models. Large directed blasts such as those at Bezymianny in 1956 and Mount St. Helens in 1980 were caused by the unloading of a magmatic and hydrothermal system by collapse of a large sector of the volcano. The blasts affected hundreds of square kilometers in a broad sector extending 25-35 km from the volcano. Therefore, hazard zones for such events can be circles of 35-km radius centered on the volcano (Figure 3.12). In the event of precursory or eruptive activity, structural changes or deformation of an edifice could indicate sectors most prone to hazards from directed blasts. At that time, more specific hazard zonation would be possible. If volcanoes were

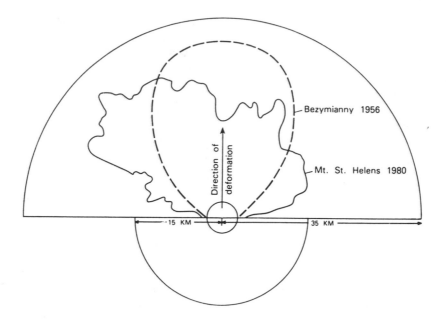

Fig. 3.12. Areas affected by two historical lateral blasts and suggested extent of a lateral-blast hazard zone for short-term planning based on these events and their precursory deformation (from Crandell and Hoblitt, 1986). The larger semicircle of 35-km radius encloses area of principal danger from pyroclastic density currents. A smaller semicircle of 15-km radius encloses area of possible impact of ballistic particles. For long-term planning, a full circle of 35-km radius could be used.

buttressed or shaped in such a way that a sector collapse and resulting explosion were unlikely on certain flanks, then the shape of the hazard zone could be modified.

On the basis of the distribution of ballistic fragments and pyroclastic-flow and surge deposits from laterally directed blasts at growing domes, Crandell and Hoblitt (1986) suggested that hazard zones for such events be a circle with a radius of 10 km, with an additional margin of safety of up to 5 km, centered on a dome or expected site of a dome (Figure 3.12). The shape of zones can be modified for domes from which blasts could have only certain orientations.

Debris avalanches and lahars. Hazard zones for debris avalanches and lahars, like those for pyroclastic flows and surges, have commonly been based on the extent and frequency of such events on the volcano of concern. Most workers have developed zones showing relative degrees of hazard based on frequency-magnitude relations. On maps that portray hazard zones for all types of flowage phenomena, lahar- and related flood-hazard zones typically extend down valleys several times farther than hazard zones for pyroclastic flows and surges (Figure 3.13). Examples include hazard-zonation maps for Mount Baker (Hyde and Crandell, 1978) and Glacier Peak (Beget, 1983), United States; Cotopaxi, Ecuador (Miller et al., 1978; Hall and von Hillebrandt, 1988a, 1988b); Nevado del Ruíz, Colombia (Parra et al., 1986); and Ruapehu, New Zealand (Houghton et al., 1987).

In contrast to hazards from pyroclastic flows and related surges, which can affect areas high above valley floors far from vents, hazards from lahars, lahar-runout flows, and floods have more sharply defined upper limits that typically are restricted to within tens of meters or less of valley floors (Figure 3.8). Studies that reconstruct the inundation levels, velocities, discharges, and flow conditions of past lahars can aid in determining quite precise hazard boundaries along valley floors. Several uncertainties exist, however. For example, the discharge, and therefore the width and depth, of a lahar can change rapidly along its course depending on its mode of origin, grain size, sediment-water ratio, channel geometry, and other factors (Scott, 1988). Also, unless the valley-floor configuration that existed prior to passage of a past lahar is known, it is difficult to estimate the inundation level of a similar lahar given current topography. In addition to evidence from past floods, existing models for flood routing can be used to assess the sizes of floods along streams once a lahar has transformed into a muddy flood flow.

Mathematical models of debris flows currently being developed may eventually lead to methods of defining lahar-hazard zones (for example, Wier, 1982; Mizuyama et al., 1987); however, at present they are not very useful. Most models are handicapped by our limited understanding of the physical processes of debris flows (Iverson and Denlinger, 1987) and the uncertainty of selecting model parameters.

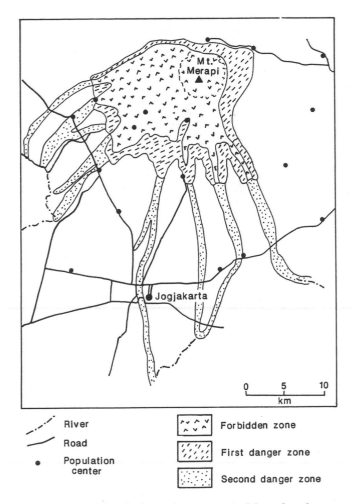

River

Road

Population
center

Forbidden zone

First danger zone

Second danger zone

Fig. 3.13. Volcanic-hazards zones at Merapi volcano, Indonesia (from Kusumadinata, 1984; simplified from Pardyanto et al., 1978). The forbidden zone is subject to pyroclastic flows and surges and thick tephra fall and extends 13 km from the summit, based on the extent of such events during the 1930 eruptions. The first danger zone is subject to ballistic particles, tephra fall, and lahars. The second danger zone is subject to lahars and floods. Rivers shown only outside of hazard zones; finger-like hazard zones follow river valleys. Almost 250,000 people live in these hazard zones.

Hazard-zonation for debris avalanches on many maps has been typically combined with that for lahars. However, a key difference in determining such hazard zones is that large-volume debris avalanches are highly mobile, can rise high on valley walls, and can overtop drainage divides and impact valleys that do not head on a volcano.

Schuster and Crandell (1984) and Siebert et al. (1987) provide data on height-to-length ratios for debris avalanches (see Figure 2.5 in CHAPTER 2) that can aid in estimating extents of future avalanches of various volumes and release points. Crandell (in press) recommends using the relationship, $L=H/f$, to estimate the length (L) of debris avalanches that have volumes greater than 1 km^3 in valleys that head on the volcano. H is the altitude difference between the volcano's summit and the floor of the valley of interest 20 km from the volcano; the distance 20 km is the median length of numerous volcanic debris avalanches with volumes greater than 1 km^3. The selection of values of the coefficient, f, can be based on the degree of conservatism desired for the hazards assessment. For example, Crandell (in press) selected values of f of 0.005, 0.075, and 0.09 to estimate extents of future debris avalanches in valleys heading on Mount Shasta and Mount Rainier.

Volcanic gases. Hazard zones for volcanic gases are typically restricted close to vents and lie within hazard zones for various flowage phenomena and thick tephra fall. More distal gas hazards are associated with tephra falls and are dealt with in tephra-hazard zonations. Gas is the major product of some types of events, especially increased activity at fumarole fields. Special zonation maps for gas hazards have been produced for such areas as the Dieng area of Java (Kusumadinata, 1984). Gas-vent locations, low-lying areas in which dense gases can accumulate, and atmospheric conditions that favor gas accumulation are all reflected in defining hazard zones.

Volcanically induced tsunamis. Hazard zones for volcanically induced tsunamis can be defined on the basis of evidence of past tsunamis, especially historical ones; however, geologic records of such events are typically meager. The limits of hazard zones need to reflect locations and mechanisms of tsunami generation, sizes of the waves produced, and estimated inundation heights along shorelines, which in many historical examples have ranged from several meters to a few tens of meters (Latter, 1981). Numerical models of tsunamis are well advanced compared to those for many volcanic processes and can be used to estimate travel times and wave heights (for example, Kienle et al., 1987). The greatest uncertainty in applying the models to long-term forecasts probably lies in predicting how a wave will be generated and how large it will be initially. However, in some cases of unfolding volcanic crises, for example structural changes that indicate an increased probability of a debris avalanche being generated, a probable mechanism and magnitude could be available for input to a model.

Regional Hazard-Zonation Maps

In addition to hazard-zonation maps of single volcanoes, maps that show the combined hazards from several volcanoes in a region are useful for land-use planning and emergency response. Certain localities may well lie in hazard zones of several volcanoes in the region. A regional map is especially useful for portraying the combined tephra hazards of several volcanoes (Mullineaux, 1976; Shipley and Sarna-Wojcicki, 1983).

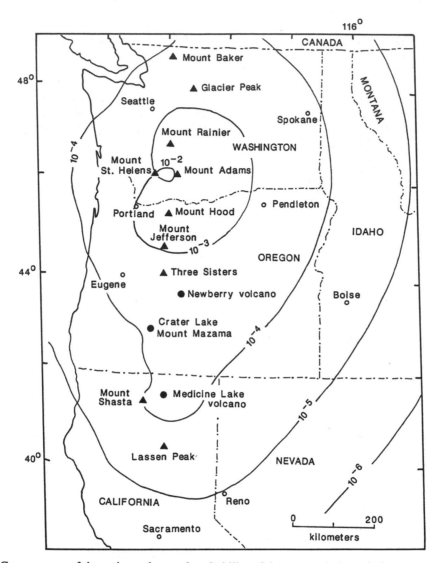

Fig. 3.14. Contour map of the estimated annual probability of the accumulation of 10 cm or more of tephra in the northwestern United States from eruptions at 13 major volcanic centers in the Cascade Range (after Hoblitt et al., 1987).

A regional tephra-hazards map was prepared for the Cascade Range as part of an assessment of potential volcanic hazards to proposed sites for nuclear-power plants by Hoblitt et al. (1987). They mapped order-of-magnitude annual probabilities of tephra falls of 1, 10, and 100 cm in the Pacific Northwest by combining the following: (1) the probabilities of each major composite volcano having a tephra eruption with a volume exceeding 0.01 and 0.1 km^3, (2) a distance-thickness relationship of historical tephra falls from a worldwide sample of eruptions of 0.01-0.1 km^3 of tephra, and (3) the probability of the wind blowing in a given direction based on recent weather records. The map showing the annual probability of accumulation of 10 cm or more of tephra is shown in Figure 3.14. Note that relatively few volcanoes, especially Mount St. Helens, dominate the tephra-fall probabilities of the entire range. Many of the Cascade volcanoes have not produced major tephra falls during the past 10,000 yr.

Hazard-zonation maps have also been prepared for the states of Washington (scale 1:1 million; Crandell, 1976) and California (scale 1:500,000; Miller, in press). They show generalized flowage-hazard and tephra-hazard zones for all potentially active volcanoes and outline regions in which monogenetic volcanoes might erupt. More generalized maps have also been prepared for the Cascade Range (scale 1:2 million, Hoblitt et al., 1987) and the western United States (scale 1:7.5 million, Mullineaux, 1976). Such maps can provide planners and civil authorities with a regional perspective on the distribution of hazard zones in areas under their jurisdiction.

Site-Specific Hazards Maps

Assessments of volcanic hazards have also been prepared for specific sites, especially critical facilities such as dams and nuclear-power plants. Few such reports are available in published form, as most were undertaken by engineering consultants for developers; however, an assessment of the volcanic hazards at the Trojan Nuclear Power Plant, which is located 50 km west of Mount St. Helens, was published by the State of Oregon following the 1980 eruption of Mount St. Helens (Beaulieu and Peterson, 1981).

Hoblitt et al. (1987) presented some general guidelines for evaluating long-term volcanic hazards at proposed nuclear-power-plant sites. Information needed for such evaluations includes: (1) frequency and magnitude of various volcanic events that are recorded in the geologic history of the site itself, or that can be postulated for the site from the geologic record elsewhere, (2) eruptive histories of each volcano that could affect the site, (3) events of a type or magnitude that are unprecedented at volcanoes near the site, but have occurred at similar volcanoes elsewhere, (4) potential effectiveness of mitigation of the hazards at a site, and (5) possible adverse secondary effects of volcanic events on the operations of a plant, such as interference with cooling systems.

CHAPTER 4. VOLCANO MONITORING AND SHORT-TERM FORECASTS

Norman G. Banks[1], Robert I. Tilling[2], David H. Harlow[2], and John W. Ewert[1]

[1]U.S. Geological Survey, Vancouver, Washington 98661

[2]U.S. Geological Survey, Menlo Park, California 94025

Introduction

Most, perhaps all, eruptions are preceded and accompanied by geophysical and/or geochemical changes in the state of the volcano. If large or otherwise conspicuous, some changes are noticed by people living nearby. Most of the changes, however, are small and subtle, but they can be detected and precisely measured by present-day techniques and instrumentation. The term "volcano monitoring" refers collectively to scientific studies that systematically observe, record, and analyze the changes-- visible and invisible--in a volcano and its surroundings. Before the 20th century, observations of active volcanoes consisted only of occasional qualitative descriptions during or following eruptions or unusual activity. With the founding of modern volcano observatories in Japan and Hawaii in 1911, seismometers and other instruments began to be used for the first time in history in the study of volcanoes.

The record of past eruptions and the nature of their products and impacts provide the basis for making long-term forecasts of future volcanic activity and associated hazards (years, decades, or longer; see CHAPTER 3). The data obtained by volcano monitoring describe a volcano's current behavior and furnish the essential information to make short-term forecasts or predictions (months, weeks, days, or hours). The terms *forecast* and *prediction* have been, but should not be, used loosely or interchangeably. For the purposes of the short course, we adopt the specific distinctions between them as recognized by the USGS' Cascades Volcano Observatory (Swanson et al., 1985, p. 397):

"*factual statement*--describes current conditions but does not anticipate future events.

forecast--is a comparatively imprecise statement of the time, place, and nature of expected activity.

prediction--is a comparatively precise statement of the time, place, and ideally, the nature and size of impending activity. A prediction usually covers a shorter time period

Published in 1989 by the American Geophysical Union.

than a forecast and is generally based dominantly on interpretations and measurements of ongoing processes and secondarily on a projection of past history."

This chapter gives an updated general introduction to the wide-ranging topics of volcano monitoring and short-term forecasts. It draws heavily on the excellent review paper of Newhall (1984), who summarized the salient data contained in the pertinent pre-1984 literature, including UNESCO (1972), Civetta et al. (1974), Decker (1978, 1986), and Tazieff and Sabroux (1983). For more specific and detailed information on the topics introduced, the interested reader is referred to the relevant studies cited (see REFERENCES).

Volcanic Unrest, Eruption Precursors, and Volcano Monitoring

Volcanic unrest reflects, directly or indirectly, the changes in the physical or chemical state of the magma-water-gas-rock system that makes up and underlies the volcano (Figure 4.1). Some changes can be recognized by the local populace, while others can only be detected by use of scientific instruments. It must be emphasized that signs of volcanic unrest do not always culminate in eruptions, but they always should be treated as possible eruption precursors and be monitored accordingly.

Observational monitoring of indicators of unrest detectable by people

Some signs of volcanic unrest, if strong, are detectable by people living on or near the volcano. The keeping of a careful record of such changes detectable by the human senses (sight, sound, smell, feel, etc.) can be called *observational monitoring*. On occasion, unusual animal behavior has been reported in connection with some eruptions; such anomalous behavior is generally attributed to the animals responding to ground motions, sounds, or smells not sensed by humans.

Changes detectable by the human sensory system include:

- The occurrence of subterranean noises, felt earthquakes and other seismic vibrations.

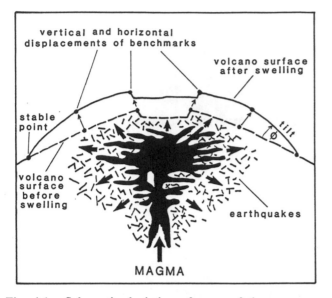

Fig. 4.1. Schematic depiction of some of the precursory indicators that can be measured by seismic and ground-deformation monitoring (see text); Ø shows the angular change in the slope of volcano surface (tilt). The change in volcano shape caused by swelling (inflation) is highly exaggerated. (Modified from Tilling et al., 1987).

- Visible signs of deformation, such as the formation or widening of ground cracks, folding or thrusting of soil and other surficial deposits, and increased occurrence of rockfalls and landslides, large-scale "bulging" of the volcano's summit or flanks.
- Increases or decreases in the volume rate, noise, color, or smell of emissions from steam vents, fumaroles, and springs.
- Changes in the mineral encrustation and deposits around fumaroles and springs.
- Changes in color, temperature, or sediment content of rivers, streams, and lakes. Unusual fluctuations in water level of wells.
- Unusual discoloration or dying of vegetation.

These signs of volcanic unrest detectable by the human senses generally only provide qualitative indicators. Nonetheless, regularly and diligently conducted observational monitoring can furnish important information useful in the design and deployment of instrumental monitoring networks. In addition, the data from observational monitoring can complement and extend instrumental monitoring data.

Instrumental monitoring of indicators of unrest

Most of the indicators of volcanic unrest, at least initially, are too subtle to be sensed by humans and can only be detected by instrumental monitoring employing sensitive scientific instruments and precise measurement techniques. These subtle indicators may begin to occur weeks, months, or even years before the onset of larger-scale changes detectable by observational monitoring. The common precursory indicators easily detectable and measurable by instrumental monitoring are described briefly below.

Volcanic seismicity. Ground vibrations are produced by the fracture of solid rocks adjacent to moving or stored magma (Figure 4.1). These vibrations, or seismic waves, may also be generated by magma movement itself, by movement or release of volcanic gases, or by changes in pressure associated with thermal heating of wallrock, water, or gas in the volcanic system. The overwhelming majority of such seismic signals are low energy and can only be detected by seismometers and recorded with seismographs or computers. Some higher energy events or processes can result in earthquakes and other ground motions strong enough to be felt by people. In the study of volcano unrest, it is important to know the locations and magnitudes of all earthquakes, whether felt or not, and these can only be determined instrumentally.

Distortion of volcano shape. Changes in the shape of the volcano--called *ground deformation*--are commonly associated with volcanic activity. These changes generally reflect the adjustments of the volcano surface in response to subsurface movement of magma into or out of the volcanic edifice (Figure 4.1).

Deformation may also be related to variations in the pressure and/or flow of fluids in the geothermal system of the volcano (see below). Whatever their cause(s), ground movements associated with volcano deformation are detectable by precise surveying techniques, utilizing instruments as simple as a precise level or "high-tech" as those used in satellite-based geodesy (e.g., Global Positioning System).

"Non-seismic" geophysical effects. Changes in temperature or the mass balance of the water, gas, solid rock, and magma components comprising the volcanic system may result in deviations in the local gravitational, geomagnetic, and geoelectrical fields. Such non-seismic geophysical effects can be quantified by measurement techniques (e.g., gravimetry, geomagnetics, induced polarization [I.P.], self potential [S.P.]) that have been adapted from those used in the geophysical exploration of water, mineral, and energy resources.

Geochemical changes in the volcano's geothermal system. All volcanic systems include a zone of heated waters and fluids --called the *geothermal system or envelope*--that surrounds the molten or solidified, but still hot, magma. Influx of new magma, or movement of existing magma within the volcanic edifice, can result in the release of distinctive gases to the atmosphere or the fluids in the geothermal envelope. In addition, disturbance of the thermal regime and hydrothermal circulation patterns can cause the geothermal system to interact to some extent with both the host rock and the local groundwater regime. Such effects ultimately appear as visible and/or instrumentally measurable geochemical changes at the volcano surface, as expressed by variations in the temperature, composition, and emission rate of gases and fluids discharged from surface vents, fumaroles, and springs.

Modern volcano monitoring

Before the emergence of volcanology as a modern science in the early 20th century, observations by people living near volcanoes were the only means of detecting possible eruption precursors. In situations where areas are subjected frequently to destructive eruptions during a human life time, or if the precursory phenomena are sufficiently terrifying, people often save themselves by spontaneously fleeing the volcano ("self-evacuation"). However, when eruptions are infrequent, when the significance of precursory phenomena is not understood by the residents, or when the precursory period becomes extended, failures in hazards mitigation are common in the absence of modern volcano monitoring. Nonetheless, careful observations, done on a regular basis by personnel having a general understanding of volcanic phenomena, provide a useful, low-cost, and sometimes the only available, source of information for some volcanoes. In fact, the most widely used monitoring technique in volcanic-hazards mitigation remains the on-site presence of trained, reliable, dedicated observers. However, because instrumental monitoring has the capability to recognize precursory activity below the threshold of human detection, it permits the earliest possible detection of departure from "normal" or baseline volcanic behavior. Thus, for this every important reason, in addition to its capability to rapidly collect quantitative data, instrumental monitoring forms the foundation of modern volcano monitoring.

Seismic and deformation monitoring methods are very amenable to systematic measurement and diagnostic interpretation of the behavioral patterns of volcanic unrest. Because of their long record of use and technology development, seismic and ground-deformation studies have been the most widely applied monitoring techniques to date and have provided the primary basis for many successful eruption forecasts. Monitoring of geochemical changes and "non-seismic" geophysical effects also has produced or assisted forecasts of eruptive activity. However, "non-seismic" geophysical monitoring methods, although being increasingly tested and improved at well-studied volcanoes, still are considered to be experimental. Currently available geochemical monitoring methods also are not yet routinely applicable, because the variations in the diagnostic gases or fluids monitored at a specific site or sites may not always or fully reflect larger-scale geochemical changes in the volcanic system as a whole. For these reasons and because of the severe time limitation of the short course, discussion will focus on seismic and ground-deformation monitoring.

Seismic Monitoring

Seismic monitoring is the primary mode of volcano surveillance today because of its long and successful use in the

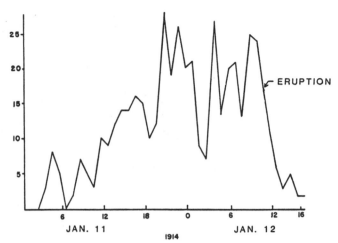

Fig. 4.2. Hourly distribution of earthquakes preceding the Sakura-jima eruption of 12 January 1914 (after Omori, 1914).

detection of anomalous volcanic behavior. Pioneering studies in Japan (Omori, 1914) and Hawaii (Wood, 1915) established seismic monitoring as an important tool for providing early warnings of eruptions. One of the first attempts to employ seismic monitoring was during the violent eruption of Sakura-jima Volcano, Japan, in 1914 (Figure 4.2). The earthquakes preceding the eruption were recorded by (today's standards) a primitive seismograph, located 11 km from the crater, with a vertical magnification of only 10. Modern high-gain seismographs would have recorded many more earthquakes and doubtless would have detected the onset of lower magnitude seismic activity much sooner before eruption.

The intrusion and movement of magma or volcanic fluids typically generate detectable earthquakes or vibrations prior to eruptive activity. The primary goal of seismic monitoring is to record, characterize, and interpret such seismicity in the short-term forecasting of future eruptions or of changes in the course of an eruption in progress. Shimozuru (1972) provides the most comprehensive summary to date of the principles, techniques, and applications of seismic monitoring. That summary is reviewed here with the addition of recent examples, subsequent refinements, and new developments in data acquisition, telemetry, and analysis.

Volcanic seismicity

Various types and categories of volcanic events that are associated with eruptive processes have been identified and classified on the basis of characteristic seismogram signatures or inferred source mechanism (e.g., Minakami, 1974; Koyanagi, 1968; Shimozuru et al., 1969; Tokarev, 1981; Schick, 1981; Malone, 1983). Today, the classification of volcanic earthquakes generally follows a scheme developed by Minakami (1960, 1974) that was developed through the experience of many eruptions and the observed changes in the different types

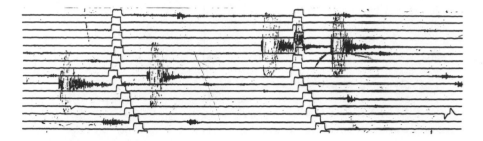

Fig. 4.3. A-type earthquakes recorded at Fuego volcano, Guatemala, 1977. (One minute between time marks.)

of events associated with these eruptions. In practice, volcano observatories often modify or expand Minakami's classification or develop their own version that better characterizes the changes in seismicity preceding and during eruptions at a particular volcano.

Some commonly used broad categories in classifying volcanic earthquakes are given below; as emphasized by Newhall (1984), the categories of volcanic seismicity may exhibit considerable gradation and overlap.

A-type. These earthquakes generally occur at depths of 1 to 10 km beneath a volcano and are characterized by high frequency seismic signatures with distinct P and S-wave phases (Figure 4.3). They are indistinguishable from short-period (or tectonic) earthquakes caused by rock fracture of non-volcanic origin. A-type earthquakes are inferred to be generated by the brittle fracture of rock in response to the intrusion and migration of magma, or to the expansion of high-pressure geothermal fluids.

B-type. B-type earthquakes generally occur at depths of 1 km or less, have a lower frequency content than A-type events, and have very emergent P and S-wave phases that are difficult to

distinguish unambiguously (Figure 4.4). These, like A-type events, are also thought to be caused by rock fracture, but the difference in signature characteristics appears to reflect path effects resulting from the passage of the seismic waves of these shallow-focus events through heterogeneous layers of ash and lava. A single sequence of multiple, overlapping B-type earthquakes has been given the name C-type earthquakes; these commonly occur during lava-dome growth (Minakami et al., 1951; Minakami, 1960, 1974).

Long-period. These earthquakes have signatures with a high-frequency A-type signal at the beginning of the event, but the signal as a whole is dominated by a long-period component that can be stable and independent of event magnitude (Figure 4.5). Theoretical modelling by Chouet (1985, 1988) indicates that long-period earthquakes, also called low-frequency or volcanic earthquakes, may be caused by resonance triggered by a pressure transient in a fluid-filled crack or conduit. The signatures of long-period events are very similar to those of B-type events, thus previous occurrences of long-period events and their implication for eruptive processes may not have been appreciated fully.

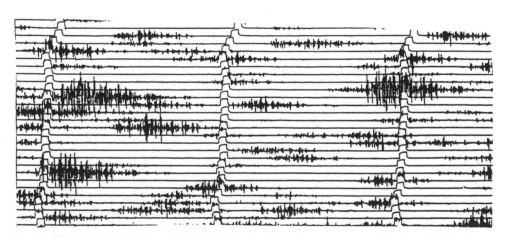

Fig. 4.4. B-type earthquakes recorded at Pacaya volcano, Guatemala, 1973. (One minute between time marks.)

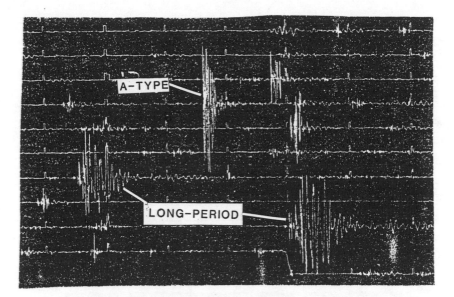

Fig. 4.5. Long-period compared to A-type earthquakes recorded at Nevado del Ruíz Volcano, Colombia, 1988. The long-period events in this seismogram have impulsive first arrivals similar to the A-type events, but the events of long-period codas are dominated by comparatively long-period signals.

Explosion earthquakes. As the name implies, these earthquakes are generated by volcanic explosions during eruptive activity. Their signatures can vary significantly depending on the strength, duration, and repetition frequency of the explosions. The small explosion earthquake shown in Figure 4.6 was recorded by a seismograph network near Fuego Volcano, Guatemala and is interesting because the later arriving air wave is clearly visible in the signatures. The explosion

earthquake in Figure 4.7 is preceded by a period of harmonic tremor (see next section).

Volcanic tremor. The term "volcanic tremor" refers to a type of volcanic seismicity commonly recorded at active volcanoes. It is characterized by an essentially continuous seismograph signature in contrast to the discrete events described above. Volcanic tremor reflects continuous ground vibration, or frequent small earthquakes whose codas overlap. At well-studied volcanoes, tremor has always been observed during eruptions. Sometimes tremor may precede an eruption, but it can also occur without eruption.

If the tremor is nearly monochromatic (i.e., of a single frequency) and has relatively constant amplitude, it is called harmonic tremor. If it varies significantly in frequency and/or amplitude, the tremor is called spasmodic tremor (Ryall and Ryall, 1983). Yet another type is periodic or banded tremor because of its distinctive appearance in seismograph records. This unusual type of tremor (Figure 4.8) has been observed prior to the 1979 phreatic eruption of Karkar volcano, Papua New Guinea (McKee et al., 1981), in conjunction with the cyclic eruptions of Old Faithful geyser, in Yellowstone National Park, Wyoming, USA (Kieffer, 1984), and prior to a phreatic eruption of Nevado del Ruíz, Colombia (Gil, 1987; Gil et al., 1987). These instances strongly suggest that periodic tremor may be caused by shallow geyser activity generated by the heat of intruding magma or volcanic fluids. Several source mechanisms appear to generate volcanic tremor and the exact nature of these sources is the focus of current research efforts (e.g., Aki et al., 1977; Aki and Koyanagi, 1981; Fehler, 1983; Chouet, 1985, 1988; Chouet et al., 1987; Koyanagi et al., 1987; Leet,. 1988).

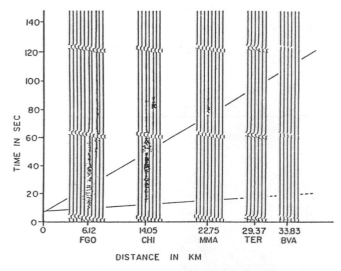

Fig. 4.6. Explosion earthquake from Fuego volcano, Guatemala, 1974. Lines mark the P-wave and the later air-wave phases. (After McNutt and Harlow, 1983.)

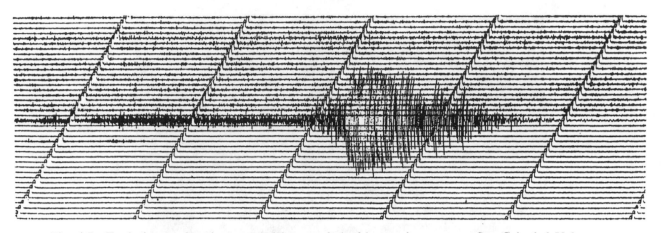

Fig. 4.7. Explosion earthquake preceded by a period of harmonic tremor at San Crístobal Volcano, Nicaragua, 1976. Note the relative seismic quiesence following the eruption.

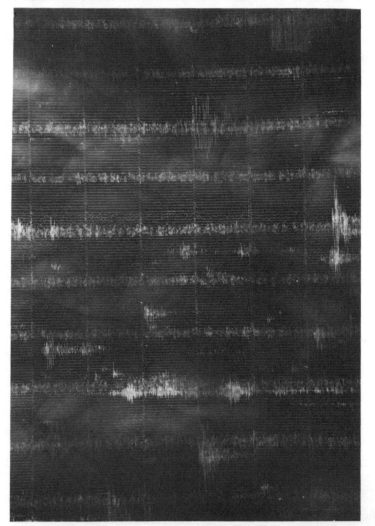

Fig. 4.8. Seismogram from Nevado del Ruíz Volcano, Colombia, 1985 showing banded or periodic tremor plus individual A- and B-type events. This seismogram was recorded about six weeks prior to a catastrophic eruption on November 13, 1985.

Earthquake signatures and precursory seismicity

Classifications of volcanic seismicity are largely descriptive and do not distinguish between earthquakes signatures caused by wave-path differences and those that reflect different source mechanisms except in obvious cases such as seismic events generated by volcanic explosions. Malone (1983) finds evidence that favors both different source mechanisms and differences caused by path effects. Current research, however, is focusing on identifying source mechanisms that may be indicated by the different types of earthquakes at volcanoes. If source mechanisms can be clearly identified, then more accurate forecasts of impending eruptive activity may be possible.

Experience indicates that the number of volcanic earthquakes typically increases as magma accumulates in the shallow reservoir. While an increased rate in volcanic seismicity, such as the occurrence of seismic swarms or flurries (the recording of hundreds of earthquakes per day), often indicates magma unrest within the volcanic edifice, this activity may not necessarily culminate in an eruption. When magma movement has occurred without eruption of material, the event is called an intrusion. For either an eruption or an intrusion, the length of time of precursory seismicity can vary widely from volcano to volcano and from eruption to eruption at the same volcano. Some precursory seismicity leads eruptions by a year or more (e.g. Krakatau, 1883; Nevado del Ruíz, 1985), but most lead times are weeks to months (e.g., Mount St. Helens, March-May, 1980). In some cases, precursory seismicity begins a few days or hours before an eruption (e.g. Krafla, Iceland, 1975-82; most eruptions of Kilauea).

Instrumentation, data analysis, and networks

The type of seismic instrumentation, recording and telemetry systems, and data processing and analysis used at active volcanoes differs widely depending on the specific objectives of the seismic studies. The most advanced systems use computer-based, real-time processing of seismic signals received at a central location to determine earthquake locations, magnitudes, and times of occurrence. Though these advanced systems can provide an immediate indication of seismic activity, less costly and easier to maintain systems can still provide adequate information to monitor and track activity. Basic principles, methods employed, and applications of seismic monitoring, including network and instrumentation design, are discussed by Shimozuru (1972) and Lee and Stewart (1981). In this section, we present below a brief discussion of the essential elements of seismic monitoring at volcanoes, expanded from Newhall's (1984) summary.

Instrumentation and data analysis. Almost all volcano observatories use electromagnetic seismometers, which convert ground shaking into changing electric voltages. Figure 4.9 illustrates the major components of modern instrumentation systems in use today. The field package consists of a seismometer, amplifier, and voltage-controlled amplifier, and telemetry interface. Seismometers are generally electromagnetic

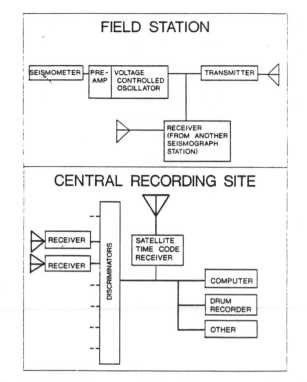

Fig. 4.9. Block diagram of the basic components of a radio-telemetered seismic-monitoring network. Power for the field station is typically provided by a battery that is kept charged by a solar panel.

and translate ground motions into electrical currents which are amplified, converted to a frequency-modulated (FM) signal by a voltage-controlled oscillator (VCO). Seismic signals can be recorded on-site or transmitted by cable, radio or satellite telemetry, to a central recording facility and processed either in analog or digital form. Seismometers used to record volcanic earthquakes and tremor should have a peak response frequency near 1 Hz and have a broad bandpass.

Analog signals from seismometers are commonly recorded on seismographs utilizing smoked paper or other types of chart paper (e.g., photographic, heat- or pressure-sensitive); they can also be recorded on photographic film systems (e.g., Develocorder). Analog recording permits immediate display of ground shaking, making possible qualitative, visual monitoring of seismicity as it happens. The recording of analog signals, usually on a drum recorder, and their processing require only basic electronic equipment and expertise. Quantitative processing of the data, however, usually takes one or more days after recording unless records are changed more frequently. The arrival times and other parameters of analog seismic data must be determined ("read") manually, and the results are then used to estimate location, depth, and magnitude, based on a known or assumed seismic-velocity model. In the past, such determinations required tedious hand calculations or graphic solutions. Seismic data now can be routinely and quickly analyzed by means of computer programs; a commonly used program is HYPOINVERSE (Klein, 1978) but there are many others.

If the analog signals are digitized at the central recording site, they can be recorded on magnetic-tape systems. Such data can later be "read" precisely and easily by computer playback. The most advanced instrumentation transmits digitized signals directly from the seismometer, and such digital recording can be transmitted over longer distances with less radio interference. In addition, digital signals provide a very broad frequency and amplitude response which further facilitates computer-based analysis of and research on the data. Today, at well established observatories, digital seismic data are fed directly into computers for quantitative location of hypocenters, determination of magnitudes, and preliminary analysis of frequencies and frequency patterns. The larger seismic events can be located automatically by such "Real Time Processing" (RTP) systems (e.g., Hill, 1984). Compared to analog seismometry, however, digital seismometry generally requires more complicated (and expensive) instrumentation and a higher level of electronic expertise to maintain the equipment.

In the past, on-line computer-based data analysis that could rapidly provide information in a crisis situation were dependent on computers that were expensive and difficult to operate without considerable high-level technical support. Their expense and operational difficulty precluded the use of computer-based systems at most of the world's volcanoes. Taking advantage of the wide availability and relative low cost of modern personal computers (PC), the U.S. Geological Survey has recently developed a PC-based seismic data and analysis system for small networks of up to 16 stations. Such a system can be implemented and maintained with modest expense and expertise. It promises an easily transportable capability to analyze seismic data from small networks on a timely basis. Figure 4.10 is a print of the monitor screen of the PC-based system showing an example of a detected earthquake. Valdes (1988) has compiled a data analysis package for the system to quickly measure parameters from individual seismic events such as arrival time, coda length, and spectral content (Figure 4.10). These versatile and portable PC-based systems permit rapid deployment in initiating or augmenting seismic monitoring at a volcano showing unrest.

Seismic networks. To locate earthquakes accurately (including depth), a volcano seismic network should have at least 4, and preferably 6 or more, stations within a 1 to 15 km radius of the vent(s), timed to within 0.05 second of each other. At least one seismic station should be located as near as possible to the center of activity, so that small earthquakes, explosions, or low-level tremor can be recorded. In some cases, relative signal characteristics at each of several seismic stations, if strategically located, can indicate the onset and progress of volcanic mudflows.

The more distant stations of a network are used to locate the origin of the seismic signals (the hypocenter) and to provide information on the attenuation of seismic signals with distance, a possible indicator of the eruptive potential of the volcano. To obtain better earthquake locations and parameters, a few seismic stations in the network should record all three components of motion--one vertical and two horizontal. Some useful guidelines for establishing seismic-network configurations to optimize earthquake locations can be found in Sato and Skoko (1965), Peters and Crosson (1972), and Uhrhammer (1980). An excellent summary of instrument characteristics and the principles of calculating earthquake hypocenters is given by Lee and Stewart (1981).

In order to permit a comparison of seismic energy release between different volcanoes, it is necessary to calibrate a seismic network by recording earthquakes of known magnitude or by recording man-made explosions of known yields and efficiencies. This can be accomplished in one of two ways: 1) use of a portable seismometer of known response characteristics, or one that has already been calibrated elsewhere, within the region of the seismic network for a period of several weeks to a few months, or 2) use of a seismometer with "standard electronics," whose characteristics are suitable to compute Wood-Anderson equivalent earthquake magnitudes. In either case, the calibration should be checked by comparison of the earthquake magnitudes determined from the seismic network and with those determined from the Worldwide Seismic Network (WWSN) or from a standard Wood-Anderson optical record (Koyanagi et al., 1977, 1978). Once a network has been calibrated, magnitudes of later volcanic earthquakes can be approximated from the duration of the signal, that is, from the coda lengths (Tsumura, 1967; Lee et al., 1972; Herrmann, 1975). Yokoyama (1988) gives a quantitative comparison of seismic energy releases associated with a number of recent eruptions.

Uses of seismic data in volcano monitoring

The pattern of volcanic seismicity that precedes and accompanies eruptions can be highly specific to an individual volcano. Thus, the question of which seismic parameters might prove to be most diagnostic in eruption forecasting can only be answered on the basis of monitoring experience and eruptive activity at the volcano being studied. Nevertheless, it might be useful here to review briefly some of the commonly used methods in the analysis of seismic data. Inherent in all these methods is the basic premise that the temporal and spatial variations in the nature, vigor, and location of the volcanic seismicity give clues to possible future behavior of the volcano.

Energy release. In general, the greater the release of seismic energy, the more likely the occurrence of an eruption or intrusion. The simplest expression of energy release is the total number of earthquakes (of all types) or bursts of volcanic tremor that occur in a given unit of time. If the quality of the data permits, such analyses also should be made according to the type of seismicity or tremor (A-type, B-type, long-period, harmonic tremor, summit vs. flank, etc.).

A more accurate estimation of energy release, however, is obtained from consideration of the magnitudes as well as the

a

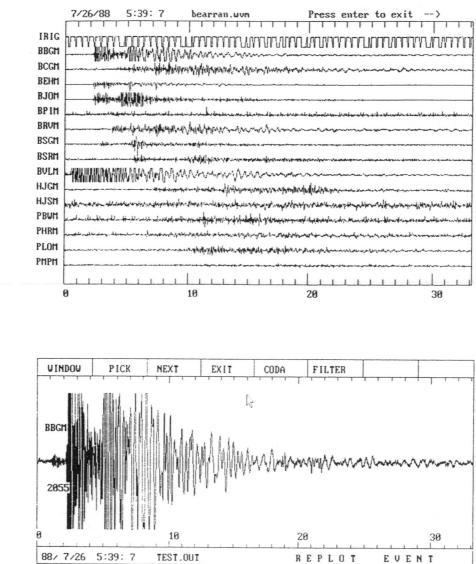

Fig. 4.10. Monitor screen of PC-based seismic-monitoring system. **A.** View of screen showing a local earthquake recorded by a network of 15 stations (the top trace is the IRIG time code). **B.** View of screen showing the single trace of an earthquake from the data-analysis program, which allows the selection of various parameters for study (e.g., phase arrivals, coda length, frequency spectra).

number of seismic events. Because the earthquake magnitude scale is exponential, the energy release of many small-magnitude events may be substantially less than that for a few larger-magnitude ones. For example, all other factors being equal, the energy released by a thousand magnitude-1 earthquakes is the same as that for a single magnitude-4 event.

Migration of seismicity. While the monitoring of seismic energy release provides important information on when an eruption or intrusion might happen, studies of volcanic seismicity in space and time may also provide clues as to where the eruption is likely to occur. For example, maps (plan view) of earthquake epicenters for different time periods may indicate the lateral migration of magma from the summit reservoir into another part of the volcano prior to an eruption or intrusion. Cross sections of earthquake hypocenters for successive time periods might show the upward migration of seismicity--a situation that generally increases the potential for eruption. Specific examples of how studies of the migration of seismicity in space and time can be used to infer active processes within a volcanic system are well documented by Klein et al. (1987) for Kilauea Volcano. This comprehensive study of Kilauea's seismicity for the period 1960-1983 graphically illustrates that not only can the paths and rates of magma migration be determined, but also the locations of possible barriers to migration and secondary magma reservoirs in addition to the summit reservoir.

Relations between the types of seismicity. The renown seismologist C.F. Richter (1958) noted an empirical relationship between earthquake magnitude and the frequency of their occurrence:

$$\log N = A - bM$$

where N is the number of events of magnitude M or greater, and A is a derived constant. The slope of this equation--commonly called "b-value"--differs with the frequency content of the earthquakes. b-values in the range from 0.6 to 1.5 are commonly observed for tectonic-type or high-frequency (including type-A) earthquakes, whereas values greater than 1.5 are commonly associated with volcanic-type or low-frequency earthquakes, such as B-type or long-period (Minakami, 1974). Figure 4.11 gives an example of the b-values observed at Mount St. Helens for high- and low-frequency earthquakes.

Certain relations between the various types of volcanic seismicity have been observed repeatedly at some well-studied volcanoes. For example, at Kilauea, A-type (tectonic) earthquakes typically increase during the build-up to an eruption or intrusion, but upon the onset of activity, they decrease sharply and cease. During the ensuing activity, the seismicity is dominated by B-type and long-period earthquakes, generally accompanied by harmonic tremor. The simple plotting of daily counts of B-type earthquakes at Asama Volcano, Japan, was used by Minakami (1960, 1974) to develop an empirical probability formula for forecasting eruptions based on the number of events that occurred during the previous five days (Figure 4.12).

Plotting of the ratios of different types of volcanic earthquakes can provide useful information. An example of this method is a plot of the ratio of the number of B-type to A-type earthquakes with time prior to the 1943-1945 eruption of Usu Volcano, Japan (Figure 4.13). As the eruption approached, the ratio increased, indicating that a higher percentage of events were occurring at shallower depths. Similar shifts in this ratio have been reported elsewhere (Minakami, 1960, 1974; Malone, 1983), suggesting that this simple analysis technique, or variations thereof, might be applied with success at other volcanoes.

Another method of analyzing seismic data is to combine the information given by the frequencies and magnitudes of volcanic earthquakes by plotting cumulative seismic energy release with time. In a plot of seismic energy versus time for a series of eruptions of Bezymianny Volcano (Tokarev, 1963), the slope of the curve increased exponentially as eruptions neared (Figure 4.14). This recurring pattern allowed quite accurate forecasts of

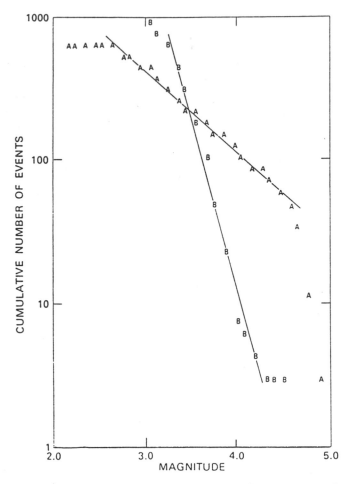

Fig. 4.11. Plot illustrating the frequency of occurrence and magnitudes of earthquakes at Mount St. Helens, March 20-May 18, 1980. The b-value for high-frequency earthquakes (A) is 0.6, and for low-frequency earthquakes (B) is 2.8 (see text). (From Endo et al., 1981, Fig. 58).

eruption onsets a few days in advance. In contrast, Shimozuru (1972) observes that the rate of seismic energy release decreases shortly before eruptions at other volcanoes. Thus, the differences in premonitory seismicity patterns indicate that great caution is needed in the formulation of eruption forecasts at volcanoes where no previous experience exists. Also, there is no guarantee that the same pattern of seismic activity will necessarily repeat itself for the next eruption of a particular volcano.

Plotting several seismic parameters together is an important monitoring at active volcanoes. Figure 4.15 is a plot of seismic parameters from the earthquake activity that preceded the cataclysmic eruption of Mount St. Helens on May 18, 1980. In this example (Endo et al., 1981), the daily frequency of earthquake declined before the eruption, but the energy-release rate remained relatively constant except for the rapid rate of

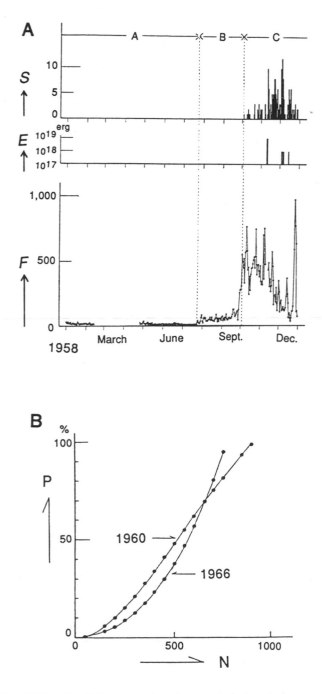

Fig. 4.12. **A.** B-type earthquakes and their relations to explosive eruptions of Asama Volcano, Japan: A = quiescent stage; B = pre-volcanic or pre-eruptive stage; C = stage of explosive eruptions; S = daily frequency of eruptions; E = eruptions larger than 10^{18} ergs in kinetic energy; F = daily frequency of B-type earthquakes. **B.** The empirical probabilities of an eruption at Asama based on the five-day frequencies of B-type earthquakes, which were derived in 1960 and in 1966. P = the probability of an eruption in the next five days. (After Minakami, 1960, 1974).

release during the first two weeks of the (phreatic) activity (Figure 4.15). As discussed in CHAPTER 5, there was no distinctive indicators--from the intensive seismic or ground-deformation monitoring--of the climactic magmatic eruption on May 18.

Seismic monitoring strategies

Proper seismic monitoring requires substantial resources in equipment and trained personnel for network maintenance and data analysis/interpretation. Because of limited economic and scientific resources, especially in the developing countries, it is impossible to conduct detailed seismic monitoring at all active or potentially active volcanoes. By necessity, the level of seismic monitoring effort at each volcano should be commensurate with the level of risk posed by each. Unfortunately, the hazards and risks are still largely unknown at many volcanoes, and some of the most dangerous volcanoes are the least studied and understood (CHAPTERS 1 and 6).

Continuous monitoring. The key to early detection of departures from "normal" behavior precursory to possible eruptive activity, or of significant shifts in activity while an eruption is in progress, is the prompt analysis and interpretation of seismic and other volcano-monitoring data. For seismic monitoring to be most useful, the network should have an adequate number of stations to record the data needed for precise determination of earthquake epicenter, depth, and magnitude. Ideally, seismic data should be received continuously, recorded at a central site, and analyzed and interpreted, at most, within a few hours of the occurrence of an earthquake. However, if economic and scientific resources are insufficient to install and maintain a multi-station, telemetered seismic network, effort should be made to conduct some type of continuous monitoring. A careful and experienced operator, using even a single seismic station, can obtain remarkably useful information about volcanic seismicity, such as, daily counts of various types of seismic events, an estimate of earthquake magnitudes and, hence, their energy release, and a measure of the time delay in the arrival of P- and S-waves, which can be used to determine distance of the source.

Monitoring with less-than-adequate networks. At present, only a few volcanoes (mostly in developed countries) are monitored by seismic networks that permit the accurate location and characterization of volcanic seismicity. Most volcanoes are monitored by less adequate networks with fewer than the requisite number of seismic stations, or they have no seismic monitoring at all. When less-than-adequate monitoring networks are used, the volcanologist should be aware of some common problems that arise:

- *Too few stations.* In this situation, many smaller-magnitude earthquakes are poorly located or not locatable, passage of significant mudflows may not be detectable, and events of tectonic origin are more likely to be confused with volcanic seismicity.

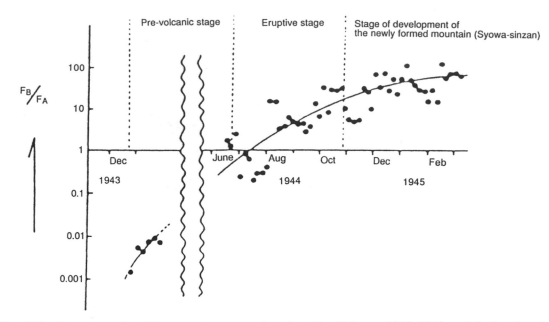

Fig. 4.13. Changing ratio of B-type to A-type earthquakes, Usu Volcano, 1943-45 (from Minakami et al., 1951; Minakami, 1974).

- *Unbalanced station arrays.* Networks with seismic stations located too close together or biased to one side of the volcano can yield poor or misleading information. As one example, this problem plagues the use of the so-called "tripartite" arrays, in which three seismic stations are located within a kilometer or so of each other on only one side of the volcano. As pointed out by Ward and Gregerson (1973), it is difficult to obtain accurate epicenters with data from such a network, because the closely spaced stations: 1) give relatively poor resolution of seismic signals, creating a false impression of a wide scatter of epicenters; and 2) cannot "focus" on the correct epicenters, sometimes resulting in an apparent concentration of epicenters on the near or far side of the volcano summit if an incorrect seismic-velocity structure is assumed.

- *Poor timing of stations.* This problem is particularly common with stations not linked by telemetry to a central recording site. An error in timing has the same effect as an incorrect assumption about seismic-velocity structure, creating a systematic bias to one or another side of the volcano summit in the location of seismic events. The timing of a new seismic network should be calibrated using man-made explosions at known locations (e.g., quarry or road-construction blasts, or explosions detonated specifically for calibration purposes).

- *Poor assumption of seismic-velocity model.* Seismic-velocity structure has been determined for only some of the world's volcanoes. Thus, in many instances, it is necessary to assume a plausible model by comparison to a

well-studied volcano thought to be similar. A poor choice in the assumed model can result in significant error and bias in hypocenter location.

Periodic monitoring. Under circumstances that preclude continuous seismic monitoring, periodic monitoring, by means of repeated seismic surveys using portable equipment and on-site recording, have been conducted at some volcanoes. Such surveys typically involve data acquisition for a period of a few weeks to months at a volcano. Commonly, such seismic surveys are conducted at regularly scheduled intervals, usually at the same time of year to minimize any possible seasonal variations in volcanic behavior. To recognize possible seasonal effects, it is recommended that one year of continuous monitoring be conducted at any one volcano before switching to a periodic mode of monitoring. By so doing, some seasonally controlled increase in seismicity would not be misinterpreted during some future brief survey at the "wrong" time.

Periodic monitoring does provide some information about volcanic seismicity during the short time covered by the survey, but this information about the level of seismic activity may not be representative of the volcano's longer term activity. A serious, and potentially dangerous, shortcoming of periodic monitoring is that it may completely miss the rapid onset and buildup of precursory seismicity to an eruption, thus providing a misleading impression of apparent volcano quiescence. This impression in turn could contribute to a false sense of complacency or unwarranted security to the surrounding population.

Accepting the premise that any monitoring of a volcano is better than none at all, then periodic seismic monitoring, nonetheless, can play a useful role until a continuous monitoring

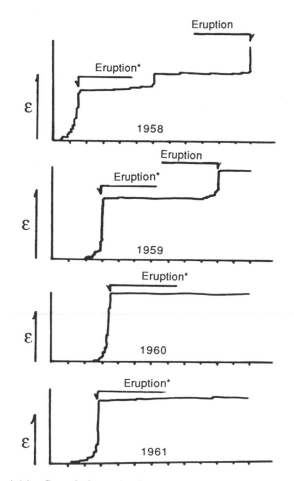

Fig. 4.14. Cumulative seismic-energy release with time for Bezymianny Volcano, Kamchatka, 1958-1961 and times of eruptions (after Tokarev, 1963).

system can be established as part of an "adequate minimum" volcano observatory (Tilling, 1982). If properly interpreted, data from repeated periodic seismic surveys can help guide the selection of sites of one or more continuously recording seismic stations and furnish background information for parts of the volcano not covered by a permanent network. Periodic monitoring can complement and supplement, but not supplant, a continuous monitoring system.

Ground-deformation Monitoring

That visible surface deformation accompanies and sometimes precedes eruptions has long been known. Some historical examples include: bulging of a farmer's field (e.g., Parícutin, Mexico [González-Reyna and Foshag, 1947]; large-scale fluctuations in sea level (e.g., Campi Flegrei, Italy [Parascandola, 1947; Corrado et al., 1977]; and Sakurajima, Japan [Kubotera and Yoshikawa, 1963]); and changes in volcano profile (e.g., Usu, Japan [Yokoyama et al., 1981]). However, such changes were noticed only when they were dramatic. Beginning in the 20th century, instrumental measurements began to be made of ground deformation (Figure 4.1) undetectable by visual observation.

The most commonly used ground-deformation monitoring methods are adapted largely from equipment and techniques employed in surveying and geodesy. Most methods are capable of detecting crustal movement of a few parts per million (ppm) or less, even though ground displacements at some volcanoes can be orders of magnitude greater. Geodetic monitoring methods applied to the study of active volcanoes have been discussed elsewhere (e.g., Decker and Kinoshita, 1972; Kinoshita et al., 1974; and Newhall, 1984), so only a brief review is given here.

Vertical displacements

Measurable changes in the vertical displacement of benchmarks or other reference markers with earthquake or volcanic activity have been long recognized. For example, large vertical (as well as horizontal) displacements associated with the 1914 eruption of Sakurajima Volcano were determined from triangulation data (Imamura, 1930). However, triangulation measurements can only detect large-scale changes. For most volcano-monitoring purposes, vertical displacements can be measured precisely by the techniques described below.

Precise levelling. The most widely used volcano-monitoring technique to measure vertical displacements is a conventional surveying technique called precise levelling, in which changes in benchmark elevations are referenced to some arbitrary datum, commonly relative to sea level or a distant benchmark (Figure 4.16). Although this technique is not new, it still has the best detection limit for elevation changes. Measured vertical displacements at large volcanic centers typically are on the order of ten centimeters to a few meters per kilometer, but only a few centimeters per kilometer at most smaller stratovolcanoes. The general principles and instrumentation used in precise levelling are well established and described in geodesy and surveying textbooks (e.g., Bomford, 1980); representative specific applications of the technique in volcano monitoring are given by Berrino et al. (1984) and by Kinoshita and others (Fiske and Kinoshita, 1969; Decker and Kinoshita, 1972; and Kinoshita et al., 1974).

Ideally, a levelling network should include some lines that radiate away from the summit of the volcano and others that encircle it; at some volcanoes, special lines across active rift zones may also be needed. In practice, however, most networks utilize existing roads and trails. The principal advantages of precise levelling are: 1) its excellent precision and the general availability, even in developing countries, of the needed equipment; 2) the measured uplift or subsidence can be portrayed as a map showing contour lines of equal vertical displacements; and 3) the data provide the best basis for modelling the volume and depth of intruding magma. If the

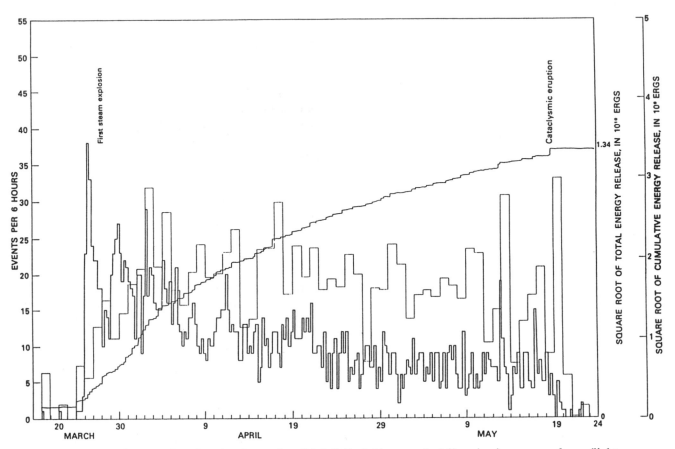

Fig. 4.15. Counts of earthquakes larger than M=2.5 (dark histogram); daily seismic energy release (light histogram); and square root of cumulative seismic energy release (curving, stepped line); from March 20 to May 24, 1980 (GMT) at Mount St. Helens. Earthquake frequency peaked on March 26, but energy release did not peak until April 2, reflecting larger earthquakes after March 27. Energy release declined more slowly than the number of earthquakes per day, again reflecting large earthquakes later in the sequence. (From Endo et al., 1981, Fig. 54).

levelling network is sufficiently dense, it is possible to identify the area(s) of maximum change (Figure 4.17). A sharply defined, nearly equi-dimensional area of maximum uplift (or subsidence) sometimes is called the inflation (or deflation) center.

Some disadvantages of precise levelling include: 1) it is labor- intensive and time-consuming, and hence expensive; 2) on steep slopes of stratovolcanoes, it is difficult to do because of the many instrument set-ups required; 3) during very rapid uplift or subsidence, it may be impossible to "close" a level loop, because the point of origin and points along the loop are rising or falling even during the survey; and 4) at some volcanoes, it is difficult, if not impossible, to repeat level lines in the winter because benchmarks are covered by snow. Therefore, to maximize repeat surveys, to the extent possible, the level lines should be established along topographically elevated areas that emerge first from snow cover with the spring thaw.

Modern precise levels and temperature-stable invar rods permit first-order levelling with measurement error of about 1 mm in 1 km. However, for volcanoes where the vertical displacements are substantially larger than measurement error, levelling to second- or third-order standards may be adequate (analytical uncertainty of several mm in 1 km). When deformation is rapid, frequently repeated (faster) third-order levelling surveys can yield more useful data than a single (much slower) first-order levelling survey. Another alternative is to conduct trigonometric levelling studies (e.g., Whalen, 1984; Rueger and Brunner, 1982), which, while slightly less precise, can measure both tilt and elevation changes (see next section). Strategies in precise levelling depend on the magnitude of expectable elevation changes and the rate of change. For a levelling network referenced to a benchmark assumed to show zero change, it is good practice to conduct levelling surveys (every few years) from that reference benchmark to one that is

LEVELING TRAVERSE

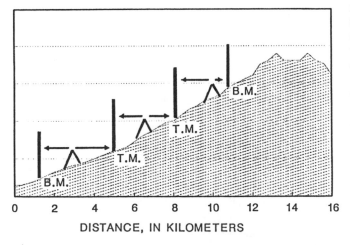

DISTANCE, IN KILOMETERS

Fig. 4.16. Illustration showing the basic measurement of elevation changes of benchmarks in precise levelling.

calibrated against tide-gauge data or some other more "absolute" datum.

Water-level changes. The level of a body of water may provide a useful reference for recognizing and measuring the relative vertical displacements of marker points or horizons on the adjacent land mass (e.g., all or parts of a volcanic edifice). Elevation changes relative to sea level, particularly useful in

monitoring island volcanoes or volcanic systems in coastal regions, can be considered "absolute," after corrections are made in the reduction of data for eustatic sea-level changes and naturally occurring tidal effects or seiches. Changes along the shoreline of an inland lake are relative only to each other unless the measured differences can be tied into mean sea level or some otherwise fixed elevation.

If the water-level changes are sufficiently large and/or rapid, the relative uplift or subsidence can be recognized visually from shore-line or near-surface modifications, such as the emergence or submergence of archeological works (e.g., monuments, docks, buildings, walls) or prehistoric geologic or geomorphic features (e.g., shell beds, coral reefs, raised beaches or terraces, wave-cut benches; see Moore and Fornari, 1984). Variations in the elevation of horizons associated with certain aquatic organisms (e.g., barnacles, algae) also furnish evidence of land-water level changes. For example, borings of sea animals on the stone columns of the ancient Roman market at Serapeo (built near Pozzuoli harbor) afford dramatic evidence of sea-level fluctuations ranging over 10 m during the past two thousand years at Campi Flegrei caldera, Italy (Parascandola, 1947; Berrino et al., 1984, Fig. 2). Changes in intertidal shell horizons also have been useful to demonstrate ground deformation at Rabaul Caldera, Papua New Guinea (de St. Ours, 1987).

In general, water-level changes in response to ground deformation are too small and gradual to be observed visually. However, such changes can be precisely measured by tide gauges (Figure 4.18), pressure transducers, or other instruments (e.g., Gutenberg, 1933; Tsuboi, 1937; Moore,

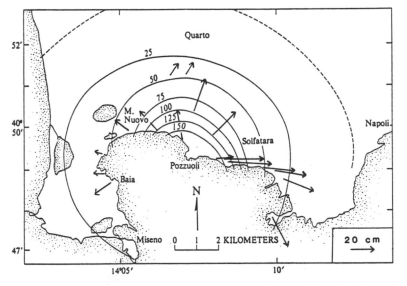

Fig. 4.17. Contours of uplift (in centimeters), determined by precise levelling, for the period January 1982 to January 1985 at Campi Flegrei caldera, west of Naples, Italy (from Decker, 1986, Fig. 10). The arrows are vectors of horizontal displacements (in centimeters), determined by EDM measurements, for the period 1980-1983 (from Berrino et al., 1984, Fig. 12). Both the vertical and horizontal displacements define an area of maximum deformation (i.e., inflation center) located at the coastal city of Pozzuoli.

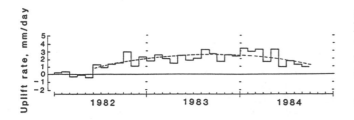

Fig. 4.18. An example of using water-level changes as an indicator of vertical displacement. The rate of the inflation at Campi Flegrei caldera is well demonstrated by the continuously recording tide gauge at Pozzuoli harbor. (From Berrino et al., 1984, Fig. 7).

1970, 1987; Otway et al., 1984, pp. 47-48; Hamilton, 1987). Tide gauges come in a variety of models, but all basically involve a float attached to a cable, which in turn drives a chart recorder. Wave and wind disturbances of the float are minimized by installation in a protected lagoon or tide pool, or by use of a stilling device (such a large-diameter barrel, pipe, or some other type of man-made cistern).

Tide-gauge data (Figure 4.18) can be recorded continuously --on a permanent basis or for a time period each year or season -- to fill out gaps between infrequent levelling surveys and obtain a complete history of uplift or subsidence. Very precise and continuous water-level monitoring may also be done with a pressure transducer fixed to the sea or lake bottom or in an near-shore stilling well. While pressure transducers have an advantage over tide gauges because they also can be used in deep water (e.g., Spiess, 1985; Spiess et al., 1987), they are much more expensive. For pressure transducers operating in sea water, fluctuations in salinity may pose a problem in data analysis and interpretation.

Even without tide gauges or other continuously recording instruments, useful information on water-level changes can be gained by periodic measurements relative to man-made or natural benchmarks using reference sticks, steel tape, plumb bob, precise-levelling methods, or specially adapted measurement systems (e.g, Lipman et al., 1981; Banks et al., 1984; Otway et al., 1984; Otway, 1986; Tryggvason, 1986, 1987). In all such periodic measurements, care must be taken in the data reduction to correct for the effects of normal tides, waves, winds, seiches, and other local factors. In well-controlled studies and under favorable weather conditions (little wind, lake surface is under ice), such as at Lake Myvatn, on Krafla Volcano, Iceland, vertical ground displacements greater than 1 mm can be reliably detected (Tryggvason, 1987). If more than three water-level stations are appropriately distributed around a lake, their periodic measurement may provide an indicator of ground tilt, with the lake itself serving as a very long-base natural tiltmeter (see next section). However, such periodic measurements are complicated by many local, transient effects (e.g., irregular rates of lake inflow and outflow, ground

slumping near stations, wind, pressure-temperature effects). For periodic water-level measurements to yield data useful for volcano monitoring, the observed variations need to be measurably larger than those associated with transient disturbances of non-volcanic origin.

Changes in volcano slope (ground tilt)

The association of changes in the inclination of the ground surface (ground tilt) with earthquake and volcanic activity was recognized Japan and Hawaii in early 20th century from records of horizontal pendulum seismometers (e.g., HVOWB, 1913 [reprinted 1988]; Omori, 1913; Jaggar and Finch, 1929). Beginning in the late 1920's, pendulum-based instruments specifically designed to measure tilt--the "clinograph" in Japan and the "clinoscope" in Hawaii--began to be developed and tested (e.g., VL, 1928, 1932). By 1933, a network of three clinoscopes, in addition to the horizontal pendulum seismometer at the volcano observatory, was being used to monitor tilt at Kilauea Volcano. However, all of these early instruments shared a serious shortcoming by having a short-base platform subject to spurious local movements not related to volcanic activity.

The water-tube tiltmeter developed by Hagiwara (1947) marked a significant technological advance, because it eliminated many of the instability problems of earlier instruments. Since then, the precise measurement of tilt, both periodically and continuously, has became an integral tool in modern volcano monitoring. For the techniques described here, tilt changes can be determined to a precision of a few microradians (10^{-6} radian). One microradian is equivalent to the angle turned (0.206 second of arc) by a 1-km-long board if one end is raised (or lowered) by 1 mm. There many different techniques to make tilt measurements, each with its own particular advantages and disadvantages, but they are all subject to a serious common problem: site stability and extraneous noise sources (see APPENDIX 4.3).

Tilt-measurement arrays ("wet" and "dry"). Early tilt-measurement systems utilized the principle of self-levelling of a liquid, most commonly water, and, hence, became known as "wet-tilt" measurements. Typically, "wet-tilt" systems involve the optical measurement of changes in water level in two or more containers ("pots") interconnected by water and air (pressure- equalization) tubes. The distance or "base" between the measurement "pots" can be "short" (a few meters apart) or "long" (tens of meters); other factors being equal, the longer the base, the greater is the precision of measurement. By using linked measurement points in either an orthogonal or triangular array, a wet-tilt system yields both the amount and direction of the tilt change between two sets of readings. Empirically, tilts of magnitudes of about 4-10 microradians can be measured reliably by this method.

Water-tube tilt measurements can be made at either permanent stations installed in a building or, better, in a underground vault to minimize temperature-related variations, as was first done at

Sakurajima Volcano. Since 1956, the short-base water-tube tiltmeter in Uwekahuna vault at the Hawaiian Volcano Observatory has been read at least daily and provides one of the longest-kept data sets on ground deformation associated with an active volcano. A portable water-tube tiltmeter (Eaton, 1959) was used successfully for many years at Kilauea Volcano. However, the Eaton system can only work for relatively flat sites, requires cumbersome equipment, is subject to temperature-related reading errors, and is inconvenient and time-consuming to use. Consequently, the so-called "dry tilt" method (also termed "spirit-level tilt") was developed in the late 1960's to supplement and replace the wet-tilt method (Kinoshita et al., 1974). The dry-tilt method is called "tilt levelling" in New Zealand.

The dry-tilt systems, which are readily portable, use a precision optical level, positioned in the center of an array of 3 or more benchmarks, to measure differential height changes of stadia rods set up on permanent benchmarks (Figure 4.19) (Kinoshita et al., 1974; Yamashita, 1981; Sylvester, 1984, 1986; Otway et al., 1984; Otway, 1986). Yamashita (1981, 1982) outlines step-by-step procedures to install a dry-tilt station and to measure and compute tilt changes. Best results are obtained on calm, overcast days, when wind and thermal disturbances are minimized. Dry-tilt measurements are nearly as precise ($\pm$ 3-5 microradians) as wet-tilt measurements, and they have some important advantages: 1) the technique can be used in slightly steeper terrain (hence increasing the number of possible measurement sites); 2) measurement is simple and rapid; and 3) the equipment is easier to transport (by vehicle and aircraft) and carry manually. The dry-tilt method provides a comparatively low-cost and effective means of monitoring many sites on a volcano that undergo relatively large tilts, on the order of tens of microradians over a period of weeks to months.

DRY TILT ELEVATION

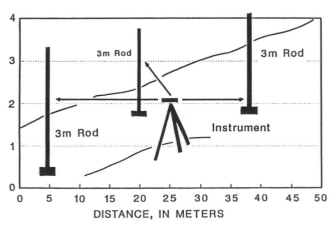

Fig. 4.19. Illustration showing a typical triangular "dry-tilt" measurement array.

TRIG-TILT ELEVATION

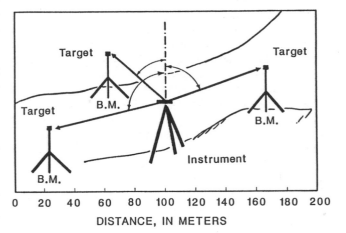

Fig. 4.20. Example of trignometric levelling array to measure ground tilt.

The triangular ("standard") dry-tilt arrays are prone to errors related to benchmark instability because of their relatively short base (40-60 m). This problem can be addressed by utilizing an array of linked, short level lines (each 100-300 meters long) containing extra benchmarks to permit isolation of areas of site instability.

Another measurement technique, employing trigonometric levelling methods (Ewert, 1989, in press), can also be used to determine ground tilt (Figure 4.20). This system uses a precision theodolite, an electronic-distance-measurement (EDM) instrument (see later section), and three reflector/target sets mounted on tripods equipped with plumb poles. Measuring tilt trigonometrically has several advantages over the standard dry-tilt method: 1) longer bases (as long as 200 meters) can be measured; 2) level ground is not necessary, thus removing a major limitation on the use of dry-tilt measurement techniques on steep-sloped composite volcanoes; 3) the system is more compact and easier to transport in difficult terrain; and 4) the system can be also be used to make other ground-deformation measurements.

Electronic tiltmeters. Portable tilt-measurement systems--wet or dry--have a disadvantage in that they provide only periodic monitoring, although this problem can be reduced by frequent reoccupation of the tilt-measurement sites. Permanent water-tube tiltmeters, if located in a near-volcano, manned observatory, provide more continuous monitoring, because they typically are read daily and, if necessary, hourly or even more often. Electronic tiltmeters, however, measure tilt changes on a truly continuous basis, 24 hours a day regardless of weather conditions. Thus, they can detect fast-developing precursory indicators that would be missed by periodic monitoring. They also offer several other useful characteristics: 1) they can detect tilts much smaller than is possible with either wet- or dry-tilt techniques; 2) they have a high and adjustable dynamic range; 3) some modern instruments are readily portable and can be used at sites difficult or impossible to monitor by other techniques; 4) the continuously recorded tilt variations can serve as a guide in scheduling reoccupation intervals of field-array networks to increase the likelihood of recording short-term tilt changes; and 5) they can provide telemetered tilt data from remote or hazardous areas with no danger to the observer.

Electronic tiltmeters, however, also have some serious disadvantages. They are very costly compared to the wet- or dry-tilt measurement techniques, in terms of initial purchase and installation as well as of later operation, maintenance, and data processing. Their short bases (a few centimeters to a few meters) make electronic tiltmeters much more susceptible to local site instability than the longer bases (tens of meters) used with tilt-measurement arrays. Another problem is that their electronic and metal parts are sensitive to ambient temperature changes, which introduce variations (diurnal, seasonal) unrelated to ground deformation. Reduction or elimination of this problem requires the installation of the tiltmeter in a thermally insulated location (e.g., underground vault, cave, lava tube) and/or the use of additional instrumental components to correct for thermal effects in the recorded data.

Many electronic tiltmeters, after initial installation, require a "settling in" period of several weeks to months before reliable data are obtained--this constitutes a major disadvantage if they are put into use in the midst of a rapidly developing volcanic crisis. Tiltmeters are also vulnerable to instrumental problems related to electronics drift or failure. Thus, each tiltmeter should be periodically calibrated against a wet- or dry-tilt station at the same or nearby site to check whether that the recorded tilt changes are genuinely related to volcano dynamics, rather than to aberrations caused by electronics, installation, or site-stability problems. Without rigorous, periodic calibration checks, data from electronic tiltmeters may be misinterpreted to indicate volcano deformation when none actually took place, thus resulting in confusion and, possibly, unnecessary anxiety. APPENDIX 4.1 gives a brief summary of some commonly used types of electronic tiltmeters.

Distribution of tilt-measurement sites

Ground tilts, determined by electronic tiltmeters or tilt-measurement arrays, will be most reliable and diagnostic if they are made at several sites on a volcano. Any single site may be located too far from the pressure source (inflation/deflation center) or may suffer from local site instability. Therefore, a network of sites should be distributed around the volcano to detect any systematic tilt changes and to establish the areal pattern of tilt. The design of a tilt or any other volcano-monitoring network is invariably a compromise between an ideal number and distribution of measurement sites and what is actually possible given the available monetary and scientific resources, terrain considerations, logistics and accessibility, etc. However, to the extent possible, tilt-measurement sites should

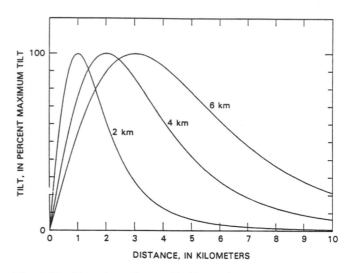

Fig. 4.21. Plot of maximum tilt (theoretical) as a function of horizontal distance from a point-pressure source for Kilauea Volcano, Hawaii. Curves labelled 2, 4, and 6 km are predicted maximum tilt for point sources (e.g., magma reservoir) at these depths; (see text for discussion). (After Dvorak and Okamura, 1987, Fig. 46.3).

be established at or near the principal vent(s) and at several distances away from them. Ideally, every 60°-sector on a composite volcano should have one or more tilt-measurement sites at various distances along radial lines from the summit (Figure 4.22B). Data from such a network would provide not only the temporal information needed for volcano-monitoring purposes, but also would constrain the location and size of the pressure source causing the tilts.

In the selection of possible tilt-measurement sites, it should be noted that, for a point-pressure source, the maximum tilt will occur at a horizontal distance from the center of inflation (usually near the summit of the volcano) equal to about one-half the depth of the magma beneath the surface. For example, maximum tilt caused by magma accumulation 2 km below the summit will occur at a distance of 1 km from the summit (Figure 4.21)--on the upper slopes of most volcanoes. Therefore, at least one tilt-measurement site (and tiltmeter) should be placed on the upper flanks to detect nearly maximum tilts related to magma intrusion at shallow depths. The more distant tilt stations would provide for early detection of magma intrusion at depth.

Horizontal displacements

Pre-eruption inflation or deflation of a volcanic edifice causes horizontal strain as well as vertical displacements (Figure 4.1). The horizontal component of ground deformation can be monitored by theodolite measurements, electronic-distance-

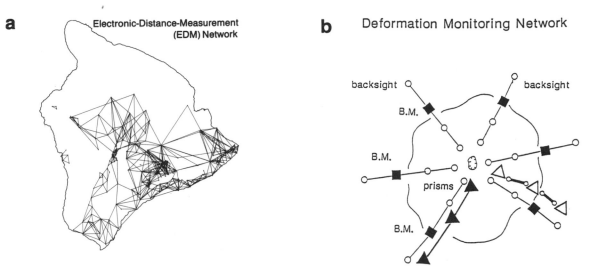

a Electronic-Distance-Measurement (EDM) Network

b Deformation Monitoring Network

Fig. 4.22. **A.** The EDM network (trilateration network) used by the Hawaiian Volcano Observatory to monitor horizontal strain at Kilauea and Mauna Loa Volcanoes. Each line represents a single EDM measurement; not all measured lines are shown. (From Heliker et al., 1986). **B.** A simple, but effective, monitoring network of radial arrays of segmented EDM lines, tilt-measurement sites, and tilt-levelling lines: solid square, EDM instrument site; open circles, permanent or mobile target reflectors; solid triangles, location of electronic tiltmeters and calibration dry-tilt arrays; open triangles, dry-tilt (or spirit-tilt) measurement sites; and heavy lines anchored by small open circles, short level lines to measure tilt. Simpler versions of this idealized network have been established at Mayon Volcano, Philippines, and several other composite volcanoes in developing countries. **C.** The EDM monitoring network at Mount St. Helens (From Swanson et al., 1981, Fig. 92). This type of network is intermediate between examples (a) and (b) in complexity and cost but probably would provide adequate coverage for most composite volcanoes.

measurement (EDM) instruments, strainmeters (extensometers), and crack lines. The EDM technique has largely supplanted angular measurements with the theodolite and perhaps provides the best measure of rapidly determining horizontal strain integrated over a wide area of the volcano, because the distances between benchmarks can be as long as tens of kilometers. However, under some circumstances, angular and distance measurements can be combined effectively (Lipman et al., 1981). A strainmeter permits continuous, precise measurement of horizontal strain at a single site, which with rare exceptions spans maximum distances of several to a few tens of meters. Individual segments of crack lines generally involve measured distances of tens of meters or less. The monitoring of horizontal strain at a volcano is best done by some combination of these techniques, depending on the areal coverage needed and the monetary and scientific resources available.

Electronic-distance-measurement (EDM). The general principles and procedures of the EDM method in volcano monitoring have been well described (Kinoshita et al., 1974; Banks, 1984). APPENDIX 4.2 discusses some important factors in the actual measurement technique. The EDM method utilizes the coherent transmission of a laser beam from the instrument set up over one benchmark to a reflector ("target") at another benchmark. The phase shift that occurs during the time

for the light to travel to the reflector and back to the transmitting instrument is proportional to the distance between the two benchmarks. Measurements are usually expressed as slope distance, the actual distance between the two benchmarks. Simple geometrical calculations can be used to determine the horizontal distance. Although some lines may involve a vertical angle as much as 25°, most are much flatter or nearly horizontal; the measured changes are loosely regarded as horizontal strain unless otherwise specified. For relatively flat lines, contraction of measured distances between benchmarks on the volcano and "baseline" benchmarks at distant, stable locations suggests inflation of the volcanic edifice. Extension of tangential and inclined radial lines between benchmarks on the edifice can also suggest inflation. If a benchmark is common to two or more intersecting lines (Figure 4.22A,C), the measured displacements can determine the bearing as well as amount of horizontal movement of that benchmark between two sets of measurements; such vectors can be computed or graphically determined (see Kinoshita et al., 1974). With an adequate number and distribution of EDM lines, the vectors of horizontal movement can define the center of inflation (e.g, Figure 4.17).

In theory, changes of less than 1 ppm (= 1 microstrain or 1 mm in 1 km) should be detectable by most instruments, if the measurements are fully corrected (Bomford, 1980); some

c

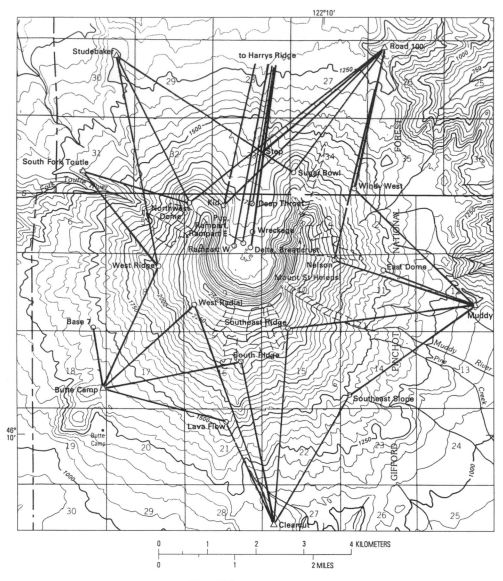

Fig. 4.22. cont.

instruments can achieve a precision of 0.1 microstrain if the measurement lines are flown. In practice, uncertainties are typically in the range of 3-8 ppm, because line lengths are generally longer than 1 km, full atmospheric corrections usually cannot be made, and operator error is inevitable. This level of precision is usually adequate to detect horizontal strains of 10^{-5} to 10^{-3} commonly observed at several well-monitored volcanoes (i.e., between 1 cm and 1 m per km of line length). If the strains are on the order of 10^{-5} (1-3 cm of change in 1 km of line length), measurements can be made with temperature and pressure readings only at the instrument end of lines and permanent reflectors at the opposite ends of the lines.

EDM measurements have the following advantages: 1) faster than tilt and levelling surveys per unit area monitored; 2) require less manpower per unit area monitored; 3) can better detect deep magma intrusion than either tilt or levelling studies; and 4) at present, provide the only practical field- portable means of acquiring horizontal strain data in volcano monitoring. Major disadvantages of EDM measurements are: 1) the equipment is expensive; 2) line-of-sight between benchmarks is necessary; 3) good atmospheric conditions are required along the entire line-of-sight for each measurement and during the entire period of network reoccupation; and 4) unless special steel towers are constructed over benchmarks, such as at Mount St. Helens

(Swanson et al., 1981), measurements are difficult, if not impossible, when benchmarks are covered by deep snow. The snow-cover problem can be overcome at some target locations by mounting a permanent reflector onto an expansion bolt embedded in a vertical or overhanging cliff face.

EDM-monitoring arrays. If possible, an EDM network should be composed of stable baselines and interlinked triangular arrays of lines, sometimes called a "trilateration" network (Figure 4.22A). However, many stratovolcanoes are too steep, too dangerous, or too remote to practically and safely permit regularly scheduled reoccupations of the benchmarks in a trilateration array. In such cases, repeated measurements of simple linear arrays of permanently emplaced reflectors can provide much of the information that can be obtained by reoccupation of a full trilateration network, and at a fraction of the cost and effort (Figure 4.22B). These radial arrays have been established at several remote and logistically difficult volcanoes (e.g., Pagan Volcano, Mariana Islands; Mayon and Bulusan Volcanoes, Philippines; and Nevado del Ruíz, Colombia). Such arrays allow daily measurement of 10 or more stations on several segmented lines from 3 or more instrument stations around the base of the volcano, using existing roads or trails to move only the instrument. Thus, frequent measurements can readily be made with relative safety to more stations with significantly less equipment, vehicles, and personnel. The disadvantages are that the displacements measured yield only apparent (not absolute) strain, and the precision of the measurements, particularly for steeper or longer lines, is degraded because the temperature and pressure at the permanent target reflector are not known.

Another, and perhaps more serious, shortcoming of an EDM network consisting of only 2 or 3 radial segmented lines is that narrowly localized, but potentially dangerous, ground deformation may go undetected. For example, a network spaced at sectors fewer than those shown in Figure 4.22B might miss a "bulge"--comparable in size to the one that existed at Mount St. Helens before the 18 May 1980 eruption--if it should happen to develop in a sector between two radial lines. Adequate coverage of a composite volcano might require a more extensive network, similar to that at Mount St. Helens (Figure 4.22C).

Strainmeters (extensometers). Strain gauges or strainmeters, largely developed for engineering applications, vary widely in design and purpose. In general, the use of strainmeters in volcano monitoring is restricted to measurement of contractions or extensions across recognizable areas of movement (fissures, faults, zones of cataclysis, etc.). Agnew (1986) has reviewed in detail the principles, workings, and limitations of the main types of instruments used in geophysical studies: rod strainmeters, wire strainmeters, laser strainmeters, and borehole hydraulic strainmeters. He concluded that a major difficulty in using strainmeters in tectonic studies was the stable attachment of the instrument to the ground to eliminate spurious or unwanted signals.

Most geophysical strainmeters are extensometers, which can detect horizontal displacements of 0.1 mm or less. They mostly are being used to measure tectonic creep, such as occurs in the San Andreas and other fault systems. While strainmeters afford the only current means of continuously measuring horizontal displacements, they to date have been little used in volcano monitoring because: 1) most instruments are very expensive to install, operate, and maintain; 2) most are not very portable; and 3) the data are highly site dependent and apply only to a small part of the volcano. Nonetheless, an inexpensive continuously recording extensometer, consisting of a modified tide gauge, has been used successfully at Kilauea Volcano to monitor the opening of cracks related to volcanic activity (Duffield and Burford, 1973; Tilling, 1976). Also, two relatively low-cost ($800), highly portable, telemetered wire-line strainmeters are currently being used with good success to monitor the lava dome at Mount St. Helens.

Hand measurements (crack lines). A simple and direct method of monitoring horizontal displacements is the periodic measurement with a standard surveyor's steel tape of distances between reference points in a linear array (sometimes called "crack lines") across one or more radial cracks, fissures, thrust faults, and other surface rupture. Such features are found most commonly in the immediate vicinity of a vent. Localized inflation that is symmetric about a point source can result in radial cracks and concentric thrust faults, as found, for example, around the base of the active dome at Mount St. Helens (Chadwick et al., 1983, 1988). Dike intrusion generally is characterized by long linear cracks and fissures.

While the method of monitoring crack width by hand-held tape measurements is less precise ($\pm$ 2-3 mm in a distance of tens of meters) than the more sophisticated ("high-tech") volcano-monitoring techniques, it is highly reliable and very cost effective. Steel-tape measurements of the rate of movement of small thrusts and radial cracks at the base of the growing lava dome have provided a remarkably successful "low-tech" technique in predicting dome-building eruptions at Mount St. Helens (Figure 4.23). Because the use of such "low-tech" techniques may require working in possibly hazardous areas close to active vents, the safety of the personnel making the measurements must be considered carefully in the design and conduct of such monitoring.

Photographic comparisons

Comparison of photographs can provide another low-cost method of detecting deformation caused by some volcanic processes. The comparison can be either qualitative or semiquantitative. An example of a qualitative comparison would be the detection of new cracks, bulging, and other indicators of deformation by comparing aerial or ground-based photographs taken before and after the activity. To yield semi-quantitative data, the photographs being compared would have to be taken from the same location, elevation, and angle, with the same

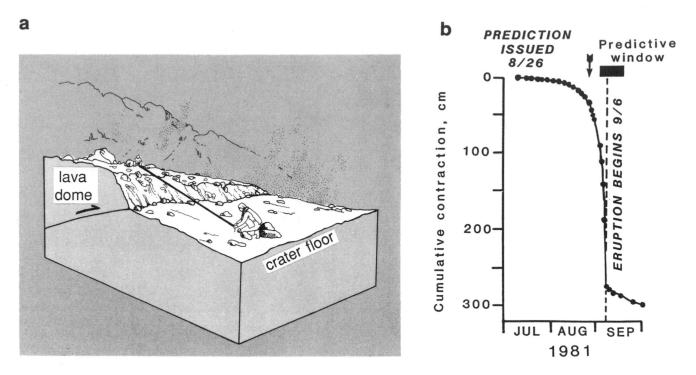

Fig. 4.23. An example of a useful "low-tech" technique to monitor horizontal displacements. **A.** Distances across the leading edges of thrust faults around the base of the lava dome within the crater of Mount St. Helens are measured periodically by means of a steel tape (from Brantley and Topinka, 1984). **B.** The cumulative contraction of the measured distances are used, along with other monitoring data (e.g., Figure 4.25), to successfully predict dome-building eruptions since June 1980. In this example, the arrow marks the issuance date of the eruption prediction, the black rectangle shows the period during which the eruption was predicted to occur ("predictive window"), and the dashed vertical line indicates the eruption onset. (Modified from Swanson et al., 1983, Fig. 3).

lens-camera system, and with some sort of included scaling factor (two or more distinct morphological features or man-made markers). Semi-quantitative monitoring might also include establishment of a number of photographic stations with benchmarks that are reoccupied periodically, with the camera set at the same tripod height and aimed at fixed references, and use of scaling factors. An example of such a situation would be the monitoring of growth of an active dome, where movements on the order of meters would be easily resolved. Another would be the monitoring of known cracking areas or fumarolic fields for changes detectable by photography.

Importance of benchmark and site stability

Inherent in any ground-deformation monitoring technique is the fundamental assumption that the changes measured truly reflect volcanic behavior, **not** local ground dislocations caused by site instability or other non-volcanic effects (e.g., ground slumps; thermal, diurnal or seasonal changes; electronic drift; instrumental bias). No matter how precise or reliable the measurement method, the data obtained are worthless unless they detect actual responses to subsurface pressures acting on the volcanic system. Thus, the two most important prerequisites in ground-deformation measurements are: 1) the proper installation of the reference marks on the surface (benchmarks), and 2) the selection of sites for benchmarks or placement of monitoring equipment (tiltmeters, strainmeters, seismometers, etc.).

Benchmarks established in bedrock are generally the most stable, if due consideration is given to avoid areas of obvious instability, such as detached or potentially detachable blocks near steep slopes and cliffs. If there is no recourse but to install benchmarks in poorly consolidated material, then every attempt should be made to establish the largest possible base to minimize possible post-installation movement related to environmental (including man-made) causes, or the inherent instability of the substrate of the benchmark. Unfortunately, some benchmarks-- in unconsolidated deposits and also at some bedrock sites-- appear initially to be good in terms of stability, but later turn out to be unstable, inert, or otherwise unresponsive to volcano-related deformation.

Some specific examples of attempts to address benchmark and instrument installation problems in tilt measurements are given in APPENDIX 4.3. However, the placement of redundant benchmarks in the monitoring network provides perhaps the best means to determine whether the benchmark installations and measurement sites are well coupled to the deforming volcano surface. Moreover, the evaluation of site stability is an empirical process, one that requires the comparison of data obtained at each site with data obtained at other sites to recognize inexplicable deviations from an otherwise coherent patterns of ground deformation. For such evaluations to be diagnostic, the monitoring data considered should span a period of time long enough, at least a few months and perhaps years, to establish baseline behavior and, ideally, to bracket several eruptions or intrusions.

At well-monitored volcanoes, adjustments are made periodically in the method of benchmark installation and in the layout of monitoring networks, as critical data become available to assess the stability and responsiveness of measurement sites. On volcanoes studied only for a short time in response to a crisis, there are no baseline data for comparison and for evaluation of benchmark and site stability. Therefore, the interpretation of deformation data must be accordingly cautious.

Interpretation of Monitoring Data and Eruption Forecasting

Most, perhaps all, eruptions and intrusions are preceded by precursory seismic activity and ground-deformation. There also may be accompanying geochemical and non-seismic geophysical changes. Many of these precursors are measurable with present-day technology, and their systematic monitoring provides the essential data needed to make short-term eruption forecasts and predictions. Volcanologists must interpret the available monitoring data to try to understand past or current volcanic behavior, and, then by extrapolation, to anticipate future behavior, including possible eruptive activity. Unequivocal interpretation of monitoring data, however, is rarely possible. While considerable advances have been made in volcano-monitoring methods and instrumentation, forecasting future volcanic behavior still remains elusive. The difficulties in this task include the following: 1) the monitoring data are insufficient and cover too short a time span for meaningful interpretation; 2) diagnostic information obtained at well studied volcanoes may not be directly transferable to poorly understood volcanoes; 3) precursory behavior is not the same from one eruption to the next, even at the same volcano; 4) eruptive behavior can change with time; and 5) with current knowledge, there are no criteria to distinguish between the precursory activity that leads to eruption and that which culminates in an intrusion (or "abortive eruption" as termed by Walker, 1982).

Assumption and basis

The fundamental assumption in interpreting monitoring data is that the measured changes in seismicity, ground deformation, and other geochemical or geophysical parameters reflect the complex rise of magma into shallow crustal levels (< 5 km depth), if not into the volcanic edifice itself (Figure 4.1; an actual magma reservoir almost certainly would not have the simple volume and geometry shown). Eruptive or intrusive activity thus is expected to result in physical displacement or pressurization of material beneath and within the volcanic edifice, which in turn initiates inflation and seismicity. At some volcanoes, such phenomena occur in cycles, such as those that have been well documented for Kilauea Volcano (Figure 4.24) and a few other well-studied volcanoes in Japan, Iceland, and elsewhere.

In general, pre-eruption inflation occurs gradually and slowly, over periods of weeks to years. Typically, such inflation is evidenced by increasing ground tilt and occurrence of short-period (A-type) earthquakes, also possibly accompanied by detectable changes in other geophysical parameters and in the geochemistry of fumaroles, springs, and lakes on the volcano. With the onset of an eruption or intrusion, rapid deflation may occur as pressure on the magma reservoir is quickly relieved. During deflation, changes in tilt and in vertical and horizontal displacements of benchmarks tend to be opposite to those during pre-eruption inflation, though not necessarily equal in magnitude. With deflation, A-type earthquakes generally diminish in numbers and size. Long-period (B-type) earthquakes can occur before eruption and commonly occur with increasing frequency, reflecting stress adjustments related to the exit of magma from the reservoir to feed the eruption or intrusion (Figure 4.24). The occurrence of volcanic tremor, which commonly precedes and accompanies other volcanic seismicity, is one of best indicators of magma or fluid movement and, hence, of possible volcanic activity. As discussed earlier, volcanic tremor occurs during all eruptions, precedes some, and can occur without culmination in eruption.

However, there are some documented cases that demonstrate neither detectable increases in seismicity nor edifice-wide deformation occurred before major eruptions. These cases represent exceptions to our general assumption and are not well understood, because the baseline monitoring data for them are limited and cover only a short time. In such cases, it seems that the edifice does not become significantly pressurized because of localized weakness (e.g., 1980 Mount St. Helens) or because the vent is already essentially open by virtue of earlier eruptions or intrusions (e.g., 1981 Pagan, Marianas; 1984 Mayon, Philippines; 1985 Ruíz, Colombia). Thus, forecasting of such eruptions may be hampered by lack of deformation monitors in critical areas, or by failure to recognize the possibility that poorly recorded or unrecorded earlier activity had already significantly weakened the edifice and/or cleared the magma conduit and vent(s).

To date, short-term forecasts and predictions have been empirical and based almost exclusively on *pattern recognition*-- recognition of a characteristic pattern of precursory behavior and its relation to an ensuing eruption. Precursory behavior can be an inflation-deflation cycle or some other distinctive, recurring

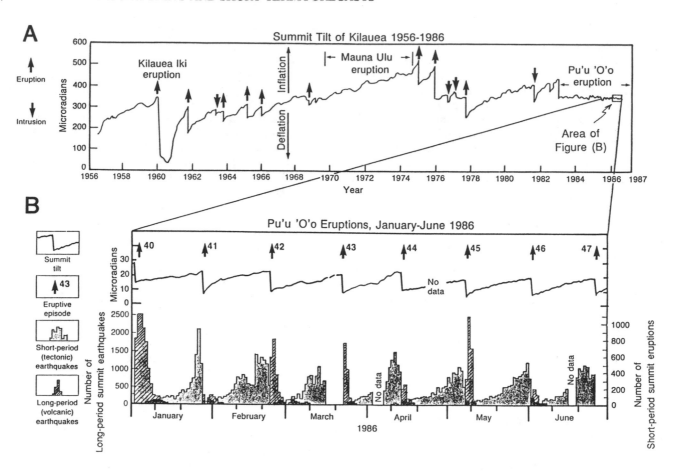

Fig. 4.24. The inflation-deflation cycle commonly observed at Kilauea Volcano, Hawaii (see text). **A.** The common pattern of gradual inflation, followed by abrupt deflation, is well demonstrated by major eruptions and intrusions. **B.** Detailed look at a 6-month segment of the tilt record shows similar inflation-deflation patterns for the high-lava fountaining episodes of the Pu'u 'O'o eruption, even though the tilt changes and time intervals are much smaller (compare with A). Also well shown are the variation patterns of the two common types of seismicity that commonly precede and accompany Kilauea eruptions. (Modified from Tilling et al., 1987).

pattern of changes in the state of the volcano. If a particular pattern is known to have preceded an earlier eruption, recurrence of that pattern suggests that another eruption might possibly occur. Reliable identification of recurring patterns of precursory behavior essential to eruption forecasting requires many years or decades of volcano monitoring between and during eruptive activity. Experience from well-studied volcanoes has amply shown that the monitoring data needed for pattern recognition and eruption forecasts are best obtained by a combination of approaches, rather than relying on any single method. Thus, optimum monitoring requires a multidisciplinary effort.

The indispensable part in recognizing possible patterns of volcanic behavior is the acquisition of baseline monitoring data for both active and presently quiet, but potentially dangerous, volcanoes. Only by knowing the range of variations (seasonal or cyclic) in the monitored parameters while a volcano is quiet is

it possible to detect unambiguously a departure from baseline or "normal" behavior that might augur renewed activity. It is important to establish baselines for even long-dormant volcanoes, because they might have eruption frequencies of many centuries and, hence, may not be considered "active" (generally defined as having erupted in historical time). For example, in the U.S., studies are underway to establish baseline data for several of the presently quiet volcanoes in the Cascade Range and for some caldera systems that have shown recent signs of unrest (e.g., Dzurisin et al., 1982, 1983a; Jachens et al., 1983; Hill, 1984; Chadwick et al., 1985; Denlinger et al., 1985; Mortensen and Hopkins, 1987; and Dzurisin and Yamashita, 1987).

The acquisition of baseline data need not to be on a continuous basis, but measurements of the baseline networks should be repeated on a regular schedule (e.g., every few years). Should the volcano begin to show increased seismicity or other signs of unrest, monitoring studies then should be accelerated and be made continuously.

Some examples

In the 20th century, considerable advances have been made in the young science of volcanology, particularly in our understanding of volcanic phenomena and in volcano-monitoring techniques. Less progress has been made in our ability to forecast or predict volcanic activity. However, for the few volcanoes that have been well studied through several eruptive episodes, volcanologists can now routinely detect and monitor precursors to possible activity. Present capability to recognize early departure from normal behavior and an increased probability of activity represents an important step toward eruption prediction. Early recognition of precursory indicators allows some lead time to increase monitoring studies and to advise and educate the emergency-management authorities, land managers, and local populace of potential activity and associated hazards. Equally important is the early recognition that an eruptive episode or a volcanic crisis is over; such recognition allows officials to declare an end to evacuation and other emergency measures, thereby minimizing the socio-economic costs and the disruption of the daily life of the region affected.

Precursory seismicity has guided observers to arrive at the outbreak locations before the onset of all eruptions at Kilauea since 1979 (Decker, 1986). Also, emergency-response officials in Hawaii routinely rely on the Hawaiian Volcano Observatory to alert them of the need to evacuate certain areas, roads, and trails, and to advise them when it is safe for the evacuated people to return. For example, based on increasing precursory seismicity and rate of summit inflation, Decker et al. (1983) forecasted that "the probability significantly increases for an eruption of Mauna Loa during the next 2 years." In March 1984, the volcano, which had been inactive since July 1975, began a 3-week eruption (Lockwood et al., 1985).

Strictly speaking, the successful anticipations of the likely sites and/or time window of eruptive activity in Hawaii were forecasts, not predictions, as defined at the beginning of the chapter, because the exact times of the actual eruptions were not stated in advance. However, the near-perfect record of successful forecasts in Hawaii and predictions of dome-building eruptions at Mount St. Helens since June 1980 (Dzurisin et al., 1983b; Swanson et al., 1983, 1985) does mark a significant advance in predictive capability. An example of a successful prediction at Mount St. Helens and related factual statements is illustrated in Figure 4.25 and Table 4.1.

It should be emphasized, however, that the forecasts in Hawaii are for a shield volcano that has been well studied for many decades and the predictions of the relatively small, non-explosive events at Mount St. Helens involve an intensive program of sophisticated monitoring. It is unreasonable to assume that the capabilities achieved in Hawaii and at Mount St. Helens can be easily achieved for, or applied to, more

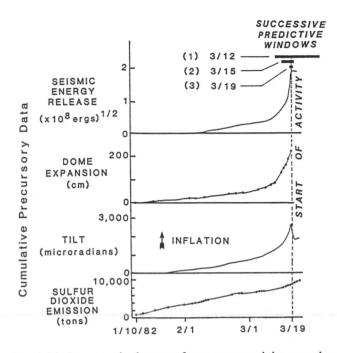

Fig. 4.25. Increases in the rate of precursory activity served as the basis for the successful prediction of the onset of the March-April 1982 eruptive episode at Mount St. Helens (modified from Swanson et al., 1985, Fig. 3). Dome expansion is measured by EDM measurements of horizontal displacements (but comparable data were obtained by crack-line measurements), tilt change by electronic tiltmeter, and sulfur dioxide emission by correlation spectrometer (COSPEC). Excerpts from the factual statements and predictions (1), (2), and (3), issued on March 12, 15, and 19 respectively, are given in Table 4.1; black bars indicate the successively narrowing predictive windows.

voluminous and explosive eruptions at other volcanoes. To date, only a few explosive eruptions have been successfully predicted, largely on the basis of seismic or ground-deformation monitoring: Tolbachik, Kamchatka, U.S.S.R. (Tokarev, 1978); Mount St. Helens, U.S.A. (Swanson et al., 1985); and Sakurajima, Japan (Ishihara, 1988).

Challenges in Volcano Monitoring and Eruption Prediction

This section builds upon the cogent discussion of this topic by Newhall (1984). While much progress has been made in recent decades, major challenges still confront volcanologists in advancing the state of the art in volcano monitoring and eruption prediction on a global basis.

TABLE 4.1. Examples of factual statements and predictions of the onset of the March-April 1982 eruptive episode at Mount St. Helens (modified from Swanson et al., 1985).

Time	Date	Factual statement or prediction issued
0900	March 5	*Factual statement*: "Seismicity...increased around 21 February and has remained at a level somewhat above background since that time...Measurements made last week (27 February) show only slow ground deformation...and no significant increase in gas emissions..."
		[Measurements after 0900 on March 5 show increased rates of deformation]
0800	March 12	*Factual statement and prediction (1)*: "Seismicity...continues at elevated levels...Rates of ground deformation in the crater have increased during the last two weeks...Based on rates of deformation, an eruption is likely within the next 3 weeks. Deformation is confined to the crater area, suggesting that renewed dome growth will occur."
		[Measurements on March 15 showed greatly greatly accelerated deformation]
1900	March 15	*Prediction updated (2)*: "...an eruption, most likely of the dome-building type, will probably begin within 1 to 5 days."
		[Rates of deformation and and seismic-energy release continued to increase rapidly]
0900	March 19	*Prediction updated (3)*: "...an eruption will begin soon, probably within 24 hours. The character of both the seismicity and deformation in the crater area indicates that the most likely type of activity is dome growth."
1927	March 19	ERUPTION BEGINS (see text)

The Need for Effective and Sustained Monitoring Efforts

More than 22,000 people perished in the 1985 volcanic disaster at Nevado del Ruíz (Colombia), even though some volcano monitoring had begun, and the potential for mudflow hazards was recognized, months before the eruption and devastating mudflows on 13 November (see CHAPTER 5). The death toll probably could have been reduced substantially, if the communications between the volcanologists and public-safety authorities and the emergency-response measures had been more effective (Herd et al., 1986; Podesta and Olson, 1988; Tomblin, 1988; Voight, 1988). A contributory factor was the failure, both nationally and internationally, to quickly develop a sustained monitoring effort at Ruíz involving experienced scientists and advanced equipment and methods during the year-long unrest before the eruption. Early international augmentation of the on-site team might have produced more precise forecasting, which in turn might have improved both understanding and concern outside the scientific community. Might the authorities and affected public have responded with alacrity had the scientists' warnings been based on more, and better, monitoring data and a more precise forecast? We will never know. Definitely the Ruíz experience establishes the fact that information from volcano monitoring and hazards-zonation mapping is wasted unless it is effectively communicated to, and swiftly acted upon, by emergency-response officials.

Only a small number of active or potentially active volcanoes are being monitored on a sustained basis, and nearly of all of these are in the developed countries (Tilling, 1989, in press). The most dangerous volcanoes remain the least studied. Thus, to mitigate effectively volcanic hazards on a global basis, adequate sustained monitoring needs to be conducted at many more high-risk volcanoes; most of these are located in the developing countries that lack sufficient economic and scientific resources for the needed studies. In the absence of in-country scientific expertise and monitoring equipment, the international community must provide rapid, adequate, and sustained assistance during a volcanic crisis or disaster (see CHAPTER 6). Also, international cooperative programs in volcanology should place greater emphasis on monitoring and related studies of explosive volcanoes identified to be high-risk, well before a crisis develops at any of them.

The Need for an Expanded Monitoring Base

The Ruíz tragedy provides a hard lesson that some minimum level of monitoring be established at every high-risk volcano.

The minimum monitoring required would be dependent on the individual volcano and the scientific resources available. In general, such monitoring might include the elements listed below [modified from a listing made by the World Organization of Volcano Observatories (WOVO), a Working Group of the International Association of Volcanology and Chemistry of the Earth's Interior (IAVCEI); Tilling, 1982]:

- Geological mapping and other studies to define the potential hazards and improve understanding of prehistoric activity.
- A seismic network of four stations, with telemetry and an alarm that sounds if seismicity exceeds a certain threshold.
- Continuously recording 2-component tiltmeters (in the near-, middle- and far-field) with telemetry and adjacent tilt-measurement stations to serve as a check and calibration of each tiltmeter.
- A mudflow alarm system (if potential mudflow hazards exist).
- A modest EDM network.
- Periodic reoccupation of the tilt and EDM networks--to establish benchmark stability and baseline data.
- Periodic observations of physical changes in the vicinity of the volcano (e.g., appearance of new fumaroles and/or changes in known fumarolic areas, ground cracking and other surface signs of instability, unaccountable changes or damage of vegetation).
- Collection and interpretation of all information resources, maps, and documentation of the volcano's past behavior.
- Collection of pertinent manuals and articles for instruments, monitoring techniques, and comparable volcano case histories.

The Need for More Observational Posts

The eventual trend in monitoring will be toward greater automation of equipment and computerized analysis of telemetered data at a central recording site. However, the value of a local observer should not be underestimated as an effective and low-cost monitor. A local observer who is intimately familiar with a volcano and who checks it frequently and carefully may still be the first to recognize some precursors to an eruption. This is especially true if the observer has been given training in basic volcanology, if the monitoring data are not analyzed and interpreted expeditiously at the central recording site, or if electronic or telemetry problems result in periods when no data are sent to the central recording site. Moreover, it may be more economical in some developing countries to have monitoring instruments read by local field observers than to have data telemetered to a central location.

One of the best examples of the utilization of local observers is in Indonesia. The establishment and operation of a network of simple observatories, manned by knowledgeable observers, has achieved considerable success in hazards mitigation. This low-cost program has been effective in reducing fatalities during the explosive eruptions of Merapi and other volcanoes in Indonesia.

However, technological advances in telemetry (including satellite telemetry), a growing need for better quality and more rapidly acquired data, and rising costs of maintaining small field stations will eventually make telemetry and centralized recording necessary and more cost effective. When technical expertise is limited, telemetry can bring real-time data directly to the few scientists in a country who have the experience to interpret it. Telemetry systems are expensive and require greater electronic skills than may be available, but an initial investment in equipment and electronics training can result in more timely and better data interpretation. Data processing in central observatories is becoming increasingly automated, permitting greater application of computer-based, real-time analysis of data from continuous seismic monitoring.

Development and/or Refining of Existing Methods and Instruments

Another major challenge in volcano monitoring is the need to improve and add to existing monitoring techniques. Seismic monitoring achieved a recent breakthrough, just beginning to be applied, in the development of a widely available, readily portable PC-based system for on-line acquisition, digitizing, and analysis of seismic data. Needed is a parallel advance in deformation monitoring, particularly in the refinement of measurement precision. Too frequently, noise in the data obscures, or is confused with, genuine indicators of precursory movement of magma. More precise, more absolute determinations of horizontal and vertical strain are needed to improve resolution of magma rise rate, volume and depth of source, and other information not easily derived from seismic data. The Global Positioning System (GPS) and other satellite-based geodetic measurements (e.g., Prescott and Svarc, 1986; Schutz, 1987) hold promise of wide application in the future, if the few parts-per-million resolution needed for volcano monitoring can be routinely attained and if the equipment and operating costs can be lowered. With wide distribution and sufficiently lowered costs, perhaps the GPS can be used at permanent telemetered sites.

Development and/or Refining of Methods and Instruments for Continuous Monitoring

Considerable progress also needs to be made in the development of reliable, continuously recording monitoring equipment. At present, such systems are routinely available only to monitor seismicity and ground tilt. At a few well-studied volcanoes, tide gauges, gravimeters, strainmeters, hydrogen gas probes, and experimental geoelectric arrays permit limited continuous monitoring of vertical and horizontal strain, geochemical parameters, and geoelectric phenomena. Continuous monitoring offers the best chance to detect short-term precursors and to determine the full variability of such activity; also, such monitoring helps to ensure that critical data can be gathered immediately before and during eruptions without undue hazard to volcanologists.

Recognizing Eruptions Precursors that are Subtle or Widely Separated in Space and Time

A prerequisite for the recognition of subtle precursors at a volcano is a database of baseline behavior; the longer the period spanned by the database, the better are the prospects of detecting subtle precursors. A general approach to creating such a database is to compile a continuous time-series record of every reported or measured change (e.g., earthquake, usual animal behavior, variations in emissions from springs and fumaroles) within several tens of km of each volcano, even if the significance of each change is not immediately understood. Too often, changes that are not understood are dismissed and forgotten, only to be seen later as significant after an eruption.

In addition, it would be important to increase communication between all parties who might have pertinent observations--other geoscientists, airline pilots, surveyors, local residents--so that volcanologists might learn of changes that they might not normally monitor, and so that each specialist can suggest significance to observations that the others might not have considered. Compilation of the precursors to historical eruptions of the world, as has been recently done for historical unrest at large calderas (Newhall and Dzurisin, 1988), provides another avenue that may reveal heretofore unrecognized relations between precursors and eruptive behavior.

Developing Techniques for Forecasting the Time of Climax of an Eruption

Some eruptions reach their climax within minutes or hours of their onset; others do not climax until months or years. For example, of 205 major historical explosive eruptions world wide, 92 of these reached their climax within the first day of eruption, many of these within the first hour (Simkin and Siebert, 1984). On the other hand, the 1815 eruption of Tambora Volcano (Sumbawa Island, Indonesia)--the largest and most deadly in history--took place nearly three years after the start of eruption. Such observations should caution volcanologists to never assume that the worse is over after the initial eruptive phase. However, are there as yet undiscovered techniques that will enable us to forecast whether an eruption is likely to climax shortly after its onset or much later? Our present state of knowledge is inadequate to address this question.

Increased Use of Other Techniques for Forecasting the Type and Magnitude of an Eruption

Volcanologists rely on pattern recognition in monitoring data and use of past eruptive behavior of volcanoes to forecast eruption type, magnitude, and timing. However, even at well-studied volcanoes, the relationship between precursors and the nature of ensuing activity can be highly complex and variable. Thus, an important objective in volcanology is to more accurately define the magma source region; potential size, volatile content, viscosity, resupply rate, and pressure of the magma supply; and the yield strength and configuration of the conduit path.

Some promising work that might apply here is precise geobarometry of petrographic studies, determination of pre-eruption volatile contents of magma, and comparison of the pre-eruption volatile contents from explosive and non-explosive eruptions, historical and prehistoric (e.g., Melson, 1983; Devine et al., 1984; Sigurdsson et al., 1985a). Are there other geochemical studies of eruptive products that might provide additional clues? Are there new ways to relate changes in magma composition and/or physical properties with observed modes of degassing, or with changing patterns of seismicity and ground deformation? Are there untested or undiscovered geophysical techniques that might address the basic questions of the generation, ascent, storage, and, ultimately, intrusion or eruption of magma?

Minimizing "False Alarms"

The occurrence of precursory activity does not always culminate in eruptions; the moving magma and/or fluids may not breach the surface, resulting only in subsurface intrusions. Currently, the best hope for distinguishing precursors that might lead to eruptions lies in careful, continuous monitoring of a volcano through many eruptive and dormant cycles, to learn its full range of characteristic patterns. However, this is a process of trial and error, in which the errors can be minimized but probably never eliminated.

Perhaps in time, as scientific knowledge about how volcanoes work improves, it may become possible to distinguish between precursory processes that cease with subsurface intrusions from those that culminate in eruptions. However, until such distinction can be made routinely and reliably, it seems prudent to treat every occurrence of unmistakable precursory activity as having the potential for eruption and to advise emergency-response officials accordingly. With this prudent approach, "false alarms" (actually aborted eruptions) will be unavoidable. A current, and much needed, partial solution to the false-alarm problem is to educate the government officials and general public about the probabilistic nature of forecasts and predictions and of the limitations inherent in the scientific information upon which they are based. However, an equally serious challenge to volcanology is to minimize false alarms through more reliable pattern recognition--a challenge that entails new developments in, and expansion of, volcano-monitoring efforts. If society wishes to maximize effective response to warnings of volcanic hazards, it must be prepared to accept the consequences of the unavoidable false alarms. False alarms themselves can provide, through objective assessment of the scientific and public response to a volcanic crisis that ended without eruption, valuable lessons useful in making or improving contingency plans for the next crisis, which could culminate in an eruption.

APPENDIX 4.1. COMMONLY USED TYPES OF ELECTRONIC TILTMETERS

Currently used electronic tiltmeters are the following common types: pendulum tiltmeter, mercury-pool tiltmeter, and bubble tiltmeter. The following general description of these systems is summarized from Banks (1984). As discovered decades ago in Japan and Hawaii, the offset of the base of a long-period horizontal pendulum seismometer provides a sensitive measurement of tilt. In theory, two such seismometers operating at right angles can resolve tilt vectors of about 0.1-0.2 microradian, but such a system has a small dynamic range, is subject to spurious motions not unrelated to volcano tilt, and is not very portable. Modern electronic pendulum tiltmeters employ a suspended pendulum and two pairs of sensors placed at right angles below it, allowing the instrument to resolve tilt vectors. Such tiltmeters have large dynamic range and can be installed in boreholes to minimize atmospheric and surficial thermal disturbances.

A mercury-pool tiltmeter in an underground vault (Uwekahuna) has continuously recorded ground tilt at Kilauea Volcano since 1967 (Decker and Kinoshita, 1972). Analogous to a water-tube tiltmeter, this type of instrument utilizes the change in level of liquid mercury in two interconnected cisterns ("pools") by continuously recording changes in capacitance between the mercury-pool surface and a capacitance plate rigidly suspended above it. Changes in the measured capacitance, which are inversely proportional to the distance between the plate and the liquid surface, are electronically processed, converted to tilt changes, and continuously plotted on an analog recorder. Mercury-pool (or mercury-tube) tiltmeters are typically single-component systems, and thus two instruments placed at right angles are required to measure the amount and direction of tilt changes. Though they can detect tilts of 0.1 microradian, mercury-pool tiltmeters have a dynamic range of only about 25 microradians. This limitation, combined with difficulty in moving or servicing them, effectively precludes the deployment of mercury-pool tiltmeters in remote sites that experience tilt fluctuations greater than such a small dynamic range.

Recent advances in microelectronics have enabled the development of simple, relatively inexpensive electronic bubble tiltmeters (e.g., Westphal et al., 1983). The configuration of the electrolytic bubble sensors can vary widely, depending on mode of installation (platform or bore hole) and design factors, but all of the instruments can resolve tilt changes of 0.1 microradian. They have large (adjustable) dynamic range and are rugged, light weight, and compact; thus, they are well suited for installation requiring backpacking to otherwise inaccessible sites high on the volcano's slope, where tilts are likely to be most pronounced. Tilt data can be recorded on site for 2-3 months duration or telemetered back to a central observatory. Bubble tiltmeters are successfully used to monitor activity of the Mount St. Helens lava dome (Dzurisin et al., 1983b). Wyatt et al. (1984) give a recent comparison of some tiltmeters commonly used to measure crustal deformation.

APPENDIX 4.2. IMPORTANT FACTORS IN EDM MEASUREMENT

The distance is determined by a phase-comparison technique, whereby the reflected light beam is converted into an electrical signal. Because a time interval proportional to the distance occurs between transmission and reception of the signal, the phase of the reference signal has advanced relative to that of the return signal. In modern EDM instruments, the phase relationship between the reference and return signals is compared by an internal microcomputer and converted into a direct readout of the distance. For older instruments, the measured distance must be computed manually from field readings of the phase offset.

The maximum distance that an EDM instrument can measure is determined by three factors: instrument design and power, type of target reflector, and atmospheric conditions. Signal strength depends on the wattage delivered to the laser generator, the wavelength of the laser light generated, and the sensitivity of the receiver electronics. In general, the ruby-colored visible light lasers (helium-neon) have more range than invisible (infrared) lasers. The maximum range can be as great as 60 km for a He-Ne laser instrument, but only 20 km or less for most infrared instruments. However, most distances measured in a typical EDM network are less than 10 km. Accessibility to and line-of-sight between benchmarks and the better precision obtained by shorter lines generally are more important considerations in network design than is how far apart benchmarks can be placed.

A target can be of any material that can reflect the laser back to the instrument in sufficient intensity to be received and processed by the optical-electrical system of the instrument. The reflector may be as simple as beaded cloth (as used in projection screens) or a plastic highway reflector. Such reflectors, however, can be used only for measurement of short distances, rarely more than 200 meters, not useful for most monitoring applications. For the greater signal intensity needed for most measurements, glass reflectors, composed either of 3 orthogonal mirrors or a corner-cube retroreflector made of high-quality, sealed optical glass, are required. One or more such reflectors are used as targets for measuring distances over 1 km; the corner cubes are more reflective but 3-5 times the cost of the orthogonal glass mirrors.

Atmospheric conditions perhaps pose the most severe constraint on use of EDM techniques. Rainy, cloudy, hazy, or fumy conditions between the benchmarks can greatly diminish the effective range of the instrument and, under the worst conditions, prevent measurement. Atmospheric factors such as absorption, scattering, and background radiation all reduce, in an exponential manner, the maximum distance that can be measured.

EDM measurements must be corrected for the index of refraction of the air through which the laser beam passes. For best precision, the index of refraction is determined along the entire light path by flying a light plane or helicopter to measure air temperature, pressure, and humidity during measurement. However, such a procedure is prohibitively expensive in many cases, even if the aircraft and needed recording equipment are available. Thus, a more common, though much less precise, procedure to compensate refraction-related errors is to assume a standard humidity (usually a 0.5 ppm correction for lines < 5 km) and to measure temperature and pressure at each end of the EDM line at the start, end, and several intervening times during the measurement. The sacrifice in precision is partly compensated by reduction in measurement time, thus allowing a greater number of measurements to be made during a given period.

For precise trilateration, a correction for earth and beam curvature needs to be made, if the distances are longer than 8.5 km, (Meade, 1969); however, for simple monitoring of line-length changes, this correction is not necessary. In recent years, an experimental "two-color" laser EDM instrument (Slater and Huggett, 1976; Langbein et al., 1982), which eliminates the need for atmospheric corrections, has been used with good results in monitoring ground deformation at Long Valley caldera (Hill, 1984; Linker et al., 1986). However, at present, the "two-color" EDM system has shorter range and is much more expensive and less available than conventional EDM instruments.

APPENDIX 4.3. BENCHMARK AND SITE INSTABILITY

Fundamental to any technique of ground-deformation monitoring are well-installed and well-located reference marks on the surface of the volcano. The reference marks are commonly called benchmarks, and the importance of their proper installation cannot be overstressed. Proper benchmark installation may require considerable effort and expense, to insure that they will move in response to subsurface volcano-induced pressures, not in response surficial instabilities. If there is any possibility that measured displacements result from frost heave, gravitational slumping, or disturbance of the benchmark by man or animal, then even the most sophisticated and precise measurements will be worthless. The uncritical interpretation of such measurement data may result in misleading, even damaging, conclusions detrimental to effective hazards-mitigation efforts.

In addition, the benchmarks must be arranged in arrays or networks that assure optimum detection of deformation in the amount and pattern expected. For example, the best arrays on conical volcanoes radiate from and surround the central vent(s); depending on the monitoring method used, the arrays should include both near-field and far-field reading and instrument stations. However, the minimum array for detecting eruptions on linear rift zones of dike injection is perpendicular to the feature, even if the array is tangential to the overall form of the volcano.

Benchmarks established in bedrock are generally the most stable, if due consideration has been made to avoid the problems of detached blocks, potentially-detachable blocks, proximity of steep slopes and cliffs, and areas subject to fault movements. When, as is the common case for stratovolcanoes, benchmarks must be established in poorly consolidated material, one should attempt to establish the largest possible base to avoid post-emplacement movement related to environmental causes or the inherent instability of the substrate of benchmark. A usually successful installation in unconsolidated substrate involves driving 4 or more heavy-gauge stainless-steel or brass rods at various angles into the deposit (ideally to a depth of no further penetration, but at least 2 to 3 meters), followed by construction of a substantial concrete pier on top of and including the array of rods (see Banks, 1984). Benchmarks or tiltmeters are then affixed to the pier. Installation of redundant benchmarks and piers is recommended to determine if the benchmark sites and installations are actually reflecting the true movement of the deforming volcano surface.

CHAPTER 5. SOME RECENT CASE HISTORIES

Raymundo S. Punongbayan

Philippine Institute of Volcanology and Seismology, Quezon City, Philippines

Robert I. Tilling

U.S. Geological Survey, Menlo Park, California 94025

Introduction

An effective program of disaster preparedness against natural hazards requires the following mutually interdependent components: preparedness planning, preparation of hazards-zonation maps, monitoring, prediction, warning and response systems. Each component consists of a network infrastructure and operational framework. The cases selected for this chapter--three from the Philippines, and one each from Indonesia, Papua New Guinea, Colombia, and United States--contrast how people and institutions have coped with volcanic and related crises. The disaster preparedness programs of these countries involved differed widely in stage of development, ranging from non-existent, through emerging and to developing, to developed.

The Taal, Mayon, and Canlaon cases (Philippines) illustrate the evolution of the country's preparedness in the monitoring, prediction and warning components in volcanic-hazards mitigation. At Galunggung (Indonesia), a pre-eruption hazards assessment and spontaneous and quick response made up for the shortcomings of a just emerging monitoring system and prediction-warning capability. The Rabaul case (Papua New Guinea) shows how a volcanic crisis was well handled, through advance preparation of hazards-zonation maps, contingency planning, and increased volcano surveillance. The Nevado del Ruíz (Colombia) disaster arose from faulty warning-communication and response systems which negated pre-event hazards-zonation mapping and monitoring efforts of concerned agencies. The United States case provides an example of relatively good response to the reawakening of Mount St. Helens in 1980 after more than a century of repose.

In this chapter, each of these volcanic crises and the general lessons learned from them will be discussed briefly.

Taal Volcano, Philippines, 1965-1977

Taal Volcano, an intracaldera stratovolcano (14.00 N, 121.00 E) located in Batangas Province, has had 33 recorded eruptions since its earliest known outburst in 1572. Its largest historical eruption was in 1911, which killed more than 1,300 people (Table 1.2). Taal then remained quiet until 1965, when it again erupted violently. The 1965 eruption and the ensuing intermittent activity through 1977 took place during a period when the country's monitoring, warning and response systems were largely undeveloped and untested.

The Events

On 28 September 1965 at 0200 (local time), Taal Volcano began to fountain incandescent materials. More than an hour later, a powerful blast occurred in the vicinity of Mt. Tabaro, forming a NE-SW-oriented deep embayment of Taal Lake in the southwestern part of Volcano Island (Figure 5.1). Later eruptions were localized along this embayment.

Continuous strong pulses built up a 20-km-high eruption column. Most of the airborne pyroclasts were deposited to the west of the eruption site. The base of the eruption column formed into an outwardly expanding ring-like cloud of hot particles and gas, the first base surge ever described during a volcanic eruption (Moore, 1967; Moore et al., 1966). Smaller explosions during the waning phases of the 1965 eruption created a cinder cone islet within the explosion crater.

Since then, Taal erupted every year from 1966 to 1970, and again in 1976 and 1977 before it finally calmed down. The 1966 eruption was a less violent cone-building phreatomagmatic eruption and filled much of the 1965 explosion crater. The succeeding 1967 outburst was an even milder phreatomagmatic event confined within the 1966 crater lake.

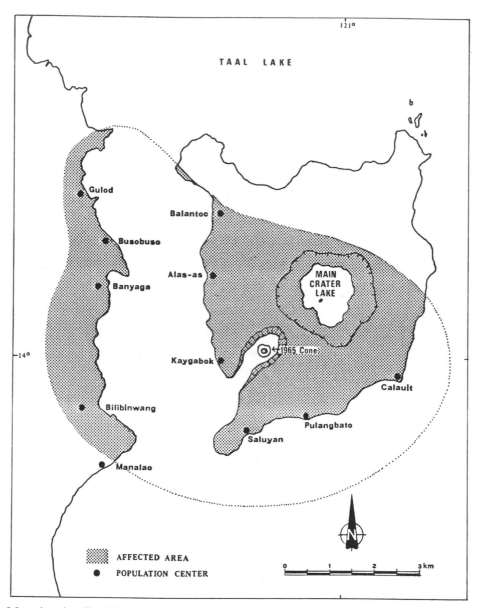

Fig. 5.1. Map showing Taal Volcano, Philippines, and the areas affected by the base surge of the 1965 eruption. Data from Moore et al. (1966).

In 1968-1969, the eruptive activity became Strombolian, characterized by spasmodic lava fountaining. Lava production was so extensive that the pre-1965 shoreline was regained by advancing lava flows. In 1970, Taal had another weak phreatomagmatic eruption that was construed to be the culminating phase of the activity that began in 1965. However, the volcano's quiescence after 1970 was short-lived as activity in the 1965 eruption site was renewed in 1976-1977, this time by phreatic eruptions. Regular explosions produced voluminous ash and lapilli deposits and formed an elongate explosion crater in the 1969 cinder cone (Ruelo, 1983).

Impacts

The heaviest impact of Taal's eruptions was felt in 1965 during the initial strong blasts which devastated the Mt. Tabaro area. An estimated volume of 40 million m^3 of volcanic deposits blanketed an area of 60 km^2 around the volcano and killed about 200 persons. Most died while fleeing the island when their boats capsized due to the combined effects of overloading, falling ejecta, and waves caused by the turbulent base surge. Barrios in the southern half of the volcano island, such as Alas-as, Kaygabok, Saluyan, Pulang-bato and Calauit were devastated. Even barrios on the mainland 7 km from the eruption site were hit by hot pyroclastic fragments, which were preferentially hurled to the west and southwest of the volcano (Figure 5.1). There were fatalities in the municipality of Agoncillo, located about 10 km from the volcano.

Crops of cassava and rice on the island were ready for harvest when the volcano erupted. More than 2,000 visitors had come to the island to enjoy the traditional harvest festival, thus adding to the permanent population of 3,000. Economic losses were incurred by burial of arable lands and crops under ash and lapilli. Barrio Kaygabok was virtually erased from the map when the explosion crater carved out its land area. Trees were uprooted and burned. Houses collapsed under the weight of accumulated ash while others were simply blasted away. Bloated carcasses of cows, carabaos and other flocks and herds littered the shore of the island. The livelihood of many inhabitants was completely ruined so that without outside aid they had nothing to start with. The costs of the ensuing evacuation of about 50,000 beleaguered inhabitants of towns around Taal Lake entirely drained the calamity fund of the national government (P12 million, or about $ 3 million [U.S.] at the 1965 exchange rate)

Pre-1965 preparedness and monitoring

In 1953, the Commission on Volcanology (COMVOL), the predecessor of the Philippine Institute of Volcanology and Seismology (PHIVOLCS), had prepared Operation Taal, a contingency plan for Taal Volcano. This plan was based on hazards associated with past eruptions of the volcano and declared the volcano island and parts of the coastal areas affected by the 1911 eruption as a Permanent Danger Zone. The plan also pointed out the need for an organization to coordinate disaster response in the country.

The Commission maintained two monitoring stations at Taal. However, the eruption in 1965 was a baptism of fire for COMVOL. At that time it had no baseline monitoring data on which to recognize possible eruption precursors and to make short-term forecasts or predictions. Also, the immediate seismic precursor (felt earthquakes) was short. Therefore, the eruption was not anticipated or predicted.

Response

The 1965 eruption of Taal created a stir in the local and national leadership. Though all the relief agencies responded quickly--such as the Social Welfare Administration (now Department of Social Welfare and Development), Red Cross, Armed Forces, and Civil Defense Administration (now Office of Civil Defense)--the evacuation process gained notoriety as a disorganized and inefficient operation (e.g., Burgos, 1965;

Cruz, 1965). Political leaders were lambasting one another, while journalists criticized these leaders for using the emergency situation for political purposes (Soliven, 1965a,b). The presidential election was only a few weeks away.

Following the onset of activity, the COMVOL personnel saved many lives by helping in the evacuation. However, the COMVOL organization was accused of negligence and incompetence for failing to predict the eruption, and for assuring people, even a few days before the eruption, that nothing untoward would happen.

As soon as the news of the eruption reached Malacañang, President Macapagal commissioned the Defense Department to organize the Task Force Vulcan, manned by hundreds of officers and enlisted men. The prime task of Vulcan was to handle the transportation requirements for relief efforts and to assure security and order in the evacuation. Governor Leviste of Batangas declared the province in a state of emergency to ensure a smoother relief operation and to make contingency resources readily accessible to afflicted families.

The eruption victims generated much sympathy from the public. National media appeals for donations were usually accompanied by emotion-laden photographs of deaths and grieving relatives and horror stories of survivors. Donations in cash and goods poured into the evacuation centers. Civic and community organizations also prominently figured as generous donors and volunteer relief workers in the evacuation centers. Carroll and Parco (1966) made a detailed study of the disaster relief and related social aspects.

The 1965 Taal eruption, and the poor response to it, exposed a serious weakness of the government, namely, its unpreparedness to handle a national emergency (Valencia, 1965), particularly one caused by a natural disaster. The crisis underscored the volcanic hazards facing people living on Taal Volcano Island and raised the issue of a long-range program of permanent relocation of the inhabitants.

The eruptions that occurred during 1966-1977 were milder and better anticipated. Also, by that time, there were fewer inhabitants in the danger zones to worry about, and those who moved back to the affected areas were henceforth always on the alert and in close touch with the Commission on Volcanology.

Mayon Volcano, Philippines, 1984

Mayon Volcano, a stratovolcano (13.26 N, 123.68 E) in the eastern part of Albay Province, has had 44 eruptions since its earliest recorded activity in 1616. The scientific and governmental response to the volcanic crisis associated with its month-long eruption in 1984 illustrates the improvement in the disaster preparedness of the Philippines since the 1965-1977 eruptions of Taal Volcano. The volcanic crisis did not culminate in a disaster because of the following: 1) the existence of a well-developed volcanic-emergency management system and procedures; 2) the gradual buildup of the volcano's eruptive force; 3) the readiness and promptness of surveillance

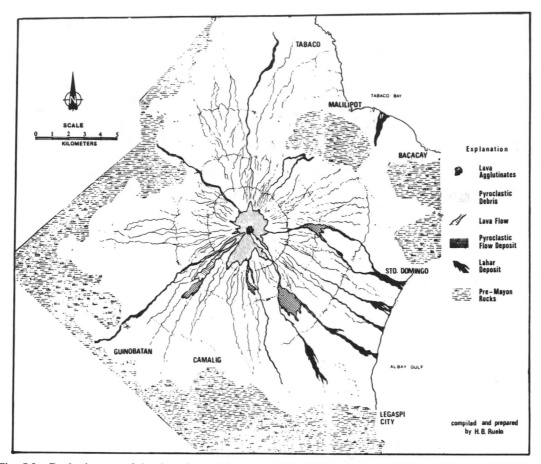

Fig. 5.2. Geologic map of the deposits and features of the 1984 eruptions of Mayon Volcano, Philippines. (Modified from Umbal, 1987, Fig. 1).

and response institutions to act; and 4) the assistance of non-government local organizations and of international scientific and relief agencies.

The Events

The 44th and most recent eruption of Mayon occurred in three phases from 9 September to 6 October 1984 (SEAN, 1984a,b). Intermittent crater glow, increased steam emission and rockfalls progressively intensified until the first eruptive phase on 9 September. The first phase was characterized by lava effusion and strong Strombolian activity with the generation of andesitic pyroclastic flows and lava flows along the NW and SW flanks of the volcano (Figure 5.2). This phase lasted until 18 September. The resurgence or second phase started on the 22 September and lasted until 29 September. During this phase, strong Vulcanian eruptions formed ash columns 16 km high and triggered pyroclastic flows. On 6 October, a minor outburst formed an eruption column nearly 2 km high and small pyroclastic flows down to 1000 m elevation around the cone.

Numerous lahars occurred during and after the eruptions (Umbal, 1987). The first mudflows formed on 14 September in the SW and NW quadrants where the new deposits had accumulated. More mudflows occurred after the activity during 23-25 September, as rain reworked the unconsolidated pyroclastic flow and ashfall deposits in the SE and E sectors.

Impacts

The destructive agents unleashed by the 1984 eruptions of Mayon Volcano were lava flows, mudflows (lahars) and ashfalls. The lava flow covered only the upper slopes of the volcano. Pyroclastic flows of the first phase were confined to the upper elevations (1800+ m), but, during the resurgence, these swept farther down toward the SE and E. The Bonga pyroclastic flows, representing the largest single pulse of the eruption, reached the 200 m elevation, about 2 km from Barangay Bonga; one lobe advanced even closer to the adjacent Barangay Matanag. Mudflows were mainly distributed along gullies and nearby lowlying residential and cultivated areas around the volcano. They reached the coastal towns on the

NE, E, and SE flanks, and as far as 8 to 13-km radius on the N, S, and W quadrants (Umbal, 1987). Ash fell on areas extending to a 20-km radius on the N, NW, and SW flanks and beyond the Tabaco Bay coastline to the NE. Most of the affected areas received only light ashfalls (< 1 mm thick). Thicker deposits of ash (5 mm, 15 mm and 20 mm) accumulated in areas mostly within a 8 to 9-km radius on the N and SE slopes.

Eighty-five barangays in the municipalities of Camalig, Daraga, Guinobatan, Ligao, Malilipot, Sto. Domingo, and Tabaco and in the city of Legaspi were affected. These were populated by more than 85,000 inhabitants at the time of the eruptions. About 21,000 hectares of prime agricultural lands were rendered non-productive by the eruptive products, and agricultural losses were estimated at P46 million or about $2.3 million (U.S.) (Tayag et al., 1984).

Infrastructures and developed properties were likewise hit by Mayon's destructive processes and products, particularly by the lahars that caused damage costing more than P15 million or $750 thousand (U.S.). Fortunately, no lives were lost as a direct result of the month-long eruption. However, the number of recorded deaths during the eruption was about 15 higher than that typical for the region during non-eruptive periods. Possibly, the higher death rate may be attributed to illnesses caused or aggravated by exposure to the elements or to harsh conditions in the evacuation centers (Tayag et al., 1984).

Pre-event Preparedness and Monitoring

Prior to the 1984 activity, a contingency plan called Operation Mayon, had already been tested in two previous eruptions (1968 and 1978). A hazards- zonation map was also available delineating the areas within a 6-km radius of the summit as a Permanent Danger Zone officially closed to permanent human habitation.

Before 1984, the Philippine Institute of Volcanology and Seismology (PHIVOLCS) was maintaining two volcanological observatories: the Mayon Resthouse and Observatory (MRHO), located about 4 km NNW from the volcano's summit at elevation 760 m (a.s.l.), and the Sta. Misericordia Station (SMS), located 8.5 km E of the summit. Both stations were equipped with a three-component Hosaka electromagnetic seismograph. The seismograph at MRHO stopped functioning on 17 August and resumed operation only on 10 September, one day after the start of the eruption. Luckily, in the early evening of 9 September, personnel on duty at MRHO observed the intense crater glow and fountaining of incandescent materials at the volcano's summit, and immediately relayed the observation to the central office of PHIVOLCS.

Institutional Response

On the night of 9 September, PHIVOLCS notified the President, the Minister of Science and Technology and the Albay Provincial Disaster Coordinating Council (PDCC) of the

eruption. The first official PHIVOLCS bulletin announcing the eruption was released the next day. On 11 September, the Albay PDCC convened, reviewed plans, and began immediate implementation of warning and contingency measures. An order was issued on 12 September to evacuate areas within the Permanent Danger Zone, to ensure compliance with restrictions barring permanent human habitation. A few days later, the evacuation order was extended to the residents on the southwestern side within a 8-km radius of the volcano (the High Risk Zone). During the first phase, a total of 23,000 persons were evacuated to safer ground.

During the second phase of the eruption, all areas around the volcano were affected: 10 barangays within the High Risk Zone and some barangays within the Probable Danger Zone (10-km radius of summit) were ordered to evacuate. The number of evacuees swelled to 73,400. A total of 49 evacuation centers were established in 47 schools or government buildings and 2 private buildings. Evacuation of beleaguered inhabitants was carried out and supervised by the Municipal Disaster Coordinating Councils (MDCC's). Security was maintained by the Philippine Constabulary-Integrated National Police (PCINP).

To provide the necessary services to the evacuees, more than 1,100 regular staff of national agencies, local governments, and volunteer workers were assigned to the evacuation centers. Services provided included the distribution of relief goods, health and medical care, information dissemination, and education on backyard gardening, sanitation, nutrition and family planning. Relief food, clothing, medicine, and other necessities were provided not only by government but also by various private civic, religious organizations and individuals. Families who lost their homes were given P200 emergency assistance.

Cash donations from government and private organizations and individuals totalled more than P231,000 by late November. A considerable volume of relief goods had also been contributed by various donors. Still, the provision of the basic necessities, services, and amenities to an average number of 50,000 persons for more than 2 months proved to be a heavy economic burden. Considering the evacuees' loss of income, their daily subsistence needs had to be mostly subsidized, requiring a daily outlay of P400,000. The food donations were inadequate to meet the needs of all the evacuees (Tayag et al., 1984).

Fifty health stations were established in the evacuation centers and 156 health personnel were deployed in the centers to provide medical services. Volunteers from private organizations and institutions, such as St. Luke's Hospital, San Miguel Corporation and Philippine Medical Association, augmented the services provided by the government health personnel.

Foreign Technical Assistance

In response to a request from PHIVOLCS, UNESCO and the Office of Foreign Disaster Assistance (OFDA) of the U.S.

Agency for International Development (USAID) sponsored the participation of a 3-man team from the U.S. Geological Survey (USGS) in monitoring and studying the eruption. The USGS team introduced and trained PHIVOLCS personnel in the use of new monitoring methods, including electronic-distance-measurement (EDM) and dry tilt techniques. Technical assistance was also provided by the Committee for Coordination of Joint Prospecting for Mineral Resources in Asean Offshore Areas (CCOP) in the study of debris-flow phenomena and their attendant hazards.

People's Response

PHIVOLCS conducted a survey of the socio-economic impacts of the 1984 eruptions of Mayon during the second week of October (Tayag et al., 1984), immediately after the eruption ended. This survey involved 118 heads of household randomly picked from the barangays within a 8-km radius of the volcano. The results of the study included the following: 1) before 9 September, 8% of the respondents already "knew"--from observational monitoring (e.g., increased heat/humidity, sulfurous odors, apprehensive animal behavior) that there would be an eruption; and 2) before 10 September, when the official bulletin of PHIVOLCS was disseminated, 47% were already certain that Mayon was erupting. The dark steam emissions (locally termed "mai-tim na usok) and the crater's fiery glow on 9 September confirmed the local inhabitants' suspicions.

By 11 September, the day the Albay PDCC met to plan the implementation of contingency measures, 44% of the respondents reported to have received an order to evacuate either from barangay captains or mayors. This finding indicates that the local officials in the municipal and barangay levels had taken the initiative to issue the evacuation order ahead of the PDCC. Discrepancies were observed between the dates the evacuation order was received by the respondents and the dates of their actual evacuation. There was also a discrepancy between the number of respondents who received an order to evacuate (82%) and the number of informants who actually evacuated (94%). These discrepancies seem to indicate that the people's response to the event was based more on their own perceptions and initiative, rather than on the advisories and information given by the warning-contingency response agencies.

Most of the inhabitants of the volcano area had experienced the two earlier eruptions of Mayon in 1968 and 1978. Their previous eruption experiences, therefore, had familiarized them with the behavior of the volcano before and during the two earlier eruptions and with the contingency measures taken. However, the survey results also indicated that the residents were largely dependent on outside assistance for mobility, shelter, and sustenance during the emergency. Though maximum efforts were exerted by response agencies to provide basic facilities for the affected inhabitants, the respondents complained of congestion, lack of water, inadequate lighting, and poor sanitation facilities at the evacuation centers.

Towards Improving Emergency Response

The failure of the concerned agencies to issue a pre-eruption warning was compensated for by the people's own perception of danger and initiative to take refuge. However, in an event wherein Mayon Volcano exhibits a behavioral pattern never experienced by the inhabitants in their lifetime, the absence of pre-eruption warning could be disastrous. PHIVOLCS has been upgrading its monitoring network in the Mayon area and its staff has been concentrating efforts on making medium- to short-term predictions. Results of these studies formed the basis of long-term forecast made in 1985 that Mayon may erupt between 1987 and 1989. On 20 August 1988, PHIVOLCS issued a medium-term forecast stating that Mayon may erupt within nine months based on monitoring data and observations of crater glow and other changes in the summit crater.

PHIVOLCS hopes to issue a short-term prediction and timely warnings the next time the volcano erupts. As of this writing (December 1988), a short-term prediction has not been made. Projects have also been proposed to upgrade the facilities of the evacuation centers. None of these, however, have been implemented as of October 1988. Another matter which should be considered is the need to improve the capability of the people to stock up for emergencies. Because most of the inhabitants have limited marketable skills and are living at a subsistence level, skills development and livelihood projects might help prepare them for future crisis, or perhaps encourage and permit them to live and work elsewhere.

None of the respondents in the PHIVOLCS survey indicated receiving any notification when it was safe to return home (Tayag et al., 1984). They went back on their own counsel. Thus, at least some evacuees may have stayed at the evacuation centers longer than necessary, thereby extending the responsibility and cost of providing for them. For future volcanic crises at Mayon, steps will be taken to *officially* cancel any warnings or evacuation orders when information and conditions indicate that the volcanic emergency is over.

Canlaon Volcano, Philippines, 1987-1988

Canlaon Volcano is a stratovolcano (10.41 N, 123.13 E) situated in the north central part of Negros Island, Philippines. To date, it has erupted 24 times; its first recorded eruption was a minor ash ejection in 1866. The Canlaon case illustrates how a developed monitoring system equipped with an adequate understanding of a volcano's activities can minimize, and perhaps prevent, unnecessary worry, emergency actions and expenditures.

The Events

The 1987-1988 activity of Canlaon Volcano started on 30 March 1987 when 9 volcanic earthquakes were recorded by the seismic stations around the volcano (SEAN, 1987a,b). Prior to this, the average number of events recorded ranged from 1 to 3. After 30 March, the daily number of volcanic earthquakes fluctuated between low (1 to 8) to moderate level (9 to 17) until 0600 on 22 April 1987, when it abruptly peaked to an alarming level (74). On 3 May, 1987, the volcano ejected ash-laden steam clouds that rose 200 m above the crater rim. The event was followed by emission of ash on 5 May. In addition, both the volume of steam being emitted and the height of the steam plume increased from 10 April to 30 May.

The heightened activity at Canlaon volcano persists up to this time of writing (October 1988). During the first quarter of 1988, seismic activity of the volcano increased, as 687 volcanic earthquakes were recorded compared to 377 during the last quarter of 1987. Fumarolic activity from the active crater generally varied from wispy to moderate steaming during the first quarter. Since 15 March, geochemical monitoring of the Mambucal hot springs disclosed decreasing pH values and increasing chloride concentrations for Aqua pool, Mud pool, and Sulfur spring, suggesting increasing HCl input into the volcano's geothermal system.

On 21 June 1988, the volcano ejected ash-laden steam clouds that rose 300 m above the crater. The next day, ash injections at 1330 and 1418 rose 600 m above the crater. These events were reflected on the seismograms as bursts of small amplitude (0.5 mm) harmonic tremor. Sulfur odor was noted by the residents on the southeast slope of the volcano. On 24 June, ejections at 1155 and 1455 were accompanied by faint rumbling sounds. Ash from the 500 m-high eruption clouds fell on the southeastern upper slopes. No eruption signal was recorded by PHIVOLCS seismic stations.

Four more ash ejections were observed on 25-27 June, accompanied by explosion earthquakes which were recorded by the seismographs. Ash-laden steam clouds reached a maximum height of 500 m and drifted to the southwest and southeast. Ashfall was concentrated on the upper SE and SW slopes of the volcano. On 28 June, harmonic tremor was recorded by the Masulog station seismograph from 1118 to 1500, followed by 14 ash ejections the next three days. These ash emissions were reflected in the seismograms as explosion-type earthquakes. The ash-laden steam clouds reached a maximum height of 1,000 m before drifting to SW, SE, and NW directions. The most recent activity (through October 1988) occurred at 0714-0719 on 2 July. An explosion-type earthquake was recorded, and ash clouds rose to a height of 500 m above the crater. Ash was deposited along the southwest upper slopes.

The above chronology of activity may be part of a protracted eruptive pattern of the volcano. In 1978, Canlaon Volcano erupted 23 times from June to September. Likewise,

in 1985 and 1986, the same protracted pattern prevailed. Taking into consideration the previous eruption history of Canlaon, it is reasonable to expect more small-volume ash ejections in the near future. Although Canlaon has not erupted violently in historic time, there is some evidence indicating larger volume explosive activity in the recent geologic past. The possibility of lava outpouring cannot be ignored but it is believed to be remote at present. This is consistent with the generally low level of steam emission, both in volume and intensity, observed at the surface, particularly, within the crater. Had magma rose close to the surface, phenomena such as crater glow, withering of vegetation, and increase in fumarolic activity would have been observed. The absence of crater glow during the June-July 1988 activity is compatible with the interpretation that the current activity at Canlaon is likely to remain generally mild and at present pose no grave danger to towns within its vicinity.

It must be emphasized, however, that the evidence for the above conclusion is permissive and that future volcanic behavior does not always follow past and/or present behavior. Two important questions cannot be answered with present knowledge: What are the processes driving the current activity? Can the present relatively weak activity quickly develop into more violent activity? Intensive monitoring continues at Canlaon.

Pre-event Preparedness and Monitoring

As early as 1979, a disaster preparedness plan called Operation Canlaon had already been prepared, including a hazards-zonation map based on past eruptions of the volcano. The hazards-zonation map was updated and revised upon completion of detailed geologic studies on the area in 1986 (Figure 5.3). At the onset of the 1987-88 activity, the Philippine Institute of Volcanology and Seismology was maintaining volcanological observatories at Canlaon, Mambucal, and Cabagnaan (Figure 5.3).

Response

The 1987-88 activity at Canlaon necessitated close surveillance. The PHIVOLCS installed a telemetered seismic station at Masulog, 3.2 km SE of the volcano's summit. Ground-deformation studies using EDM, tilt and precise leveling were conducted. The existing survey lines were reoccupied and new ones were established. Additional permanent EDM reflector stations were installed on the SE slope of Canlaon Volcano. A water-tube tiltmeter was installed at Cabagnaan Station. Repeated gravity surveys were conducted to complement the ground-deformation techniques.

On 22 April 1987, PHIVOLCS notified the President about its abnormal condition and likewise informed the Secretary of the Department of Science and Technology (DOST), the Provincial Disaster Coordinating Council (PDSS) and other concerned agencies to make the necessary preparation in case

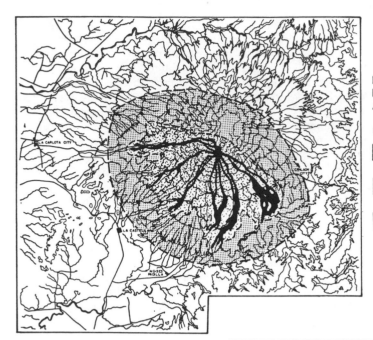

a

HAZARD ZONE MAP FOR
PYROCLASTIC FLOWS, ASH CLOUD
AND PYROCLASTIC SURGES*

EXPLANATION

HIGH DANGER AREAS FOR
ASH CLOUD AND PYROCLASTIC /
SURGES.

PROBABLE PATH AND HIGH
DANGER AREAS FOR PYROCLASTIC
FLOWS.

PROBABLE AREAS WHICH
MAY BE AFFECTED BY
PYROCLASTIC FLOWS SURGES
AND ASH CLOUD.

* *Based on the assumption that the
eruption shall take place at or near the
vicinity of the present active crater.*

b

HAZARD ZONE MAP FOR AIRFALL
TEPHRA & BALLISTIC PROJECTILES*

EXPLANATION

HIGH DANGER AREA FOR
BALLISTIC PROJECTILES.

AREAS AFFECTED BY ASHFALL
FOR ERUPTIONS SIMILAR TO
1969, 1978 AND 1985.

AREAS AFFECTED BY ASHFALL
FOR ERUPTIONS SIMILAR TO
1906.

* *Based on the assumption that the
eruption shall take place at or near the
vicinity of the present active crater.*

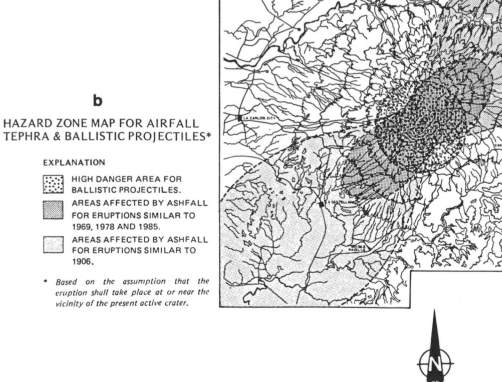

N

0   5   10   15   20 Km

CONTOUR INTERVAL 200m

Fig. 5.3. Hazard-zone maps for Canlaon Volcano, Philippines: **A**, pyroclastic flows and surges and associated ash clouds; **B**, tephra and ballistic projectiles; **C**, lahars and floods; and **D**, lava flows. (Unpublished data, Philippine Institute of Volcanology and Seismology).

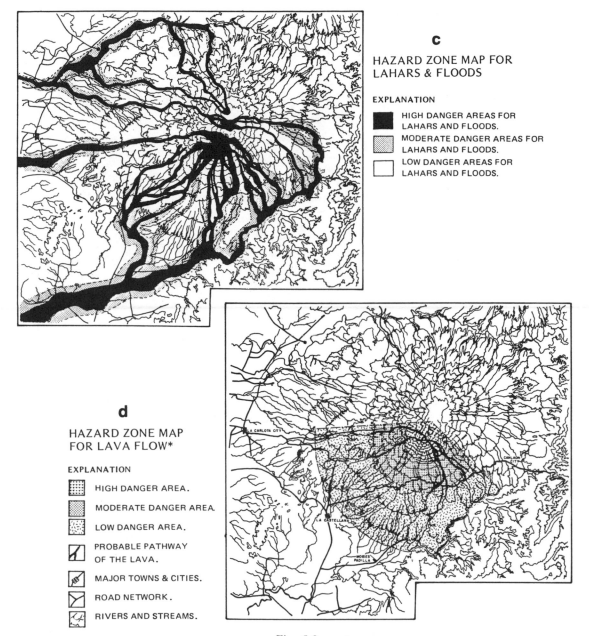

c

HAZARD ZONE MAP FOR LAHARS & FLOODS

EXPLANATION

■ HIGH DANGER AREAS FOR LAHARS AND FLOODS.

▨ MODERATE DANGER AREAS FOR LAHARS AND FLOODS.

☐ LOW DANGER AREAS FOR LAHARS AND FLOODS.

d

HAZARD ZONE MAP FOR LAVA FLOW*

EXPLANATION

▦ HIGH DANGER AREA.

▨ MODERATE DANGER AREA.

▩ LOW DANGER AREA.

◩ PROBABLE PATHWAY OF THE LAVA.

◪ MAJOR TOWNS & CITIES.

◩ ROAD NETWORK.

◩ RIVERS AND STREAMS.

Fig. 5.3. cont.

the volcano's condition should become more active. After further evaluation by PHIVOLCS of the volcano's status, evacuation was not deemed necessary. The damage caused by the ash ejection later proved minimal as the ashfalls affected only the upper, largely uninhabited slopes of the volcano. Unnecessary evacuation and emergency actions would have cost the government considerable money, time and effort. By not ordering emergency measures, undue socio-economic disruption and needless expenses on the part of the government were avoided.

As of this writing (December 1988), Canlaon does not appear to pose any significant hazards. However, with the 1985 Ruíz tragedy in mind, weak phreatic activity, with little or no immediate premonitory indicators, can sometimes lead to destructive magmatic eruptions. Also the present state of the art in volcano monitoring generally is inadequate to determine the type or magnitude of an impending eruption. The possibility that the decision in 1987 not to evacuate was simply lucky must not be discounted. Thus, the systematic monitoring of Canlaon continues to detect any signs of

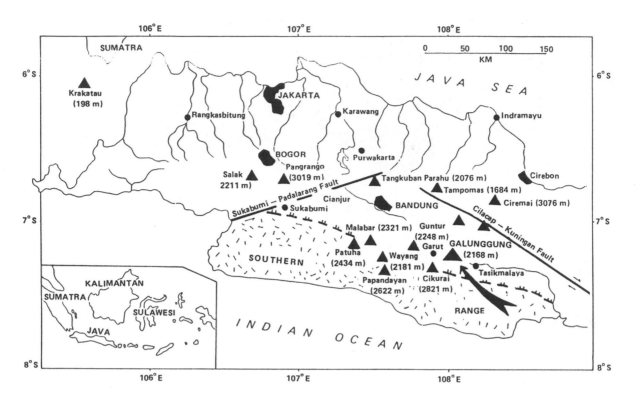

Fig. 5.4. Location of Galunggung Volcano (2168 m), indicated by arrow, with respect to principal cities and some other volcanoes in West Java. (From Katili and Sudradjat, 1984, Fig. 1).

departures from the current, relatively mild phreatic activity. One needs to determine the driving forces for the present activity, before one can decide whether Canlaon is a threat or not in the near future.

Galunggung Volcano, Indonesia, 1982-1983

Galunggung Volcano (108.05 E, 7.25 S) is located in the southeastern part of West Java, about 350 km southeast of Jakarta (Figure 5.4). It rises 1820 m above the plain or 2168 m above sea level. The 1982-83 Galunggung eruption illustrates the value of hazards zonation and immediate response by the beleaguered public, concerned institutions and foreign disaster assistance agencies.

The Events

The following description of the 1982-83 activity is taken from the summary of Yokoyama et al. (1984); more comprehensive accounts are given by Katili and Sudradjat (1984), Sudradjat and Tilling (1984), and (Katili et al., 1986).

Before 1982, Galunggung had erupted in 1822, 1894, and 1918. On 5 April 1982, explosions began with virtually no short-term precursors; there were no long-term precursors. The activity then continued intermittently until early January

1983. The first of three phases lasted from 5 April to 19 May and was characterized by partial destruction of the 1918 lava dome in the summit crater. The next two phases were characterized by ash and bomb ejection. The second phase (20 May to mid-November) was dominated by Vulcanian and Strombolian activity, and the final phase (lasting through early January 1983) by Strombolian and effusive activity. During the most vigorous activity (mid-May through August 1982), eruption columns reached heights of 20 km, nuée ardentes swept down the Cibanjaran and Cikunir Rivers (Figure 5.5), and ash even fell lightly on the capital city of Jakarta. Rainfall-induced lahars developed during or following some eruptions. A minimum volume estimate for tephra produced by the entire eruption was about 300 million m^3 (uncompacted).

Impacts

The first explosions of Galunggung awakened some 200,000 people living close to the volcano, and the ensuing series of major and minor eruptions prompted about 80,000 people to flee to nearby population centers at the foot of the volcano. Most of these evacuees eventually returned home when conditions permitted, but about 35,000 were left homeless and had to be provided with emergency shelter, food, and means of support. Many hundreds of homes, schools, and other structures were destroyed, mostly by lahars

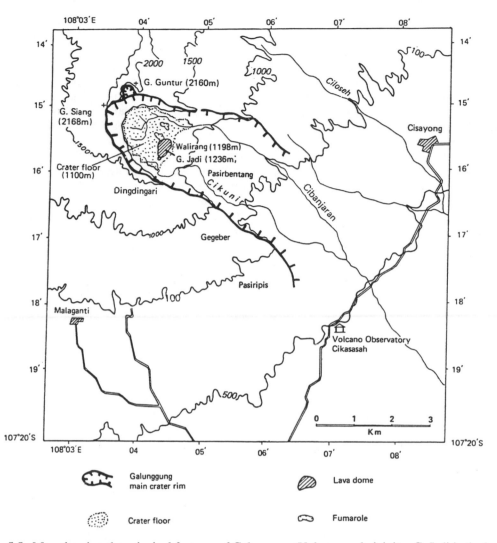

Fig. 5.5. Map showing the principal features of Galunggung Volcano and vicinity; G. Jadi is the lava dome formed in the 1918 eruption. (From Katili and Sudradjat, 1984, Fig. 2.).

and tephra falls; systems of transportation, communications, and commerce were disrupted. Around 200,000 hectares of cultivated land were severely affected, drastically reducing agricultural production. Conservative estimates placed total physical damage at US $100 million.

Because the first eruptions were relatively mild, people were to able to flee the affected areas without danger. There were no reported deaths directly attributable to the eruption, but 18 deaths were attributed to throat and lung infections caused or aggravated by volcanic ash. Nonetheless, the 9-month Galunggung eruption--unusually long for Indonesian volcanoes--caused severe socio-economic impact and disrupted the daily lives of more than 600,000 people in West Java. Nearly half of these people faced food shortages for months and, in many areas, fresh water was scarce or polluted by volcanic ash.

Pre-eruption Preparedness

From its record of historic eruptions, Galunggung was recognized as a potentially dangerous volcano, and preliminary volcanic hazard maps were drawn some 15 years before the 1982-83 eruptions. These were revised after further field studies made in 1981. It was very fortunate that, on the basis of these hazard maps and general preparedness plans, the Volcanological Survey of Indonesia (VSI) foresaw the possibility of nuées ardentes, which in fact occurred on April 8 and during some subsequent eruptions. It had recommended evacuation from the highest hazard zones prior to the eruption, thereby avoiding a repetition of a disaster on the scale of the 1822 eruption, which killed about 4,000 people. The VSI is the designated responsible body for providing information and evaluations concerning volcanic hazards to Indonesia's

National Co-ordinating Body for Natural Disaster (BAKORNAS).

Monitoring, Predictions, and Hazards Assessments During the Eruption

The VSI conducted intensive volcano monitoring throughout the protracted eruption. Technical assistance was extended by, among others, the United States Geological Survey (USGS), the Japanese Government, the Office of the United Nations Disaster Relief Co-ordinator (UNDRO), and the French Government. The government of Indonesia asked UNDRO to coordinate international assistance, issue an appeal, and assist in the diagnosis of current volcanic activity as well as the evaluation of additional monitoring needs. A National Workshop on Mt. Galunggung Volcanic Risk Management was held in Bandung on 20-25 September to find ways to best cope with problems raised by the continuing Galunggung eruption. Volcanologists and disaster-relief experts from Japan, United States, Australia, France, the United Kingdom, and other countries participated in the workshop. The results of the workshop were used by the Indonesian government to draft contingency plans to apply in mitigating the volcanic hazards posed by the seemingly unending Galunggung activity.

Before the 1982 eruption, Galunggung had been sporadically monitored. Just before a program of permanent monitoring was scheduled to start, Galunggung erupted. Thus, it was possible to initiate seismic monitoring by means of a tripartite array only two days after the first eruption. This was later augmented by additional seismic equipment contributed by Japan. A radio-telemetered seismic network, provided through a USAID-supported cooperative VSI-USGS program in existence at the time, became fully operational by September. Geophysical and geochemical monitoring techniques, including dry tilt measurements, EDM, and measurement of SO_2 emission (by means of the correlation spectrometer [COSPEC]), were also introduced. Some of the eruptions after 21 April were successfully predicted based on the results obtained by various monitoring methods. Although the prolonged Galunggung eruption strained the limited scientific resources of the VSI, it also provided an opportunity to apply an integrated combination of monitoring techniques (seismic, ground deformation, geochemical) not previously attempted on Indonesian volcanoes.

Disaster Response

Relief and various other forms of assistance came from several United Nations organizations, including UNDRO, UNDP, UNICEF, WHO (World Health Organization), WFP (World Food Program), and ILO; from other countries including USA, Australia, Canada, ASEAN countries, New Zealand, Holland, Sweden, and Switzerland; and from a number of international agencies. Donations, aid, and technical assistance totalled more than US $4 million. Eighteen emergency shelters were built in Garut and 334 in Tasikmalaya for a total cost of US $0.8 million. Refugees were provided with food, medical and health supplies, clothing and blankets, tents and straw mattresses, kitchen utensils, water pumps, gas lamps, farming tools, sports equipment, and religious materials such as the Qu'ran. A daily rice ration was issued at first but later general field kitchens were established. When a coupon system was instituted, the number of patrons dropped (presumably other refugees were staying with friends and relatives). This coupon system also discouraged the sale of donated goods in the markets.

Several lahar-control structures were built on the slopes of Galunggung in 1982. Efforts to build lahar pockets before the 1982-83 wet season drew together the largest assembly of heavy equipment seen in Indonesia. A September 1982 survey established the number of evacuees in the camps at 17,500. It was believed that 45% of these were capable of looking after themselves or could be relocated to other villages where their merchant and laboring services were needed. The remaining 55%, mainly poor peasants, were encouraged to transmigrate to southern Sumatra, Kalimantan and Sulawesi.

Post-eruption Assessment

Given the large number of organizations and people involved, it was inevitable that some leadership conflicts and jurisdictional disputes would develop. However, these problems were relatively minor and apparently did not impair the overall Galunggung disaster-relief efforts. In general, the Galunggung eruption and the response to it represented a case of largely successful mitigation. The value of pre-eruption hazards-zonation mapping was demonstrated, and the authorities and population were well aware (relatively) of the hazards and reacted appropriately.

Rabaul Caldera, Papua New Guinea, 1983-1985

The port city of Rabaul is sited somewhat precariously within a caldera (4.27 S, 152.20 E) that is open to the sea on its eastern side, forming an excellent sheltered harbor (Figure 5.6). Several satellite volcanoes are scattered along the northeastern rim of the caldera. The response to the so-called "Rabaul seismo-deformational crisis of 1983-85" (Lowenstein and Mori, 1987) provides an illustrative example of careful, detailed pre-disaster planning and good emergency management.

The Events

The following description of events is taken largely from the summary of Yokoyama et al. (1984); for detailed accounts of the 1983-85 seismo-deformational crisis at Rabaul, see McKee et al. (1984, 1985) and Lowenstein (1988).

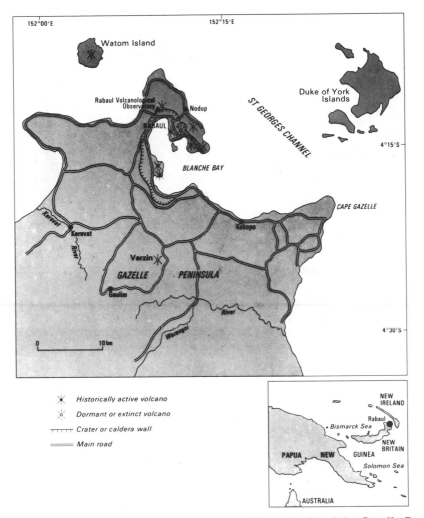

Fig. 5.6. Map showing the location of Rabaul Caldera, northeastern tip of the Gazelle Peninsula, New Britain, Papua New Guinea. The Rabaul Volcanological Observatory is on the northern rim. (From McKee et al., 1985, Fig. 1).

The number of shallow earthquakes beneath Rabaul caldera doubled in August 1971, from less than 50 to about 100 per month. During the next 10 years, there were several, 3 months-long seismic swarms, each successively more intense (Figure 5.7). Through 1983, the earthquake epicenters defined a ring-like zone along the presumed boundaries of a block that subsided during the eruption that formed Rabaul caldera 1,400 years ago (Mori and McKee, 1987). Ground-deformation studies and the uplift of beaches showed that the central part of caldera had risen 1 to 2 meters.

In August 1983, the seismicity and rate of ground deformation increased dramatically. The monthly count of shallow earthquakes in August was about 330, in September was 2135, and by 1984 exceeded 10,000. The rate of deformation also accelerated in September. Maximum tilt rates increased to between 50 and 100 microradians a month, and the uplift rate near the inflation center increase to 50 - 100 mm a month. The acceleration of seismicity and uplift in 1983 was regarded by the scientists at Rabaul and elsewhere to be a possible, if not likely, prelude to an eruption (McKee et al., 1984). However, after peaking in April 1984, the seismicity and caldera deformation declined abruptly without eruption, and returned to 1982 levels by mid-1985 (Figure 5.7).

Pre-crisis Preparedness and Monitoring

For Rabaul, volcano monitoring and hazard mapping studies are carried out by the Rabaul Volcanological Observatory (RVO), which is part of the Geological Survey of Papua New Guinea. Seismological surveillance began in Rabaul in 1940, when RVO was established following the

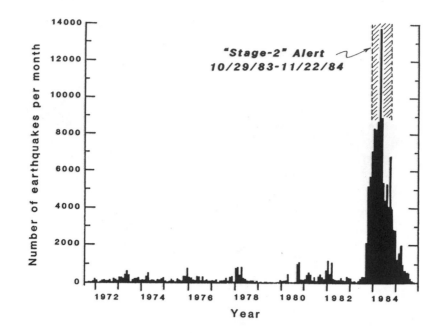

Fig. 5.7. Monthly totals of shallow earthquakes located beneath Rabaul Caldera, 1971-1985. (From Mori and McKee, 1987).

destructive eruption of 1937; in 1967, a network of seismic stations was installed around the northern part of Blanche Bay.

Since 1973, to complement the seismic monitoring, ground deformation has been measured using tilt measurements, precise leveling, gravity surveys, and sea-level changes. The changes observed in seismicity and deformation led to the interpretation that Rabaul has been building up to an eruption. Moreover, the frequency of historical eruptions within the caldera is two or three per century, so that an eruption could be expected at Rabaul before the end of the century. However, the exact pattern of events preceding historical Rabaul eruptions is not well known. Thus it is not yet possible to predict whether the next eruption will be benign or catastrophic, or whether it will happen in a year, a decade, or a century.

Hazards-zonation maps have been prepared for Rabaul (McKee, 1981; McKee and Lowenstein, 1981). Zones that are likely to be affected by the various hazards have been identified, and the scale of activity that the people of Rabaul should be prepared for is assumed to be most likely that of the 1937 Vulcan event. During the 1937 Vulcan eruption, more than 500 people were killed as a result of pyroclastic flows and surges, impact by bombs, asphyxiation, and collapse of tephra-covered houses (Johnson and Threlfall, 1985). Other types of volcanic and related hazards that pose a threat to the people of Rabaul are pumice rafts, volcanic gas discharges, tsunami, lightning strikes, the fall of mud rain, torrential run-off, and mudflows triggered by heavy rains.

Contingency Planning

A contingency plan was developed rapidly, before the events reached a critical level, and it was evident to the population that scientific and government authorities were taking all reasonable measures to ensure public safety. McKee et al.(1985) discussed the contingency plan for Rabaul Caldera in case of an eruption. Evacuation of the residents living on and around Rabaul Volcano could be carried out either by land, sea or air. Each mode, however, was fraught with difficulties. Because no roads extend more than 50 km from the caldera, any possible refuge points accessible by existing roads from Rabaul cannot be considered completely safe during eruption (Figure 5.6). Any new roads built should be directed to the south or southeast, so that evacuees could move to safer distances from the caldera. The safest and most suitable area around the caldera presently accessible by land is possibly the outermost coast of the Gazelle Peninsula near Cape Gazelle. Evacuation by air, though the fastest, might be seriously hampered by large number of evacuees and the fact that there are only two existing airstrips at Rabaul, one of which is inside the caldera. Evacuation by sea is another alternative. However, the absence of a wharf extending out over water depth suitable for large ships and overcrowding in assembly areas remain a big problem. McKee et al. (1985) proposed a two-pronged evacuation scheme. The population of Rabaul township and people of the northern and eastern flank of the caldera would be evacuated by ships and the residents west and

TABLE 5.1. One possible scheme of ranking stages of alert for volcanic eruptions (from UNDRO/UNESCO, 1985, Table 3). The scientists and officials during the 1983-1985 volcanic crisis at Rabaul, Papua New Guinea, used a scheme based largely on this one.

Alert stage	Phenomena observed	Interpretation--violent eruption possible within a period of:	Action by Disaster Control Committee and by Departments
I	Abnormal local seismic activity; some ground deformation; fumarole temperature increase.	Months or years	Inform all responsible officials. Review and update emergency plans.
II (Yellow)	Significant increase in local seismicity, rate of deformation, etc.	Weeks or months	Check readiness of personnel and equipment for possible evacuation Check stocks of materials and relief supplies.
III (Orange)	Dramatic increase in above anomalies, locally felt earthquakes, mild eruptive activity	Days or weeks	Public announcement of possible emergency and of measures taken to deal with it. Mobilization of personnel and equipment for possible evacuation. Temporary protective measures against ash falls.
IV (Red)	Protracted seismic tremor, increased eruptive activity.	Hours or days	Evacuation of population from hazard zones.

south of the caldera would move overland in a general southeasterly direction.

Response

On 29 October 1983, acting on information from RVO on the increasing seismicity and rate of deformation, government officials declared a Stage-II Alert, which implies that an eruption would occur within a few months. The stages of alert for volcanic eruptions used by scientists and officials at Rabaul were patterned after those shown in Table 5.1. The RVO began to expand and improve its monitoring capability, including the installation of telemetered tiltmeter and tide-gauge networks, the establishment of a 21-line EDM network, and the upgrading of its seismic network. In this effort, RVO personnel were assisted by a 2-man team from the U.S. Geological Survey (USGS); OFDA/USAID, USGS, and the New Zealand Ministry of Foreign Affairs contributed to the acquisition of the needed monitoring and telemetry equipment.

Under the auspices of the East New Britain's Provincial Disaster Control Committee (PDCC), a detailed disaster contingency plan was drawn. Volcanologic expertise and current information on the status of Rabaul is provided to the PDCC by the chief scientist of RVO, who serves as a non-voting member. In accordance with the Stage-II Alert, the PDCC implemented the appropriate emergency measures outlined in Table 5.1. Zones considered to be most vulnerable to volcanic hazards and subject to possible immediate evacuation, if necessary, were designated. Roads to serve as principal evacuation routes were improved and cleared of bordering trees, which might fall to impede or block vehicular transit. A simplified evacuation plan for Rabaul was published, and several evacuation exercises, some involving limited public participation, were conducted to test and improve this plan.

Meanwhile, the RVO scientists began an intensive effort to educate the local populace and officials on potential hazards should an eruption take place, as expected. During the crisis, the RVO issued more than 300 situation reports, information bulletins, and other advice to government authorities (Lowenstein, 1988). Some disagreement arose over the extent to which the public and news media should be informed of events during the early stages of an emergency. During some minor emergencies at volcanoes elsewhere in the world, the over-dramatization of early public statements have caused problems to both the officials and scientists (e.g., Fiske, 1984). Therefore, the authorities decided that at Rabaul no

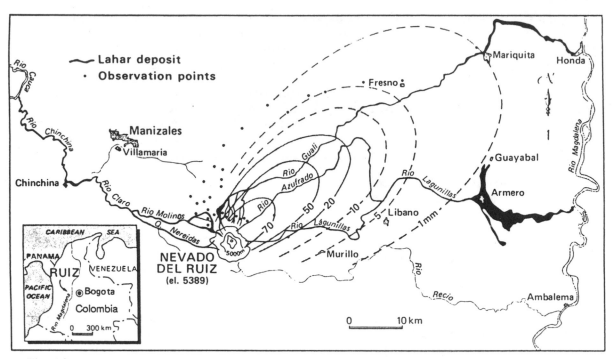

Fig. 5.8. Map showing the location of Nevado del Ruíz (inset) and distribution of tephra fall and lahar deposits from its 13 November 1985 eruption. Lahars are shown in black, and the isopachs of the tephra fall (in mm) are shown by dashed and solid lines. (From Naranjo et al., 1986, Fig. 1).

announcements be made to the press or public until a Stage-III Alert is declared. Such a stage of alert would entail the actual mobilization of personnel and equipment for possible evacuation (Table 5.1). The government's policy of information dissemination, however, proved to be unrealistic and unworkable. Given the preparations already in progress in response to the Stage-II Alert, the absence of official communications left the public anxious and the news media dissatisfied. Ultimately, it became necessary to give full information to the public throughout all stages of the emergency as they developed.

Post-crisis Situation

With the abrupt decline in seismicity and deformation rate beginning in May 1984, the stage of alert was downgraded to Stage-I on 22 November 1984. By mid-1985, Rabaul caldera returned to a pre-crisis level of activity (Figure 5.7). For the moment at least, the volcanic crisis at Rabaul has abated. However, the RVO scientists realize that the Rabaul story may still be unfolding and are maintaining a close surveillance of the volcano, with a substantially improved monitoring capability resulting from the response to the 1983-85 crisis. Ironically, with the lifting of the Stage-II Alert and the continuing relative quiet through the time of this writing (October 1988), some preparedness measures begun during the crisis, when public concern was high, remain unfinished. Complacency has

replaced concern because no eruption occurred and the situation is now calm. Yet, the large increases in insurance premiums and restrictions on insurance coverage that resulted from the 1983-85 crisis still remain in effect, slowing a return to normal economic development in the Rabaul region (Lowenstein, 1988).

Nevado del Ruíz, Colombia, 1984-1985

Nevado del Ruíz (75.37 W, 4.88 N) is located in the Cordillera Central of west-central Colombia, about 100 km west of Bogotá (Figure 5.8) . It is the northernmost active volcano in the Andes; its glacier-capped summit rises to an elevation of 5,389 m (a.s.l.). In November 1985, mudflows generated by a very small magmatic eruption at its summit killed more than 22,000 people, perhaps as many as 27,000 (Podesta and Olson, 1988). This volcanic disaster was the worst in the recorded history of Colombia and the worst in the world since the 1902 eruption of Mont Pelée (Table 1.2). The Ruíz disaster illustrates the shortcomings in a warning-communications network and an inadequate awareness on the part of the local populace and officials of the hazards posed by the volcano.

The following discussion of the pre-disaster activity and of the 13 November tragedy draws largely from the detailed accounts of Herd et al. (1986) and Voight (1988). Other accounts of the 1985 Ruíz eruption and its impacts are given also in several recent papers (e.g., Naranjo et al., 1986; Lowe et al., 1986; Tomblin, 1988; Williams and Meyer, 1988).

Pre-disaster Volcanic Activity

The signals of volcanic unrest--felt earthquakes, increased fumarolic activity, phreatic explosions--were first noticed in November 1984. Increased seismicity and fumarolic activity continued intermittently into 1985, and, largely through the coordination of UNDRO, efforts were made to initiate volcano surveillance. On 11 September, the largest of the pre-November phreatic eruptions occurred. This eruption produced measurable ash fall at Manizales, the capital of Caldas Province (population 230,000), and several mudflows in the valleys of Río Azufrado and Río Gualí. People living in the valley of Río Azufrado were placed on alert but were not evacuated, as the lahar harmlessly dissipated its energy after travelling about 27 km along the river's winding course. Seismicity briefly increased in late October to several tens of earthquakes per day and then returned to 3 - 10 events/day by early November. Meanwhile, intermittent phreatic activity occurred, but at a level considerably less than the 11 September eruption.

The 13 November 1985 Eruption and its Impacts

The 13 November eruption began at 1506 (local time) and began to deposit a thin ash layer around the summit crater (Arenas) and to the NNE. The strongest explosions occurred about 2108, producing pyroclastic flows and surges as well as tephra falls. The hot ejecta scoured and melted the ice and snow of Ruíz's glacial cap, and the resulting melt water mixed with the erupting and older volcanic debris to form mudflows. These highly mobile mudflows raced down the steep, narrow valleys on the upper slopes of the volcano. One major mudflow moved W along the Río Claro valley to the town of Chinchiná, and several others travelled down several valleys on the eastern flank of the volcano (Figure 5.8).

The largest mudflows travelled down the valleys of Río Azufrado and Río Lagunillas, merging downstream to form a 40 m-deep mass moving at 30-40 km/hr toward the town of Armero. The peak discharge of the mudflow in Río Lagunillas as it approached Armero was estimated to have reached 47,500 m^3/sec. The combined volume of all the mudflows was more than 6 x 10^7 m^3, of which 2-3 x 10^7 m^3 was water derived principally from melting of glacial ice. Studies showed that 8-10 % of the summit ice cap was removed by the 13 November eruption, which produced only about 3.5 x 10^{10} kg of magmatic eruptive products (Naranjo et al., 1986). This eruptive volume is smaller by more than an order of magnitude than that ejected during the 18 May 1980 eruption of Mount St. Helens (Sarna-Wojcicki et al., 1981a), or during the March-April 1982 eruption of El Chichón Volcano, Mexico (Duffield et al., 1984; Luhr and Varekamp, 1984; Carey and Sigurdsson, 1986).

Mudflows swept into the populated areas in the affected river valleys shortly after 2230. They caused massive destruction and killed more than 21,000 people in Armero and another 1,000 in Chinchiná. In addition, the mudflows caused serious injury to another 5,000 people, left about 10,000 homeless, and resulted in an economic loss totalling $ 212 million (U.S.).

Pre-disaster Response and Monitoring

As the intermittent phreatic activity, which began in November 1984, continued into 1985, largely through the persistence of a staff member (a seismologist) of UNDRO, efforts were made to increase volcano surveillance. Recommendations were made to civil-defense officials and to INGEOMINAS (Instituto Nacional de Investigaciones Geológico-Mineras) to install a portable seismograph on the volcano at the earliest date. Through the combined efforts of INGEOMINAS, UNDRO, and the USGS, a small network of four portable, nontelemetered seismographs began to acquire seismic data in mid-July. Also during July, the Comité de Vigilancia del Riesgo Volcánico del Ruíz (Ruíz Volcanic Risk Committee) was formed in Manizales. A fifth portable seismograph was added to the network in August.

It was not until the 11 September phreatic eruption, however, that the level of concern about the volcanic crisis increased, and additional scientific assistance was requested by the Colombian government. Following a meeting of national representatives of emergency and civil-defense groups in Bogotá on 17 September, INGEOMINAS was given national responsibility for coordinating volcano monitoring and hazards assessment. Under the guidance of a New Zealand gas geochemist, local scientists began in late September to periodically sample and analyze fumarolic gases in the summit crater. INGEOMINAS and other Colombian scientists, with assistance from several foreign scientists supported by UNDRO, OFDA, and USGS, prepared and released a preliminary version of the Ruíz hazards-zonation map on 7 October. The map stressed the hazard from lahars and accurately identified the areas of highest risk, including the towns of Armero and Chinchiná. A generalized version of this map was published in color on the front page of the newspaper El Espectador on 9 October.

Later in October, under the auspices of the World Organization of Volcano Observatories (WOVO) and UNESCO, a specialist from the Observatorio Vulcanológico y Sismológico de Costa Rica arrived to initiate tilt measurements, using both an electronic tiltmeter and dry-tilt arrays. That same month, surveying crews from the Instituto Geográfico "Agustin Codazzi" (IGAC) began to establish a geodetic polygon for detailed ground-deformation measurements. On 16 October, an Italian team of volcanologists, invited by the Colombian government to evaluate the situation and provide advice to local authorities and scientists, reported that the monitoring program at Ruíz was still seriously inadequate and unable to provide rapid warning of changing conditions. The Italian team was not aware of the UNDRO-USGS preparations underway at the time to send a telemetered seismograph to Ruíz; this instrument, unfortunately, did not arrive until after 13 November.

Following the release of the preliminary hazards-zonation map on 7 October, which was criticized by some government officials as "too alarming," involved Colombian scientists met with local authorities to discuss the map and brief them on potential hazards. Efforts were made by the Civil Defense and other agencies to improve public awareness of the hazards and evacuation procedures in the high-risk areas during the month preceding the disaster. On 10 November, the final version of the hazards-zonation map was issued; on 11 November, INGEOMINAS made a statement that Armero could be evacuated in 2 hours without danger; ironically, this statement was published in *El Tiempo* the day after the disaster (Voight, 1988).

Responses the Day of the Disaster and Aftermath

About an hour after the start of the 13 November eruption (at 1506), the Civil Defense of Tolima Province was advised by INGEOMINAS to prepare Armero and Honda for immediate evacuation. At about 1700, an emergency meeting of the Emergency Committee of Tolima began at Ibagué, the provincial capital located 70 km from Armero. The committee was briefed by INGEOMINAS on the eruptive activity and discussed the evacuation of Armero, Mariquita, and Ambalema and measures needed to detect possible mudflow activity. The police stations in Armero and neighboring towns were alerted. The committee meeting ended about 1930, but apparently without any decisions regarding emergency measures. Following the meeting, INGEOMINAS representatives went to the Red Cross and insisted that Armero, Mariquita, and Honda be prepared for evacuation, and reportedly the Red Cross ordered the evacuation of Armero.(Herd et al., 1986).

What safety measures, if any, were taken during the next several hours--with the most vigorous activity beginning shortly after 2100--is not clear from available information. Apparently there was little or no response to the scientists' warnings or the authorities' calls to evacuate, and there is some question whether the citizens of Armero actually received a general order to evacuate (Herd et al., 1986). According to Tomblin (1988, p. 10), the new explosions at 2108 "were not adequately described as significantly larger," so that the reports of their occurrence were "met with skepticism from local authorities and populations over the need to evacuate." Moreover, the people were confused by conflicting advisories given by the authorities and news media. While the calls for evacuation presumably were being made, the public-address systems of some churches and Radio Armero asked people to remain calm, to stay indoors and be protected from the falling ash. The fact that it also was raining heavily at the time might be a factor. In any case, Voight (1988, p. 30) concludes that

the Ruíz tragedy "was not produced by technological ineffectiveness or defectiveness, nor by an overwhelming eruption of unprecedented character...", but was caused by "cumulative human error--by misjudgment, indecision, and bureaucratic shortsightedness." In an attempt to reconstruct what went wrong at Ruíz, a group of Latin American geoscientists and social scientists is currently studying the scientific, emergency- management, and citizen-response aspects of the catastrophe.

Technical and humanitarian response to the disaster was swift and world-wide. At least thirty countries responded, and the assistance included, among others, rescue of survivors, and provision of health and sanitation services, food, shelter and clothing. Several scientific teams arrived to help document the impact of the eruptive phenomena and to assist in volcano monitoring. Because the 13 November eruption was small, there was serious scientific concern that larger eruptions might follow.

In February 1986, in response to the Ruíz disaster, the Colombian government, with substantial financial support of OFDA/USAID and technical guidance from the USGS, established the Observatorio Volcanológico Nacional at Manizales, under the management of INGEOMINAS. Scientists at this well-equipped modern facility are monitoring the continuing intermittent, but weak, eruptive activity at Nevado del Ruíz and conducting preliminary studies of nearby potentially dangerous volcanoes as well. With the help of the Japanese government, there are now two ground-telemetered mudflow detectors in operation at Ruíz. Since 1985, a number of the Colombian volcanologists have received training at volcano observatories in the U.S. and Iceland.

Mount St. Helens, United States, 1980

Mount St. Helens (46.20 N, 122.18 W), southwestern Washington, is one of the stratovolcanoes in the Cascade Range of the Pacific Northwest; this volcanic chain stretches from northern California to British Columbia, Canada. Prior to 1980, it erupted several times in the period 1831-1857 and then remained quiet for more than 120 years. It reawakened on 27 March 1980 following a week of premonitory seismicity. The climactic eruption occurred on 18 May 1980 and caused the worst volcanic disaster in the recorded history of the United States.

The Events and Impacts

The eruptions of Mount St. Helens in 1980 have been well documented in USGS Professional Papers 1249 and 1250 (Foxworthy and Hill, 1982; Lipman and Mullineaux, 1981) and hundreds of other scientific works. The following brief account is taken largely from overviews of Tilling (1981, 1984) and Yokoyama et al. (1984), in places verbatim.

A magnitude 4.2 earthquake on 20 March 1980 initiated the precursory seismicity, which then increased dramatically

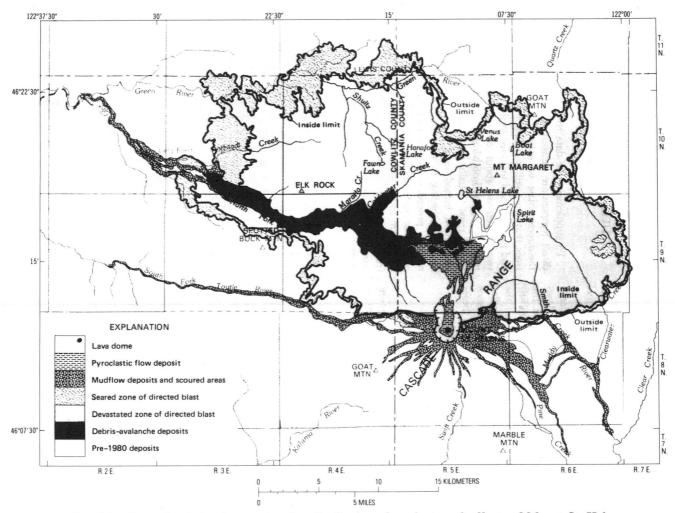

Fig. 5.9. Generalized sketch map showing distribution of products and effects of Mount St. Helens eruptions, 18 May 1980 through October 1980; the map largely reflects the catastrophic activity of 18 May. (From Lipman and Mullineaux, 1981, Plate 1).

during the following week. At about 1236 (local time) on 27 March, a phreatic eruption began. The initial explosions sent an ash plume about 2 km above the volcano and formed an 80 m-wide crater within the preexisting snow- and ice-filled summit crater. During the ensuing intermittent phreatic activity through 17 May, volcano monitoring of the volcano was greatly intensified. Of greatest concern was a large "bulge" on its north flank--reflecting the intrusion of magma high into the volcanic cone--that was moving subhorizontally at an average rate of 1.5 m/day.

At 0832 on 18 May, a magnitude 5.1 earthquake occurred about 2 km beneath the volcano. About 20 seconds later, the bulged, unstable north flank of Mount St. Helens began to collapse, triggering a rapid chain of events that culminated in violent eruption (Figure 5.9). The first minute of the catastrophic eruption produced a massive (2.7 km^3) debris avalanche, a lateral blast that devastated an area of 550 km^2,

pyroclastic flows, and an ash column that rose 24 km into the atmosphere. About 1.1 km^3 (uncompacted) of ash was ejected during the next 9 hours of plinian eruption. The eruption also produced destructive mudflows in several of the valleys draining the volcano. At the mountain itself, the eruption formed an amphitheatre-shaped crater, about 1.5 x 3 km wide and 650 m deep, and lowered the summit (formerly 2549 m a.s.l.) by 400 meters.

The 18 May eruption resulted in the loss of 57 lives, scores of injuries, more than $ 1 billion damage, and disruption of transportation and communications systems. Since May 1980, the activity of Mount St. Helens has been dominated by processes related to the emplacement and growth of a composite lava dome within the enlarged summit crater (see Swanson et al., 1987). At present, mudflows and floods constitute the greatest hazards related to the continuing, intermittent volcanic activity.

Pre-disaster Preparedness, Hazards Assessment, and Monitoring

Many years before the reawakening of Mount St. Helens, the USGS undertook geologic mapping and radiocarbon dating studies of the Cascade volcanoes. The basic geoscience data so obtained provided the basis for hazards assessments of several of the Cascade volcanoes (e.g., Crandell and Mullineaux, 1967, 1975; Crandell et al., 1979) as part of the U.S. Geological Survey's Volcano Hazards Program. From these studies, USGS scientists concluded that Mount St. Helens was the youngest and most active and explosive of the Cascade volcanoes, one which could be expected to erupt again. Crandell et al. (1975, p. 441) made a long-term forecast that Mount St. Helens will "erupt again, perhaps before the end of this century." In a later more detailed report, Crandell and Mullineaux (1978) amplified their earlier conclusions, augmenting them with a hazards-zonation map delineating the most hazardous areas, should Mount St. Helens erupt. Two years later, their forecast came true.

In 1974, Congress passed legislation ("Disaster Relief Act of 1974," P.L. 93-288) designating the USGS as the responsible Federal agency to provide reliable and timely warnings of volcanic and related hazards. Thus, with the detection and location of the 4.0 magnitude earthquake on 20 March 1980, the USGS in cooperation with seismologists at the University of Washington (Seattle) worked around-the-clock to expand the seismic monitoring network at Mount St. Helens. During the week before the initial eruption, USGS specialists in volcanic-hazards assessment and volcano monitoring arrived on the scene to meet with local authorities and to increase volcano surveillance. By the time the eruption was into its second week of phreatic activity, the scientific team had grown to more than 25 people. By 31 March, an on-site volcanic-hazards assessment was presented at a meeting of all involved emergency-management agencies, and the next day a large-scale hazards zonation map was prepared for use by these agencies and the general public.

USGS scientists participated in daily meetings with U.S. Forest Service (USFS), the principal land manager for Mount St. Helens, and other officials, and provided them updates of potential hazards, advice on the locations of roadblocks to control access to hazardous areas, etc. (Miller et al., 1981). However, all decisions regarding access and restricted areas were the responsibility of the land managers. USGS and other specialists contributed geotechnical and volcanic-hazards information essential for the preparation of the "Mount St. Helens Contingency Plan" issued by the U.S. Forest Service on 9 April. The early recognition of the potential hazards of the "bulge" on the north flank of the volcano and the systematic monitoring of its extremely rapid movement led USGS scientists to advise USFS and Washington State officials to further restrict access and to expand the closure zones to those in effect on 18 May. Had these measures not been taken, considerably greater human loss and injury would have resulted.

Unfortunately, the intensive pre-disaster volcano monitoring during the phreatic eruptive phase failed to detect any immediate precursors to permit a short-term forecast of the 18 May magmatic eruption. Diligent analysis of the seismic and ground-deformation data after the disaster also yielded no diagnostic clues. In hindsight, some of the scientists involved in the volcano monitoring have speculated that the slope of the linear growth curve of the "bulge" (see Lipman et al., 1981, Fig. 97) might have shown some precursory inflection prior to failure, if the ongoing deformation process had not been "short-circuited" by the earthquake that triggered eruption. In any case, the possibility of a major avalanche, and a large magmatic eruption triggered by it, were recognized by the scientific team at Mount St. Helens and explained to officials before 1 May (Miller et al., 1981; Decker, 1986).

Response to the Disaster

Many Federal and local agencies and volunteers responded swiftly to the Mount St. Helens disaster and provided search and rescue, medical care, and emergency shelter. Officials and people in areas downwind from Mount St. Helens, affected only by ash fall, mounted massive clean-up efforts to remove and dispose ash from highways, roads, buildings, and airport runways. These tasks took many weeks to months to accomplish and posed an unexpected financial burden on local governments.

Initial public reaction to the disaster dealt a temporary blow to tourism, an important industry in Washington. However, Mount St. Helens, perhaps because of renewed eruptive activity, has regained its appeal for tourists. In August 1982, President Reagan signed into law setting aside 110,000 acres around the volcano as the Mount St. Helens Volcanic Monument, preserving some the best sites for scientific studies, education, and recreation.

The U.S. Congress passed a supplemental appropriation of $ 951 million for disaster relief, of which the largest share went to the Small Business Administration, U.S. Army Corps of Engineers, and the Federal Emergency Management Agency to restore commerce and vital transportation and communication links. With a significant expansion of its Volcano Hazards Program, the USGS established a permanent regional office at Vancouver, Washington. On 18 May 1982, the Vancouver facility was formally designated the David A. Johnston Cascades Volcano Observatory (CVO), in memory of the USGS volcanologist killed by the climactic eruption 2 years earlier. The CVO not only monitors the continuing activity at Mount St. Helens, but also serves as the headquarters for studies of other Cascade volcanoes.

Lessons Learned

The response to a particular volcanic crisis or disaster can be variable and, by necessity, is conditioned by local circumstances prevailing at the time (state of knowledge about the volcano, amount of scientific and economic resources available, stage of development of disaster preparedness, peculiarities of volcanic behavior, social or cultural factors, etc.). Nonetheless, some general lessons can be drawn from the case histories reviewed in this chapter.

(1) It is important to have baseline monitoring data for any volcano considered to have potential for future eruptive activity, as determined by studies of its historic and prehistoric record. Any type of systematic monitoring--by high-tech and/or low-tech techniques (see CHAPTER 4)--is better than no monitoring. The longer the period spanned by the baseline data, the more reliable is the early detection of departures from "normal" behavior that might indicate precursory signals.

The lack of any baseline data was a serious problem in the case of the 1965-1977 Taal activity. At Galunggung in 1982-1983, the lack of pre-1982 baseline data hampered the interpretation of the relatively abundant monitoring data acquired during the long eruption. In the case of Nevado del Ruíz, the pre-disaster monitoring was simply a matter of too little, too late. Even for the Mount St. Helens case, there were few monitoring data prior to the onset of precursory seismicity on 20 March 1980.

(2) It is essential to make hazards assessments, including hazards-zonation maps, before the onset of volcanic unrest. Such maps, even if rudimentary and preliminary, provide the basic information in the preparation of contingency plans. The value and the effective use of hazards-zonation maps is well illustrated in the Mayon, Galunggung, and Mount St. Helens case histories. Unfortunately, in the case of the Nevado del Ruíz disaster, the hazards-zonation map, which correctly identified the areas vulnerable to mudflows, apparently was not adequately understood and/or considered by the authorities. Had the map been completed more quickly, there might have been more time to educate the officials and general public, and to make them more aware of the potential hazards and of possible measures to mitigate them.

(3) Contingency plans are likely to become outdated, forgotten, and, hence, ineffective unless they are periodically rehearsed, tested, and updated by a national organization designated to coordinate disaster response. Although a contingency plan was prepared for Taal Volcano more than 10 years before the onset of its 1965 eruption, it proved to be largely unsuccessful, because the government at the time lacked an adequate disaster-response system.

(4) Monitoring and hazards-assessment efforts before or during a volcanic crisis *are effective only if* they are well coordinated with, and backed up by, well-organized and decisive actions by emergency-management authorities. In this regard, the case histories for Mayon, Canlaon, Galunggung, Rabaul, and Mount St. Helens represent examples of fair to good coordination and interaction between scientists and officials in the mitigation of the hazards. In contrast, the Taal case and, especially, the Nevado del Ruíz case are tragic reminders of largely unsuccessful mitigation efforts. Some actions that scientists can take to improve volcanic-emergency management and to heighten public awareness of volcanic phenomena and associated hazards are discussed in next chapter.

CHAPTER 6. SCIENTIFIC AND PUBLIC RESPONSE

Robert I. Tilling

U.S. Geological Survey, Menlo Park, California 94025

Raymundo S. Punongbayan

Philippine Institute of Volcanology and Seismology, Quezon City, Philippines

Introduction

Scientific studies (e.g., basic geoscience research, hazards assessment, volcano monitoring) constitute only the first step in mitigating the risk from volcanic hazards. The scientific findings must be communicated effectively, quickly, and clearly to the civil authorities responsible for planning and implementing hazards-mitigation measures. However, the responsibility of the geoscientists does not end with the transmittal of the scientific information to the proper authorities. In addition, the geoscientists, in concert with the authorities, must work actively to inform and educate the news media and the affected populace on volcanic phenomena in general and the nature of possible hazards in particular. A well-informed public is less likely to panic and more likely to act rationally in responding to governmental advisories and contingency measures in the event of a volcanic emergency.

The effective mitigation of potential volcanic hazards from future eruptions requires a constructive scientific and public response and involves cooperative interaction between all concerned parties: scientists, land managers, public-safety officials, news media, and the general public.The role of geoscientists in responses to volcanic hazards and how scientists might influence improvements in such responses have been treated in several recent publications (e.g., Fiske, 1984; Newhall, 1984; Souther et al., 1984; Yokoyama et al., 1984; Peterson, 1986, 1988; and Tilling, 1989, in press). The brief discussion in this chapter is adapted largely from these studies.

Interactions Between Geoscientists, Authorities, and the Public

Because volcanologists are the most qualified to interpret the significance of the observations and measurements on a restless volcano, they appropriately serve as the connecting link in the

flow of information to all the groups of people who need to be informed about volcanic phenomena and associated hazards (Figure 6.1). Yet, Figure 6.1, along with Figure 1.3, shows that hazards-mitigation policies and measures are generally made by the appropriate civil officials and land managers, who must weigh the volcanologic information together with socio-economic and political factors in reaching their decisions. The more accurate, timely, and understandable the information about the volcano the geoscientists can provide, the better the decision makers and the general public are served.

Before a Volcanic Crisis Arises

Volcanologists obviously play an active public role during a volcanic disaster or crisis, but they and other geoscientists can use quiescent periods to provide background information to the public. In addition to conducting the scientific studies needed to prepare adequate hazards assessments and to establish the baseline monitoring networks, they must also participate in public relations and educational activities to make the authorities and the general public more aware of the volcanoes and their potential hazards. While the volcano is in a calm stage, geoscientists should try to develop good lines of communications and working relationships with the authorities under normal conditions. Good relationships can be fostered by attending public meetings and hearings on regional zoning, giving lectures to civic and school groups, writing non-technical articles and pamphlets, being available for talk shows and media interviews, and taking advantage of all appropriate opportunities to increase public awareness of volcanic phenomena. In particular, the scientific community must work harder to persuade government officials and land managers to include consideration of volcanic-hazards factors in land-use planning. Many, perhaps most (?), geoscientists--by training, personality, or inclination--prefer to avoid the public limelight.

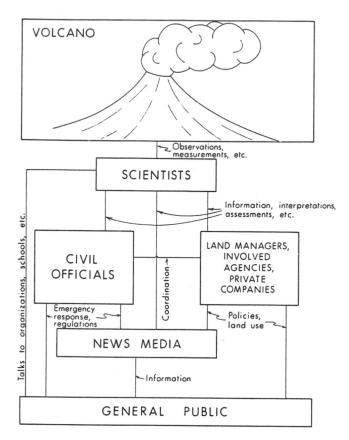

Fig. 6.1. Schematic diagram illustrating the flow of volcanologic information about Mount St. Helens to the civil authorities and the general public. Such a system of information flow, with minor modifications, probably can be generally applied to other volcanoes. (From Peterson, 1987, Fig. 13; reprinted in Peterson, 1988, Fig. 1).

However, it seems clear that we must play a more active and visible role to promote a better understanding and greater awareness of volcanic hazards by the civil authorities and populations in volcanically active regions.

During a Volcanic Disaster or Crisis

When a volcanic disaster strikes or a volcanic crisis arises, volcanologists are thrust into public prominence. They appropriately are called upon to provide accurate and current possible scientific information and advice on the status of the volcano (Figure 6.1). If groundwork is laid in establishing or improving lines of communications and public awareness before the onset of an emergency, the geoscientists' role as the principal supplier of volcanic-hazards information is likely to be more effective. It is difficult to establish good rapport with civil authorities and the public within a short time under crisis circumstances.

Experience has shown that it is important that a single institution or group be designated by the authorities to be responsible for the scientific response to the volcanic hazards. Such designation should be made by the government long before a volcanic emergency arises. During the 1976 volcanic crisis at Soufrière (Guadeloupe, F.W.I.), the two rival scientific teams on site had major differences in their interpretations of the volcanic activity. These differences were exploited by sensationalistic journalists, causing confusion and discord among the authorities and the affected populace (Fiske, 1984). In the United States, the U.S. Geological Survey (USGS) was designated by the Congress through the Disaster Relief Act of 1974 (Public Law 93-288) as the scientific organization responsible for providing timely warnings of volcanic and related hazards (Tilling and Bailey, 1985). Such designation does not mean that the USGS is the only scientific organization involved in hazards-mitigation studies, but rather that it coordinates all studies and serves as the official source for scientific information. For example, the seismic monitoring of Mount St. Helens and several other Cascade volcanoes is a cooperative effort between the USGS and seismologists at the University of Washington (Seattle).

In Japan, the responsibility for volcanic-hazards assessments and monitoring studies is shared among several universities and various government agencies, principally the Japan Meteorological Agency (JMA) and the Geological Survey of Japan (GSJ). The Japanese program of volcanic-hazards mitigation is under the auspices of a Coordinating Committee for the National Program for the Prediction of Volcanic Eruptions (Shimozuru, 1981). The JMA observatories are involved mainly with systematic volcano monitoring, whereas the university observatories are more concerned with "pure" research on volcanic phenomena; most volcanic-hazards assessments are prepared by the GSJ. Other countries have systems of responding to volcanic eruptions and associated hazards that differ from those of the U.S. and Japan. Such differences are to be expected and reflect each country's cultural background, scientific heritage, and mode of government. Unfortunately, some countries with active or potentially active volcanoes do not have any institution(s) specifically designated to be responsible for volcanic-hazards studies.

Peterson (1988, p. 4167) has ably summarized the observations and recommendations of Fiske (1984) pertinent to improving relations between scientists, journalists, and the public during a volcanic crisis:

"1. Gather background information about geologic and geophysical behavior of the volcano before a crisis develops to provide a basis for assessing the behavior during new unrest.

2. An experienced and respected chief scientist should coordinate the various activities into a single group effort. While not suppressing scientific disagreements or differing interpretations, he would assure that unified and consistent information reaches civil officials and the news

media. This should help reduce the possibility of irresponsible competition for media attention between scientific groups.

3. Individual scientists should convey their separate activities as part of the team effort, especially during interviews by journalists. Their remarks should be confined to their own area of expertise.

4. During times of crisis, journalists must realize that scientists need to discuss among themselves assorted speculative possibilities, and these conversations must not be monitored by outsiders who could easily misinterpret them.

5. When a crisis reaches major proportions, an information scientist should be designated to interact with the news media, with the full concurrence of the chief scientist. Such an assignment reduces media interference with scientific work and enables the effectiveness of the designated scientist to improve with experience."

Need for Improved Global System to Respond to Volcanic Crises

The preceding discussion assumes that, in a volcanic disaster or crisis, the country or region struck is fully capable in coping with it; that is, the country is self-sufficient in volcanic-emergency management. However, as has been generally recognized (e.g., Yokoyama et al., 1984; Tilling and Newhall, 1987), most of the world's high-risk volcanoes are found in the developing countries, which lack sufficient economic and scientific resources to study and monitor them adequately. Thus, increased efforts to mitigate volcanic hazards should be concentrated in the developing countries, especially those in the circum-Pacific region that are densely populated.

One obvious way to confront volcanic hazards would be for the affected developing country to inaugurate or accelerate research and related educational programs (upgrade equipment and facilities, train scientists and technicians, etc.) to attain self-sufficiency in volcanology and hazards mitigation. This solution, however, is necessarily costly and long-term, requiring decades, perhaps longer. In the interim, the developed nations and international organizations must work actively to develop improved global programs of volcanic-hazards mitigation focused toward developing countries. Such programs should provide: 1) rapid response and mutual assistance during volcanic crises; 2) technical assistance in the preparation of hazards assessments; 3) acquisition of baseline monitoring data at high-risk volcanoes; and 4) training/education for scientists, emergency-management officials, media people, and the threatened populace.

To date, existing bilateral or international programs are limited, not well coordinated, and generally "too little-too late" responses to volcanic disasters. However, in recent years, a few modest pre-disaster projects have been undertaken, with support of UNESCO and/or the Office of Foreign Disaster Assistance (U.S. Agency for International Development), to augment volcanic-hazards studies in several developing countries (e.g., Indonesia, Mexico, Nicaragua, Guatemala, and Ecuador) by use of "mobile teams" of scientists specializing in various aspects of volcano monitoring or hazards assessments (Banks, 1985, 1986, 1987a). While these recent efforts are helpful, they are inadequate to address the problem on the required global scale. Some proposed interim global programs are relatively low cost but must have stable funding to achieve effective and permanent results. For example, the average annual budget ($ 195,000, U.S.) for a five-year program proposed to UNESCO (Yokoyama et al., 1984) represents only a small fraction of the daily helicopter costs during the disaster-relief operations at Ruíz in 1985. As of 1989, this proposed program remains unfunded. Because the host countries must request these interim international programs, the scientific communities in the developing countries must vigorously encourage their foreign ministries to initiate such requests.

While the dispatch of "mobile teams" of specialists to developing countries provides needed short-term assistance, such teams must operate under the direction of the officially designated scientific institution in the host country that is responsible for volcanic-hazards studies. Otherwise, confusion in information flow to emergency-management officials and the news media might arise. Unfortunately, inappropriate and insensitive remarks made to journalists by a few "foreign experts" have caused difficulties for local scientists and officials during some recent volcanic emergencies. The participants at three regional workshops in 1983 sponsored by UNESCO unanimously agreed that: "Data and associated interpretations by the Mobile Team will only be given to, and discussed with, members of the national scientific team. No member of the Team is permitted to discuss the eruptive activity and its possible consequences with local or international news media, or with local civil defense officials, unless specifically authorized to do so by the national government authorities." (Yokoyama et al., 1984, p. 28).

Major Challenges to the Geoscience Community

Future accomplishments in volcanic-hazards mitigation, on a global basis, are most likely to be achieved by wider application of existing technology to as yet poorly understood high-risk volcanoes in the developing countries, rather than by technological advances alone (Tilling and Newhall, 1987; Tilling, 1989, in press). If this premise is valid, then some major challenges to the geoscience community include the following (largely adapted from Tilling, 1989, in press):

1) Apart from their regular work on volcanic phenomena and/or hazards studies, geoscientists must play a much more active and visible role in increasing public awareness of volcanoes and their potential hazards. Indeed, volcanologists have "an ethical obligation to convey effectively their knowledge to benefit all of society." (Peterson, 1988, p. 4161).

2) For potentially dangerous volcanoes in regions still not yet heavily populated or developed, geoscientists must prepare the best possible hazards assessments as available data permit and must identify major gaps in information needed to prepare more detailed assessments. Then they must work closely with decision makers and the public, to encourage and persuade them to consider the volcanic-hazard zonation maps in local or regional land-use planning.

3) For volcanically active areas already densely populated and that have land-use practices locked in by economic demand, culture, or tradition, the only available options in hazards mitigation are to develop improved monitoring and predictive capabilities to enable scientists to give timely warnings of impending eruptions to officials. Geoscientists also must interact closely with civil authorities to devise and periodically rehearse contingency measures before any volcanic crisis develops.

4) The convening of more international meetings and workshops to develop or refine general strategies and recommendations in the planning of global programs of volcanic-hazards mitigation is likely to yield diminishing returns. Geoscientists must convince decision makers in funding agencies that monies earmarked for such purposes might be more productively used for specific activities outlined in projects or programs already proposed, but still unfunded. Such activities, for example, could include making a hazards-zonation map or baseline monitoring measurements at a restless, high-risk volcanic in a developing country.

5) Higher priority must be placed on the preparation of general-interest publications, movie films, videotapes, training manuals, and other audio-visual aids in a concerted program to educate the emergency- management officials and the general public on the types and nature of volcanic and associated hazards and their destructive potential. In 1988, under the auspices of the International Association of Volcanology and Chemistry of the Earth's Interior (IAVCEI), efforts were begun to secure funding to produce two 25-minute video source-tapes on volcanic hazards and their adverse impact. These videotapes will be used by volcanologists to assist in educating decision makers and the affected public about the nature of the hazards and some protective measures that can be taken.

6) Many scientists in the developed countries are reluctant to become involved in efforts to promote and develop the needed interim international programs to help train scientists in developing countries, or to try to educate officials and the public. Sometimes scientists are so narrowly dedicated to their own research that they are disdainful of any non-research activity, even though their research may be funded by hazards-reduction programs.

7) Scientists in the developing countries must persistently encourage their governments to give stronger support to basic geoscience studies of volcanoes. The long-range goal is for their country to achieve self-sufficiency in volcanology. In the interim, geoscientists should urge their governments to request increased participation in shorter term international programs to augment volcanic-hazards studies of their highest risk volcanoes.

In summary, the developed countries and international organizations need to increase technical assistance, via bilateral or international programs, until the developing countries attain economic and scientific self-sufficiency. Meanwhile, the most pressing problem for both the scientific community and the decision-making bodies is to prevent volcanic crises from turning into volcanic disasters.

REFERENCES

Agnew, D.C., Strainmeters and tiltmeters, *Rev. Geophys., 24, no. 3,* 579-624, 1986.

Aki, K., and R.Y. Koyanagi, Deep volcanic tremor and magma ascent mechanism under Kilauea, Hawaii, *J. Geophys. Res., 86, no. B8,* 7095-7109, 1981.

Aki, K., M. Fehler, and S. Das, Source mechanism of volcanic tremor: fluid-driven crack models and their application to the 1963 Kilauea eruption, *J. Geophys. Res., 2,* 259-287, 1977.

Alcayde, M., editor, *Proceedings, Symposium on Volcán Chichónal,* VI National Geologic Convention of Sociedad Geológica Mexicana, September 1982, Mexico City, Instituto de Geología, Universidad Autónoma de México, Mexico City, 120 pp. (in Spanish), 1983.

Alzwar, Muziel, G. Kelut, *Berita Berkala Vulkanologi, Edisi Khusus, no. 108,* 58 pp., map scale 1:167,000, Direktorat Vulkanologi (Volcanological Survey of Indonesia), 1985.

Anderson, Tempest, and Flett, J.S., Report on the eruptions of the Soufrière in St. Vincent, 1902, and on a visit to Montagne Pelée, in Martinique, *Phil. Trans. Royal Soc. London, Series A, 200,* 353-553, 1903.

Apple, R.A., Thomas A. Jaggar, Jr. and the Hawaiian Volcano Observatory, *in* Volcanism in Hawaii, edited by R.W. Decker, T.L. Wright, and P.H. Stauffer, *U.S. Geol. Surv. Prof. Paper 1350,* pp. 1619-1644, 1987.

Aramaki, Shigeo, Asama volcano, Japan, in *Source-Book for Volcanic-Hazards Zonation: Natural Hazards 4,* edited by D.R. Crandell, Basil Booth, K. Kusumadinata, D., Shimozuru, G.P.L. Walker, and D. Westercamp, pp. 60-64, UNESCO, Paris, 1984.

Aramaki, Shigeo, and S. Akimoto, Temperature estimation of pyroclastic deposits by natural remnant magnetism, *Amer. J. Sci., 255,* 619-627, 1957.

Armienti, P., and M.T. Pareschi, Automatic reconstruction of surge deposit thicknesses. Applications to some Italian volcanoes, *J. Volcanol. Geotherm. Res., 31,* 313-320, 1987.

Armienti, P., G. Macedonio, and M.T. Pareschi, A numerical model for simulation of tephra transport and deposition: Applications to May 18, 1980, Mount St. Helens eruption, *J. Geophys. Res., 93, no. B6,* 6463-6476, 1988.

Baker, V.R., Flood erosion, in *Flood Geomorphology,* edited by V.R. Baker, R.C. Kochel, and P.C. Patton, pp. 81-96, John Wiley and Sons, New York, 1988.

Baker, V.R., and R.C. Kochel, Flood sedimentation in bedrock fluvial systems, in *Flood Geomorphology,* edited by V.R. Baker, R.C. Kochel, and P.C. Patton, pp. 123-138, John Wiley and Sons, New York, 1988.

Baker, V.R., R.C. Kochel, and P.C. Patton, editors, *Flood Geomorphology,* 503 pp., John Wiley and Sons, New York, 1988.

Banerjee, S.K., The Holocene paleomagnetic record in the United States, in *Late-Quaternary Environments of the United States, Volume 2, The Holocene,* edited by H.E. Wright, Jr., pp. 78-85, University of Minnesota Press, Minneapolis, 1983.

Banister, J.R., Pressure wave generated by the Mount St. Helens eruption, *J. Geophys. Res., 89, no. D3,* 4895-4904, 1984.

Banks, N.G., Measuring and interpreting deformation of volcanoes, *Notes for UNESCO Training Course,* Legaspi City and Manila, Philippines, 55 pp. (xeroxed), 1984.

Banks, N.G., Expanded monitoring capabilities and rapid response to volcanic crises through mobile volcano observatories, *Abstracts, IAVCEI Scientific Assembly on Potassic Volcanism - Mt. Etna Volcano, Giardini-Naxos, Italy, September 1985,* 35, 1985.

Banks, N.G., Hazard mitigation and rapid response to volcanic crises with mobile volcano observatories [abstract]: *Eos, Trans. Amer. Geophys. Union, 76,* 398, 1986.

Banks, N.G., U.S. Volcano Assistance Program, *Episodes, 10, no. 1,* 49, 1987a.

Banks, N.G., Preliminary assessment of the volcano hazards of Pacaya volcano, Guatemala, Instituto Nacional de Sismología, Vulcanología, Meteorología e Hidrología (INSIVUMEH, Guatemala), 20 pp., map scale 1:120,000. 1987b.

Banks, N.G., and R.P. Hoblitt, Summary of temperature studies of 1980 deposits, *in* The 1980 eruptions of Mount St. Helens, Washington, edited by Lipman, P.W., and D.R. Mullineaux, D.R., *U.S. Geol. Surv. Prof. Paper 1250,* pp. 295-313, 1981.

Banks, N.G., R.Y. Koyanagi, J.M. Sinton, and K.T. Honma, The eruption of Mount Pagan Volcano, Mariana Islands, 15 May 1981, *J. Volcanol. Geotherm. Res., 22, no. 3/4,* 225-269, 1984.

Barberi, F., F. Innocenti, L. Lirer, R. Munro, T. Pescatore, and R. Santacroce, The Campanian ignimbrite: A major prehistoric eruption in the Neapolitan area (Italy), *Bull. Volcanol., 41*, 10-32, 1978.

Barberi, Franco, M. Rosi, R. Santacroce, and M.F. Sheridan, Volcanic hazard zonation: Mt. Vesuvius, in *Forecasting Volcanic Events*, edited by Haroun Tazieff and J.-C. Sabroux, pp. 149-161, Elsevier, Amsterdam, 1983.

Beaulieu, J.D., and N.V. Peterson, N.V., Seismic and volcanic hazard evaluation of the Mount St. Helens area, Washington, relative to the Trojan Nuclear site, Oregon, *Oregon Department of Geology and Mineral Industries Open-File Report 0-81-9*, 80 pp. (A summary of this report was published in *Oregon Geology, 43, no. 12*, 159-169, 1981).

Beget, J.E., Glacier Peak volcano: A potentially hazardous Cascade volcano, *Environ. Geol., 5*, 83-92, 1983.

Belousov, A.B., and G.E. Bogoyavlenskaya, Debris avalanche of the 1956 Bezymianny eruption [abstract]: *Abstracts Volume, Kagoshima International Conference on Volcanoes*, 352, 1988.

Berger, G.W., Thermoluminescence dating of volcanic ash, *J. Volcanol. Geotherm. Res., 25*, 333-347, 1985.

Berger, G.W., Thermoluminescence dating of the Pleistocene Old Crow tephra and adjacent loess, near Fairbanks, Alaska, *Canadian J. Earth Sci., 24*, 1975-1984, 1987.

Berger, G.W., Dating Quaternary events by luminescence, in Dating Quaternary Sediments, edited by D.J. Easterbrook, *Geol. Soc. Amer. Special Paper 227*, 13-50, 1988.

Berrino, G., C. Corrado, G. Luongo, and B. Toro, Ground deformation and gravity changes accompanying the 1982 Pozzuoli uplift, *Bull. Volcanol., 47-2*, 187-200, 1984.

Beverage, J.P., and J.K. Culbertson, Hyperconcentrations of suspended sediment, *J. Hydraulics Division, American Society of Civil Engineers Proceedings, v. 90, no. HY6*, 117-128, 1964.

Birkeland, P.W., *Soils and geomorphology*, 372 pp., Oxford University Press, New York, 1984.

Blinman, Eric, P.J. Mehringer, Jr., and J.C. Sheppard, Pollen influx and the deposition of Mazama and Glacier Peak tephra, in *Volcanic Activity and Human Ecology*, edited by P.D. Sheets and D.K. Grayson, pp. 393-426, Academic Press, New York, 1979.

Blong, R.J., Some effects of tephra falls on buildings, in *Tephra Studies*, edited by S. Self and R.S.J. Sparks, pp. 405-420, NATO Advanced Study Institutes Series, D. Reidel Publishing Company, Boston, 1981.

Blong, R.J., *The time of darkness: Local legends and volcanic reality in Papua New Guinea*, 257 pp., Australian National University Press, Canberra, 1982.

Blong, R.J., *Volcanic hazards: A Sourcebook on the Effects of Eruptions*, 424 pp., Academic Press, Orlando, Florida, 1984.

Bogoyavlenskaya, G.E., O.A. Braitseva, I.V. Melekestsev, V. Yu. Kiriyanov, and C.D. Miller, C.D., Catastrophic eruptions of the directed-blast type at Mount St, Helens, Bezymianny, and Shiveluch volcanoes, *J. Geodynamics, 3*, 189-218, 1985.

Bolt, B.A., W.L. Horn, G.A. Macdonald, and R.F. Scott, *Geological Hazards*, 328 pp., Springer-Verlag, New York, 1977.

Bomford, G., *Geodesy*, 4th edition, 855 pp., Clarendon Press, London, 1980.

Booth, Basil, Assessing volcanic risk, *J. Geol. Soc. London, 136*, 331-340, 1979.

Booth, Basil, Ronald Croasdale, and G.P.L. Walker, Volcanic hazard on São Miguel, Azores, in *Forecasting Volcanic Events*, edited by Haroun Tazieff and J.-C. Sabroux, pp. 99-109, Elsevier, Amsterdam, 1983.

Bradley, R.S., *Quaternary Paleoclimatology*, 472 pp., Allen and Unwin, Boston, 1985.

Brakenridge, G.R., 1988, River flood regime and floodplain stratigraphy, in *Flood Geomorphology*, edited V.R. Baker, R.C. Kochel, and P.C. Patton, pp. 157-168, John Wiley & Sons, New York, 1988.

Brantley, S.R., and R.B. Waitt, Interrelations among pyroclastic surge, pyroclastic flow, and lahars in Smith Creek valley during first minutes of 18 May 1980 eruption of Mount St. Helens, U.S.A., *Bull. Volcanol. 50, no. 5*, 304-326, 1988.

Brantley, Steve, and Lyn Topinka, Volcanic studies at the U.S. Geological Survey's David A. Johnston Cascades Volcano Observatory, Vancouver, Washington, *Earthquake Information Bull., 16, no. 2*, 44-122, 1984.

Brantley, Steven, David Yamaguchi, Kenneth Cameron, and, Patrick Pringle, Tree-ring dating of volcanic deposits, *Earthquakes and Volcanoes, 18, no. 5*, 184-194, 1986.

Bullard, F.M., *Volcanoes of the Earth*, 629 pp., 2nd edition, University of Texas Press, Austin, 1984.

Burgos, J.G., Chaos mar aid work, *Manila Times*, October 1, 1965.

Cameron, K.A., and P.T. Pringle, A detailed chronology of the most recent major eruptive period at Mount Hood, Oregon, *Geol. Soc. Amer. Bull., 99, no. 12*, 845-851, 1987.

Capaldi, Giuseppe, and Raimondo Pece, On the reliability of the ^{230}Th-^{238}U dating method applied to young volcanic rocks, *J. Volcanol. Geotherm. Res., 11*, 367-372, 1981.

Capaldi, Giuseppe, Massimo Cortini, and Raimondo Pece, On the reliability of the ^{230}Th-^{238}U dating method applied to young volcanic rocks--reply, *J. Volcanol. Geotherm. Res., 26*, 369-376, 1985.

Carey, S.N., and Haraldur Sigurdsson, Influence of particle aggregation on deposition of distal tephra from May 18, 1980, eruption of Mount St. Helens volcano, *J. Geophys. Res., 87*, 7061-7072, 1982.

Carey, S., and H. Sigurdsson, The 1982 eruptions of El Chichón volcano, Mexico (2): Observations and numerical modelling of tephra-fall distribution, *Bull. Volcanol., 48, no. 2/3*, 127-142, 1986.

Carey, Steven, and R.S.J. Sparks, Quantitative models of the fallout and dispersal of tephra from volcanic eruption columns, *Bull. Volcanol., 48*, 109-125, 1986.

Carroll, J.J., and S.A. Parco, *Social organization in a crisis situation: The Taal disaster*, Philippine Sociological Society monograph, Manila, 58 pp., 1966.

Cas, R.A.F., and Wright, J.V., *Volcanic Successions-- Modern and Ancient*, 528 pp., Allen and Unwin, London, 1987.

Cassidy, J., C.A. Locke, and I.E.M. Smith, Volcanic hazard in the Auckland region, in Volcanic hazard assessment in New Zealand, edited by J.G. Gregory.and W.A. Watters, *New Zealand Geol. Surv. Record 10*, pp. 60-64, 1986.

Cepeda, Hector, Ricardo Mendez, Armando Murcia, and Heyley Vergara, Mapa preliminar de riesgos volcánicos potenciales del Nevado del Huila, Colombia, *Ministerio de Minas y Energía (INGEOMINAS) Informe No. 1981*, 59 pp., map scale 1:25,000, 1986.

Chadwick, W.W., Jr., D.A. Swanson, E.Y. Iwatsubo, C.C. Heliker, and T.A. Leighley, Deformation monitoring at Mount St. Helens in 1981 and 1982, *Science, 221*, 1378-1380, 1983.

Chadwick, W.W., E.Y. Iwatsubo, D.A. Swanson, and J.W. Ewert, Measurements of slope distances and vertical angles at Mount Baker and Mount Rainier, Washington, Mount Hood and Crater Lake, Oregon and Mount Shasta and Lassen Peak, California, *U.S. Geol. Surv. Open-File Report 85-205*, 95 pp., 1985.

Chadwick, W.W., Jr., R.J. Archuleta, and D.A. Swanson, The mechanics of ground deformation precursory to dome-building extrusions at Mount St. Helens 1981-1982, *J. Geophys. Res., 93, no. B5*, 4351-4366, 1988.

Champion, D.E., Holocene geomagnetic secular variation in the western United States: Implications for the global geomagnetic field, *U.S. Geol. Surv. Open-File Report 80-824*, 277 pp., 1980.

Chouet, B., Excitation of a buried magmatic pipe: A seismic source model for volcanic tremor, *J. Geophys. Res., 90*, 1881-1893, 1985.

Chouet, B., Resonance of fluid-driven crack: Radiation properties and implications for the source of long-period events and harmonic tremor, *J. Geophys. Res., 93, no. B5*, 4375-4400, 1988.

Chouet, B., R.Y. Koyanagi, and K. Aki, Origin of volcanic tremor in Hawaii: Part II, Theory and Discussion, *in* Volcanism in Hawaii, edited by R.W. Decker, T.L. Wright, and P.H. Stauffer, *U.S. Geol. Surv. Prof. Paper, 1350*, pp. 1259-1280, 1987.

Christiansen, R.L., and D.W. Peterson, Chronology of the 1980 eruptive activity, *in* The 1980 eruptions of Mount St. Helens, Washington, edited by P.W. Lipman, and D.R. Mullineaux, *U.S. Geol. Surv. Prof. Paper 1250*, pp. 17-67, 1981.

Civetta, L., P. Gasparini, G. Luongo, and A. Rapolla, editors, *Physical Volcanology, Developments in Solid Earth Geophysics, 6*, 333 pp., Elsevier Scientific Publishing Company, Amsterdam, The Netherlands, 1974.

Collins, B.D., T. Dunne, and A.K. Lehre, Erosion of tephra-covered hillslopes north of Mount St. Helens, Washington, *Zeitschrift für Geomorphologie, Supplement Bd 46*, 103-121, 1983.

Colman, S.M., 1981, Rock-weathering rates as functions of time, *Quaternary Research, 15, no. 3*, 250-264, 1981.

Colman, S.M., and K.L. Pierce, Weathering rinds on andesitic and basaltic stones as a Quaternary age indicator, western United States, *U.S. Geol. Surv. Prof. Paper, 1210*, 56 pp., 1981.

Condomines, Michel, Age of the Olby-Laschamp geomagnetic polarity event, *Nature, 276*, 257-258, 1978.

Corrado, G. and G. Luongo, Ground deformation measurements in active volcanic areas using tide gauges, *Bull. Volcanol., 44-3*, 505-511, 1981.

Corrado, G., I. Guerra, A. Lo Bascio, G. Luongo, and R. Rampoli, Inflation and microearthquake activity of Phlegraean Fields, Italy, *Bull. Volcanol., 40-3*, 1-20, 1977.

Costa, J.E., Physical geomorphology of debris flows, in *Developments and Applications of Geomorphology*, edited by J.E. Costa and P.J. Fleisher, pp. 268-317, Springer-Verlag, New York, 1984.

Costa, J.E., and R.L. Schuster, The formation and failure of natural dams, *Geol. Soc. Amer. Bull., 100, no. 7*, 1054-1068, 1988.

Crandell, D.R., Postglacial lahars from Mount Rainier volcano, Washington, *U.S. Geol. Surv. Prof. Paper 677*, 73 pp., 1971.

Crandell, D.R., Map showing potential hazards from future eruptions of Mount Rainier, Washington, *U.S. Geol. Surv. Miscell. Geol. Invest. Map I-836*, scale 1:250,000., 1973.

Crandell, D.R., Preliminary assessment of potential hazards from future volcanic eruptions in Washington, *U.S. Geol. Surv. Miscell. Field Studies Map MF-774*, 1976..

Crandell, D.R., Recent eruptive history of Mount Hood, Oregon, and potential hazards from future eruptions, *U.S. Geol. Surv. Bull. 1492*, 81 pp., 1980.

Crandell, D.R., Potential hazards from future volcanic eruptions on the Island of Maui, Hawaii, *U.S. Geol. Surv. Miscell. Invest. Series Map I-1442*, scale 1:62,500, 1983.

Crandell, D.R., Deposits of pre-1980 pyroclastic flows and lahars from Mount St. Helens, Washington, *U.S. Geol. Surv. Prof. Paper 1444*, 91 pp., 1988.

Crandell, D.R., Gigantic debris avalanche of Pleistocene age from ancestral Mount Shasta volcano, California, and debris-avalanche hazard zonation, *U.S. Geol. Surv. Bull. 1861*, 32 pp., in press.

Crandell, D.R., and D.R. Mullineaux, Volcanic hazards at

Mount Rainier, *U.S. Geol. Surv. Bull., 1238,* 26 pp., 1967.

Crandell, D.R., and D.R. Mullineaux, Potential geologic hazards in Lassen Volcanic National Park, California, *U.S. Geol. Surv. Administrative Report,* 54 pp., 1970.

Crandell, D.R., and D.R. Mullineaux, Pine Creek volcanic assemblage at Mount St. Helens, Washington, *U.S. Geol. Surv. Bull. 1383-A,* 23 pp., 1973.

Crandell, D.R., and D.R. Mullineaux, Technique and rationale of volcanic-hazards assessments in the Cascade Range, northwestern United States, *Environ. Geol., 1,* 23-32, 1975.

Crandell, D.R., and D.R. Mullineaux, Potential hazards from future eruptions of Mount St. Helens Volcano, Washington, *U.S. Geol. Surv. Bull. 1383-C,* 26 pp., 1978.

Crandell, D.R., and R.P. Hoblitt, Lateral blasts at Mount St. Helens and hazard zonation, *Bull. Volcanol., 48,* 27-37, 1986.

Crandell, D.R., D.R. Mullineaux, and M. Rubin, Mount St. Helens Volcano: Recent and future behavior, *Science, 187,* 438-441, 1975.

Crandell, D.R., D.R. Mullineaux, and C.D. Miller, Volcanic-hazards studies in the Cascade Range of the western United States, in *Volcanic Activity and Human Ecology,* edited by P.D. Sheets and D.K. Grayson, pp. 195-219, Academic Press, New York, 1979.

Crandell, D.R., B. Booth, K. Kusumadinata, D. Shimozuru, G.P.L. Walker, and D. Westercamp, *Source-Book for Volcanic-Hazard Zonation,* 97 pp., UNESCO, Paris, 1984.

Cruz, J.V., Tasteless exploitation of the Taal disaster, *Manila Times,* October 1, 1965.

Davies, D.K., M.W. Quearry, and S.B. Bonis, Glowing avalanches from the 1974 eruption of volcano Fuego, Guatemala, *Geol. Soc. Amer. Bull., 89,* 369-384., 1978a.

Davies, D.K., R.K. Vessell, R.C. Miles, M.G. Foley, and S.B. Bonis, Fluvial transport and downstream sediment modifications in an active volcanic region, *in* Fluvial Sedimentology, edited by A.D. Miall, *Canadian Soc. of Petrol. Geol. Memoir 5,* 61-84, 1978b.

de Saint Ours, P.J., Potential hazards at Manam Island, *Geol. Surv. Papua New Guinea Report 82/22,* 16 pp., 1982.

de St. Ours, Patrice, Inflation of Rabaul caldera since its 1937 eruption as revealed by emergence of intertidal shell horizons [abstract], *Abstracts Volume, Hawaii Symposium on How Volcanoes Work, Hilo, Hawaii, January 1987,* 220, 1987.

Decker, R.W., State of the art in volcano forecasting, in *Geophysical Predictions,* pp. 47-57, Geophysics Study Committee, National Research Council, National Academy Press, Washington, D.C., 1978.

Decker, R.W., Forecasting volcanic eruptions, *Ann. Rev. Earth Planet. Sci., 14,* 267-291, 1986.

Decker, R.W., and W.T. Kinoshita, Geodetic measurements, in *The Surveillance and Prediction of Volcanic Activity,* pp. 47-74, UNESCO, Paris, 1972.

Decker, R.W., R.Y. Koyanagi, J.J. Dvorak, J.P. Lockwood, A.T. Okamura, K.M. Yamashita, and W.R. Tanigawa, Seismicity and surface deformation of Mauna Loa Volcano, *Eos, Amer. Geophys. Union Trans., 64, no. 37,* 545-547, 1983.

DeNevi, Don, *Earthquakes,* 230 pp., Celestial Arts, Millbrae, California, 1977.

Denlinger, R.P., F.P. Riley, J.K. Boling, and M.C. Carpenter, Deformation of Long Valley, Caldera between August 1982 and August 1983, *J. Geophys. Res., 90, no. B-13,* 11,199-11,209, 1985.

Devine, J.D., H. Sigurdsson, A.N. Davis, and S. Self, Estimates of sulfur and chlorine yield to the atmosphere from volcanic eruptions and potential climatic effects, *J. Geophys. Res., 89,* 6309-6325, 1984.

Dibble, R.R., I.A. Nairn, and V.E. Neall, Volcanic hazards of North Island, New Zealand--overview, *J. Geodynamics, 3,* 369-396, 1985.

Disaster Prevention Bureau, *Volcanic Disaster Countermeasures in Japan,* Disaster Prevention Bureau, National Land Agency, Prime Minister's Office, Tokyo, 23 pp., 1988a.

Disaster Prevention Bureau, *Natural Disasters and International Cooperation: The Abstract of A White Paper on Disaster Countermeasures in 1988 Toward the IDNDR,* Disaster Prevention Bureau, National Land Agency, Prime Minister's Office, Tokyo, 32 pp., 1988b.

Djumarma, A., S. Bronto, I. Bahar, F.X. Suparban, R. Sukhyar, C.G. Newhall, R.T. Holcomb, N.G. Banks, T. Torley, J.P. Lockwood, R.I. Tilling, M. Rubin, and M.A. del Marmol, Did Merapi Volcano (Central Java) erupt catastrophically in 1006 A.D.? [abstract], *Abstracts, International Volcanological Congress, Auckland-Hamilton-Rotorua, New Zealand, February 1986,* 236, 1986.

Dorn, R.I., Cation-ratio dating: A new rock varnish age-determination technique, *Quaternary Research, 20,* 49-73, 1983.

Dorn, R.I., D.B. Bamforth, T.A. Cahill, J.C. Dohrenwend, B.D. Turrin, D.J. Bonahue, A.J.T. Jull, A. Long, M.E. Macko, E.B. Weil, D.S. Whitley, and T.H. Zabel, Cation-ratio and accelerator radiocarbon dating of rock varnish on Mojave artifacts and landforms, *Science, 231,* 830-833, 1986.

Duffield, W.A., and R.O. Burford, An accurate invar-wire extensometer, *U.S. Geol. Surv. Jour. Res., 1, no. 5,* 569-577, 1973.

Duffield, W.A., C.R. Bacon, and G.R. Rocquemore, Origin of reverse-graded bedding in air-fall pumice, Coso Range, California, *J. Volcanol. Geotherm. Res., 5, no. 1,* 35-48, 1979.

Duffield, W.A., L. Stieltjes, and J. Varet, J., Huge landslide blocks in the growth of Piton de la Fournaise, La Reunion, and Kilauea volcano, Hawaii, *J. Volcanol. Geotherm. Res., 12*, 147-160, 1982.

Duffield, W.A., R.I. Tilling, and R. Canul, Geology of El Chichón Volcano, Chiapas, Mexico, *J. Volcanol. Geotherm. Res., 20*, 117-132, 1984.

Dvorak, J.J., and A.T. Okamura, A hydraulic model to explain variations in summit tilt rate at Kilauea and Mauna Loa Volcanoes, *in* Volcanism in Hawaii, edited by R.W. Decker, T.L. Wright, and P.H. Stauffer, *U.S. Geol. Surv. Prof. Paper, 1350*, pp. 1281-1296, 1987.

Dzurisin, D., and K.M. Yamashita, Vertical surface displacements at Yellowstone caldera, Wyoming, 1976-1986, *J. Geophys. Res., 92*, 13,307-13,714, 1987.

Dzurisin, D., D.J. Johnson, T.L. Murray, and B. Myers, Tilt networks at Mount Shasta and Lassen Peak, California, *U.S. Geol. Surv. Open-File Report 82-670*, 42 pp., 1982.

Dzurisin, D., D. J. Johnson, and R. B. Symonds, Dry tilt networks at Mount Rainier, Washington, *U.S. Geol. Surv. Open-File Report 83-277*, 19 pp., 1983a.

Dzurisin, Daniel, J.A. Westphal, and D.J. Johnson, Eruption prediction aided by electronic tiltmeter data at Mount St. Helens, *Science, 221*, 1381-1383, 1983b.

Easterbrook. D.J., editor, Dating Quaternary Sediments, *Geol. Soc. Amer. Special Paper 227*, 165 pp., 1988.

Eaton, G.P., A portable water-tube tiltmeter, *Bull. Seismol. Soc. Amer., 49*, 301-316, 1959.

Eichelberger, J.C., and D.B. Hayes, D.B., Magmatic model for the Mount St. Helens blast of May 18, 1980, *J. Geophys. Res., 87*, 7727-7738, 1982.

Ekren, E.B., D.H. McIntyre, and E.H. Bennett, High-temperature, large-volume, lavalike ash-flow tuffs without calderas in southwestern Idaho, *U.S. Geol. Surv. Prof. Paper 1272*, 76 pp., 1984.

Endo, E.T., S.D. Malone, and L.L. Noson, and C.S. Weaver, Locations, magnitudes, and statistics of the March 20-May 18 earthquake sequence, *in* The 1980 eruptions of Mount St. Helens, Washington, edited by P.W. Lipman and D.R. Mullineaux, *U.S. Geol. Surv. Prof. Paper 1250*, pp. 93-107, 1981.

Ewert, John, A trignometric method for monitoring ground tilt using small aperture arrays, *U.S. Geol. Surv. Open-File Report 89-???*, 1989, in press.

Fedotov, S.A., and Ye. K. Markhinin, editors, *The Great Tolbachik Fissure Eruption*, 341 pp., Cambridge University Press, Cambridge, 1983.

Fehler, M., Observations of volcanic tremor at Mount St. Helens volcano, *J. Geophys. Res., 88*, 3476-3484, 1983.

Fisher, R.V., Proposed classification of volcaniclastic sediments and rocks, *Geol. Soc. Amer. Bull., 72*, 1409-1414, 1961.

Fisher, R.V., Puu Hou littoral cones, *Geologische Rundschau, 57*, 837-864, 1968.

Fisher, R.V., Features of coarse-grained, high-concentration fluids and their deposits, *J. Sediment. Petrology, 41, no. 4*, 916-927, 1971.

Fisher, R.V., Models for pyroclastic surges and pyroclastic surges, *J. Volcanol. Geotherm. Res., 6*, 305-318, 1979.

Fisher, R.V., Flow transformations in sediment gravity flows, *Geology, 11*, 273-274, 1983.

Fisher, R.V., and Grant Heiken, Mount Pelée, Martinique: May 8 and 20, 1902, pyroclastic flows and surges, *J. Volcanol. Geotherm. Res., 12*, 339-371, 1982.

Fisher, R.V., and H.-U. Schmincke, *Pyroclastic Rocks*, 472 pp., Springer-Verlag, New York, 1984.

Fisher, R.V., H.X. Glicken, and R.P. Hoblitt, May 18, 1980, Mount St. Helens deposits in South Coldwater Creek, Washington, *J. Geophys. Res., 92, no. B10*, 10,267-10,283, 1987.

Fiske, R.S., Volcanologists, journalists, and the concerned local public: A tale of two crises, in the eastern Caribbean, in *Explosive Volcanism: Inception, Evolution, and Hazards*, Geophysics Study Committee, National Research Council, National Academy Press, Washington, D.C., pp. 170-176, 1984.

Fiske, R.S., and W.T. Kinoshita, Inflation of Kilauea Volcano prior to its 1967-68 eruption, *Science, 165*, 341-349, 1969.

Fiske, R.S., and J.B. Shepherd, Deformation studies on Soufrière, St. Vincent, between 1977 and 1981, *Science, 216*, 1125-1126, 1982.

Forjaz, V.H., Mapa de risco sismovulcanico Ilha de São Miguel: Ponta Delgada, *Servico Regional de Proteccao Civil and Direccao Regional dos Assuntos Culturais and Universidade dos Acores (Departamento de Geosciencias)*, scale 1:50,000, 2 sheets, 1985.

Fournier d'Albe, E.M., Objectives of volcanic monitoring and prediction, *J. Geol. Soc. London, 136*, 321-326, 1979.

Foxworthy, B.L., and Mary Hill, Volcanic eruptions of 1980 at Mount St. Helens: The first 100 days, *U.S. Geol. Surv. Prof. Paper, 1249*, 125 pp, 1982.

Francis, P.W., The origin of the 1883 Krakatau tsunamis, *J. Volcanol. Geotherm. Res., 25*, 349-363, 1985.

Francis, Peter, and Stephen Self, The eruption of Krakatau, *Scientific American, 281*, 172-187, 1983.

Friedman, Irving, and John Obradovich, Obsidian-hydration dating of volcanic events, *Quaternary Research, 16, no. 1*, 37-47, 1981.

Fritts, H.C., *Tree Rings and Climate*, 567 pp., Academic Press, London, 1976.

Gil C., F., Analysis preliminar de tremor y eventos de largo periodo registrados en el Volcán Nevado del Ruíz, *Revista CIAF, 11*, 13-50, Bogotá, Colombia, 1987.

Gil C., F., H. Meyer, B. Chouet, and D. Harlow, Observations of long-period events and tremor at Nevado del Ruíz volcano 1985-1986 [abs.], *Abstract Volume, Hawaii Symposium on How Volcanoes Work, Hilo, Hawaii*, 90, 1987.

Gillot, P.Y., J. Labeyrie, C. Laj, G. Valladas, G. Guerin, G. Poupeau, and G. Delibrias, Age of the Laschamp geomagnetic polarity excursion revisited, *Earth Planet. Sci. Letters, 42*, 444-450, 1979.

González Reyna, Jenaro, and W.F. Foshag, The birth of Parícutin, in *Smithsonian Institution Annual Report for 1946*, pp. 223-234, Washington, D.C., 1947.

Gorshkov, G.S., Gigantic eruption of the Bezymianny volcano, *Bull. Volcanol., 20,* 77-109, 1959.

Gorshkov, G.S., Directed volcanic blasts, *Bull. Volcanol., 26,* 83-88, 1963.

Goudie, Andrew, editor, *Geomorphological Techniques*, 395 pp., Allen and Unwin, London, 1981.

Grootes, P.M., Radioactive isotopes in The Holocene, in *Late-Quaternary Environments of the United States, Volume 2, The Holocene*, edited by H.E. Wright, pp. 86-105,, University of Minnesota Press, Minneapolis, 1983.

Guest, J.E., and J.B. Murray, An analysis of hazard from Mount Etna volcano, *J. Geol. Soc. London, 136,* 347-354, 1979.

Gutenberg, B., Tilting due to glacial melting, *J. Geol., 41,* 449-467, 1933.

Hagiwara, T., Observations of changes in the inclination of the earth's surface at Mt. Tsukuba, *Bull. Earthquake Res. Inst., 25,* 27-32, 1947.

Hall, Minard, and Ramon Vera, La actividad volcánica del Volcán Tungurahua: Sus peligros y sus riesgos volcánicos, *Escuela Politécnica Nacional, Monografía de Geología 4, 10, no. 1,* 91-144, 1985.

Hall M.L., and C.G. von Hillebrandt M., Mapa de los peligros volcánicos potenciales asociados con el Volcán Cotopaxi, zona sur, *Instituto Geofísico de la Escuela Politécnica Nacional, Quito, Ecuador*, scale 1:50,000, 1988a.

Hall, M.L., and C.G. von Hillebrandt M., Mapa de los peligros volcánicos potenciales asociados con el Volcán Cotopaxi, zona norte, *Instituto Geofísico de la Escuela Politécnica Nacional, Quito, Ecuador*, scale 1:50,000, 1988b.

Hamidi, S., I. Suryo, P. Djuhara, P. Kasturian, and D. Sumpena, Volcanic hazard map Kelut volcano, East Java (Indonesia), *Volcanological Survey of Indonesia*, scale 1:100,000, 1985.

Hamilton, W.L., Water level records used to evaluate deformation within the Yellowstone caldera, Yellowstone National Park, *J. Volcanol. Geotherm. Res., 31, no. 3/4,* 205-215, 1987.

Hay, R.L., Formation of the crystal-rich glowing avalanche deposits of St. Vincent, British West Indies, *J. Geology, 67,* 540-562, 1959.

Hays, W.W., and C.F. Shearer, Suggestions for improving decisionmaking to face geologic and hydrologic hazards, in Facing geologic and hydrologic hazards: Earth-science considerations, edited by W.W. Hays, *U.S. Geol. Surv. Prof. Paper 1240-B*, B103-B108, 1981.

Heliker, Christina, J.D. Griggs, T.J. Takahashi, and T.L. Wright, Volcano monitoring at the U.S. Geological Survey's Hawaiian Volcano Observatory, *Earthquakes and Volcanoes (formerly Earthquake Information Bulletin), 18, no. 1,* 3-69, 1986.

Hemond, Christophe, and Michel Condomines, On the reliability of the ^{230}Th-^{238}U dating method applied to young volcanic rocks--discussion, *J. Volcanol. Geotherm. Res., 26,* 365-376, 1985.

Herd, D.G., and the Comité de Estudios Vulcanológicos, The 1985 Ruíz Volcano disaster, *Eos, Trans. Amer. Geophys. Union, 67, no. 19,* 457-460, 1986.

Herrmann, R.B., The use of duration as a measure of seismic moment and magnitude, *Bull. Seismol. Soc. Amer., 64, no. 4,* 899-913, 1975.

Hill, D.P, Monitoring unrest in a large silicic caldera, the Long Valley-Inyo Craters Volcanic Complex in East-Central California, *Bull. Volcanol., 47, no. 2,* 371-396, 1984.

Hoblitt, R.P., Observations of the eruptions of July 22 and August 7, 1980, at Mount St. Helens, Washington, *U.S. Geol. Surv. Prof. Paper, 1335*, 44 pp., 1986.

Hoblitt, R.P., and K..S. Kellogg, Emplacement temperatures of unsorted and unstratified deposits of volcanic rock debris as determined by paleomagnetic techniques, *Geol. Soc Amer. Bull., 90, no. 7,* 633-642, 1979.

Hoblitt, R.P., and C.D. Miller, Comment on Walker and McBroome, 1983, *Geology, 12,* 692-693, 1984.

Hoblitt, R.P., C.D. Miller,.and J. Vallance, J., Origin and stratigraphy of the deposit produced by the May 18 directed blast, *in* The 1980 eruptions of Mount St. Helens, Washington, edited by P.W. Lipman and D.R. Mullineaux, *U.S. Geol. Surv. Prof. Paper 1250*, pp. 401-419, 1981.

Hoblitt, R.P., R.L. Reynolds, and E.E. Larson, Suitability of nonwelded pyroclastic-flow deposits for studies of magnetic secular variation: A test based on deposits emplaced a Mount St. Helens, Washington, in 1980, *Geology, 13, no, 4,* 242-245, 1985.

Hoblitt, R.P., C.D. Miller, and W.E. Scott, Volcanic hazards with regard to siting nuclear-power plants in the Pacific Northwest, *U.S. Geol. Surv. Open-File Report 87-297*, 196 pp., 1987.

Holcomb, R.T., Eruptive history and long-term behavior of Kilauea volcano, *in* Volcanism in Hawaii, edited by R.W. Decker, T.L. Wright, and P.H. Stauffer, *U.S. Geol. Surv. Prof. Paper 1350*, pp. 261-350, 1987.

Houghton, B.F., J.H. Latter, and W.R. Hackett, W.R., Volcanic hazard assessment for Ruapehu composite volcano, Taupo volcanic zone, New Zealand, *Bull. Volcanol., 49,* 737-751, 1987.

HVOWB, Weekly Bulletin of Hawaiian Volcano Observatory, October 5, 1913, in *The Early Serial Publications of the Hawaiian Volcano Observatory, vol. 2*, edited by Darcy Bevens, T.K. Takahashi, and T.L. Wright, pp. 47-50, Hawaii Natural History Association, Hawaii National Park, Hawaii, 1988.

Hwang, F.S.W., Thermoluminescence dating applied to volcanic lavas, *Modern Geology, 2,* 231-234, 1971.

Hyde, J.H., and D.R. Crandell, Postglacial deposits at Mount Baker, Washington, and potential hazards from future eruptions, *U.S. Geol. Surv. Prof Paper, 1022-C*, 17 pp., 1978.

Imai, Noboru, Koichi Shimokawa, and Michio Hirota, ESR dating of volcanic ash, *Nature, 314*, 81-83, 1985.

Imamura, A., Topographical changes accompanying earthquakes or volcanic eruptions, *Publications of Earthquake Invest. Comm. in Foreign Languages (Tokyo), no. 25*, 143 pp., 1930.

Inman, D.L., Measures for describing the size distribution of sediments, *J. Sediment. Petrology, 22*, 125-145, 1952.

Ishihara, Kazuhiro, Prediction of summit eruption by tilt and strain data at Sakurajima Volcano, Japan [abstract], *Abstracts Volume, Kagoshima International Conference on Volcanoes, July 1988*, 44, 1988.

Ivanovich, M., and R.S. Harmon, editors, *Uranium Series Disequilibrium: Application to Environmental Problems*, 571 pp., Clarendon Press, Oxford, 1982.

Iverson, R.M., and R.P. Denlinger, The physics of debris flows--a conceptual assessment, *in* Erosion and Sedimentation in the Pacific Rim, edited by R.L. Beschta, T. Blinn, G.E. Grant, G.G. Ice, and F.J. Swanson, pp. 155-165, *Inter. Assoc. of Hydrological Sciences Publication No. 165*, 1987.

Jachens, R.C., D. Dzurisin, W.P. Elder, and R.W. Saltus, Precision gravity networks at Lassen Peak and Mount Shasta, California, *U.S. Geol. Surv. Open-File Report 83-192*, 20 pp., 1983.

Jaggar, T.A., and R.H. Finch, Tilt records for thirteen years at the Hawaiian Volcano Observatory, *Bull. Seismol. Soc. Amer., 19, no. 1*, 38-51, 1929.

Janda, R.J., K.M. Scott, K.M. Nolan, and H.A. Martinson, Lahar movement, effects, and deposits, *in* The 1980 eruptions of Mount St. Helens, Washington, edited by P.W. Lipman and D.R. Mullineaux, *U.S. Geol. Surv. Prof. Paper, 1250*, pp. 461-478, 1981.

Japan Sabo Association, *Sabo Works for Active Volcanoes in Japan*, Tokyo, Japan Sabo Association, 88 pp., 1988.

Johnson, R.W., and N.A. Threlfall, *Volcano town: The 1937-43 eruptions at Rabaul*, 151 pp., Robert Brown & Associates, Bathurst, Australia, 1985

Judd, J.W., On the volcanic phenomena of the eruption, and the nature and distribution of the ejected materials, *in* The Eruption of Krakatoa, and Subsequent Phenomena, edited by G.J. Symons, Report of the Krakatoa Committee of the Royal Society of London, pp. 1-56, Trübner and Co., London, 1888.

Katili, J.A., Adjat Sudradjat, and K. Kusumadinata, editors, *Letusan Galunggung 1982-1983*, Volcanological Survey of Indonesia, Bandung, 693 pp., 1986. [A collection of 28 papers on various aspects of the 1982-1983 Galunggung eruption; 7 of the papers are in English, the rest are in Indonesian].

Katili, J.A., and Adjat Sudradjat, *Galunggung: The 1982-1983 eruption*, Volcanological Survey of Indonesia, Bandung, 102 pp., 1984.

Katsui, Yoshio, and H.R. Katz, Lateral fissure eruptions in the southern Andes of Chile, *J. Faculty of Science, Hokkaido University, series IV, 13, no. 4*, 433-448, 1967.

Keller, E.A., 1986, Investigation of active tectonics: Use of surficial earth processes, in *Active Tectonics*, Washington, D.C., National Academy Press, pp. 136-147, 1986.

Kent, D.V., D. Ninkovich, T. Pescatore, and R.S.J. Sparks, Paleomagnetic determination of emplacement temperature of Vesuvius A.D. 79 pyroclastic deposits, *Nature, 290*, 393-396, 1981.

Kieffer, S.W., Fluid dynamics of the May 18 blast at mount St. Helens, *in* The 1980 eruptions of Mount St. Helens, Washington, edited by P.W. Lipman and D.R. Mullineaux, *U.S. Geol. Surv. Prof. Paper, 1250*, pp. 379-400, 1981.

Kieffer, S.W., Seismicity at Old Faithful geyser: An isolated source of geothermal noise and possible analog of volcanic seismicity, *J. Volcanol. Geotherm. Res., 22*, 59-95, 1984.

Kienle, Jurgen, and S.E. Swanson, Volcanic hazards from future eruptions of Augustine volcano, Alaska, *University of Alaska Geophysical Institute Report UAG R-275*, 126 pp., 1980

Kienle, Jurgen, Zygmunt Kowalik, and T.S. Murty, Tsunamis generated by eruptions from Mount St. Augustine volcano, Alaska, *Science, 236*, 1442-1447, 1987.

Kinoshita, W.T., D.A. Swanson, and D.B. Jackson, The measurement of crustal deformation related to volcanic activity at Kilauea Volcano, Hawaii, in *Physical Volcanology*, edited by L. Civetta, P. Gasparini, G. Luongo, and A. Rapolla, pp. 87-115, Elsevier Scientific Publishing Company, Amsterdam, The Netherlands, 1974.

Klein, F.W., Hypocenter location program HYPOINVERSE, *U.S. Geol. Surv. Open-File Report 78-694*, 113 pp., 1978.

Klein, F.W., R.Y. Koyanagi, J.S. Nakata, and W.R. Tanigawa, The seismicity of Kilauea's magma system, *in* Volcanism in Hawaii, edited by R.W. Decker, T.L. Wright, and P.H. Stauffer, *U.S. Geol. Surv. Prof. Paper, 1350*, pp. 1019-1185, 1987.

Kling, G.W., M.A. Clark, H.R. Compton, J.D. Devine, W.C. Evans, A.M. Humphrey, E.J. Koenigsberg, J.P. Lockwood, M.L. Tuttle, and G.N. Wagner, The 1986 Lake Nyos gas disaster in Cameroon, west Africa, *Science, 236*, 169-175, 1987,

Kochel, R.C., and V.R. Baker, Paleoflood analysis using slackwater deposits, in *Flood Geomorphology*, edited by V.R. Baker, R.C. Kochel, and P.C. Patton, pp. 357-376, John Wiley & Sons, New York, 1988.

Koyanagi, R.Y., Earthquakes from common sources beneath Kilauea and Mauna Loa Volcanoes in Hawaii from 1962 to 1965, *U.S. Geol. Surv. Prof. Paper, 600C*, C120-C125, 1968.

Koyanagi, R.Y., B. Chouet, and K. Aki, Origin of volcanic tremor in Hawaii: Part I, Data from the Hawaiian Volcano Observatory 1969-1985, in Volcanism in Hawaii, edited by

R.W. Decker, T.L. Wright, and P.H. Stauffer, *U.S. Geol. Surv. Prof. Paper, 1350*, pp. 1221-1257, 1987.

Koyanagi, R.Y., P. Stevenson, E.T. Endo, and A.T. Okamura, *Hawaiian Volcano Observatory Summary 74, January to December 1974, U.S. Geol. Survey, Menlo Park, California*, 1977.

Koyanagi, R.Y., K. Meagher, F.W. Klein, and A.T. Okamura, *Hawaiian Volcano Observatory Summary 75, January to December 1975, U.S. Geol. Survey, Menlo Park, California*, 1978.

Kubotera, A., and K. Yoshikawa, Prediction of volcanic eruption at Aso and Sakurazima and some related geophysical problems, *Bull. Volcanol., 26*, 297-317, 1963.

Kuntz, M.A., D.E. Champion, E.C. Spiker, and R.H. Lefebvre, Contrasting magma types and steady-state, volume-predictable basaltic volcanism along the Great Rift, Idaho, *Geol. Soc. Amer. Bull., 97, no. 5*, 579-594, 1986.

Kusumadinata, K., Indonesia, in *Source-Book for Volcanic-Hazards Zonation: Natural Hazards 4*, edited by D.R. Crandell, B. Booth, K. Kusumadinata, D. Shimozuru, G.P.L. Walker, and D. Westercamp, pp. 55-60, UNESCO, 1984.

Lacroix, A., 1904, *La Montagne Pelée et ses eruptions*, 662 pp., Masson et Cie., Paris, 1904.

Langbein, J.O., M.F. Linker, A. McGarr, and L.E. Slater, Observations of strain accumulation across the San Andreas Fault near Palmdale, California, using a two-color geodimeter, *Science, 218*, 1217, 1982.

Latter, J.H., Tsunamis of volcanic origin, *Bull. Volcanol., 44*, 467-490, 1981.

Le Guern, F., H. Tazieff, and R. Faivre Pierret, An example of health hazard, people killed by gas during a phreatic eruption: Dieng Plateau (Java, Indonesia), February 20, 1979, *Bull. Volcanol., 45, no. 2*, 153-156, 1982.

Lee, W.H.K., and S.W. Stewart, Principles and applications of microearthquake networks, *Advances in Geophysics, Supplement, no. 2*, 293 pp., Academic Press, New York, 1981.

Lee, W.H.K., R.E. Bennett, and K.L. Meagher, A method of estimating magnitude of local earthquakes from signal duration, *U.S. Geol. Surv. Open-File Report*, 28 pp., 1972.

Leet, R.C., Saturated and subcooled hydrothermal boiling in groundwater flow channels as a source of harmonic tremor, *J. Geophys. Res., 93, no. B5*, 4835-4849, 1988.

Lehre, A.K., B.D. Collins, and, T. Dunne, Post-eruption sediment budget for the North Fork Toutle River drainage, June 1980-June 1981, *Zeitschrift für Geomorphologie, Supplement Bd. 46*, 143-163, 1983.

Linker, M.F., J.O. Langbein, and A. McGarr, Decrease in deformation rate observed by two-color laser ranging in Long Valley Caldera, *Science, 232*, 213-216, 1986.

Lipman, P.W., and N.G. Banks, Aa flow dynamics, Mauna Loa 1984, *in* Volcanism in Hawaii, edited by R.W. Decker,

T.L. Wright, and P.H. Stauffer, *U.S. Geol. Surv. Prof. Paper, 1350*, pp. 1527-1568, 1987.

Lipman, P.W., and D.R. Mullineaux, editors, The 1980 eruptions of Mount St. Helens, Washington, *U.S. Geol. Surv. Prof. Paper, 1250*, 844 pp., 1981.

Lipman, P.W., J.G. Moore, and D.A. Swanson, Bulging of the north flank before the May 18 eruption--geodetic data, *in* The 1980 eruptions of Mount St. Helens, Washington, edited by R.W. Decker, T.L. Wright, and P.H. Stauffer, *U.S. Geol. Surv. Prof. Paper, 1250*, pp. 143-155, 1981.

Locke, W.W., J.T. Andrews, and, P.J. Webber, A Manual for Lichenometry, *British Geomorphological Research Group, Technical Bulletin 26*, 1979.

Lockwood, J.P., and P.W. Lipman, Recovery of datable charcoal beneath young lavas--lessons from Hawaii, *Bull. Volcanol., 43, no. 3*, 609-615, 1980.

Lockwood, J.P., and Romolo Romano, Diversion of lava during the 1983 eruption of Mount Etna, *Earthquake Information Bulletin, 17, no. 4*, 124-133, 1985.

Lockwood, J.P., and P.W. Lipman, Holocene eruptive history of Mauna Loa volcano, *in* Volcanism in Hawaii, edited by R.W. Decker, T.L. Wright, and P.H. Stauffer, *U.S. Geol. Surv. Prof. Paper, 1350*, pp. 509-536, 1987.

Lockwood, J.P., N.G. Banks, T.T. English, L.P. Greenland, D.B. Jackson, D.J. Johnson, R.Y. Koyanagi, K.A. McGee, A.T. Okamura, and J.M. Rhodes, The 1984 eruption of Mauna Loa Volcano, Hawaii, *Eos, Trans. Amer. Geophys. Union, 66, no. 16*, 169-171, 1985.

Lockwood, J.P., H.J. Moore, E. Robinson, and Sherman Wu, Lava diversion structures to protect the Mauna Loa Observatory, Hawaii [abstract], *Geol. Soc. Amer. Abstracts with Programs, 19, no. 6.*, 399, 1987.

Lockwood, J.P., J.E. Costa, M.L. Tuttle, J. Nni, and S.G. Tebor, The potential for catastrophic dam failure at Lake Nyos maar, Cameroon, *Bull. Volcanol., 50, no. 5*, 340-349, 1988.

Lombard, R.E., M.B. Miles, L.M. Nelson, D.L. Kresh, and P.J. Carpenter, The impact of mudflows of May 18 on the lower Toutle and Cowlitz Rivers, *in* The 1980 eruptions of Mount St. Helens, Washington, edited by P.W. Lipman and D.R. Mullineaux, *U.S. Geol. Surv. Prof. Paper, 1250*, pp. 693-699, 1981.

Lowe, D.R., S.N. Williams, Henry Leigh, C.B. Connor, J.B. Gemmell, and, R.E. Stoiber, Lahars initiated by the 13 November 1985 eruption of Nevado del Ruíz, Colombia, *Nature, 324*, 51-53, 1986.

Lowenstein, P.L., Problems of volcanic hazards in Papua New Guinea, *Geol. Surv. Papua New Guinea, Report 82/7*, 62 pp., 1982.

Lowenstein, P.L. The Rabaul seismo-deformational crisis of 1983-85: Monitoring, emergency planning and interaction with the authorities, the media and the public [abstract], *Abstracts Volume, Kagoshima International Conference on Volcanoes, July 1988,* 504, 1988.

Lowenstein, P.L., and B. Talai, Volcanoes and volcanic hazards in Papua New Guinea, *Geol. Surv. Japan, Rept. 263*, 315-331, 1984.

Lowenstein, P.L., and J. Mori, The Rabaul seismo-deformational crisis of 1983-85: Monitoring, emergency planning and interaction with the authorities, the media, and the public [abstract], *Abstracts V. 2, XIX General Assembly, IUGG, Vancouver, Canada, August 9-22*, 429, 1987.

Luhr, J.F., and J.C. Varekamp, editors, El Chichón Volcano, Chiapas, Mexico, *Special Issue, J. Volcanol. Geotherm. Res., 23, no. 1/2*, 1-191, 1984.

Macdonald, G.A., The 1959 and 1960 eruptions of Kilauea volcano, Hawaii, and the construction of walls to restrict the spread of lava flows, *Bull. Volcanol., 24*, 249-294, 1962.

Macdonald, G.A., *Volcanoes*, 510 pp., Prentice-Hall, Inc., Englewood Cliffs, New Jersey, 1972.

Macdonald, G.A., and Alcaraz, Arturo, Nuées ardentes of the 1948-1953 eruption of Hibok-Hibok, *Bull. Volcanol., 18*, 169-178, 1956.

Machado, Frederico, W.II. Parsons, A.F. Richards, and J.W. Mulford, Capelinhos eruption of Fayal volcano, Azores, 1957-1958, *J. Geophys. Res., 67*, 3519-3529, 1962.

Mahaney, W.C., editor, *Quaternary Dating Methods*, 428 pp., Elsevier, New York, 1984.

Mahood, Gail, and Wes Hildreth, Nested calderas and trapdoor uplift of Pantelleria, Strait of Sicily, *Geology, 11*, 722-726, 1983.

Major, J.J., and C.G. Newhall, Effects of historical volcanic eruptions on snow and ice--a global review [abstract], *Eos, Trans. Amer. Geophys. Union, 68, no. 44*, 1550, 1987.

Major, J.J., and C.G. Newhall, Snow and ice perturbation during historical volcanic eruptions and the formation of lahars and floods--a global review, Bull. Volcanol., in press.

Major, J.J., and K.M. Scott, Volcaniclastic sedimentation in the Lewis River valley, Mount St. Helens, Washington--processes, extent, and hazards, *U.S. Geol. Surv. Bull. 1383-D*, 38 pp., 1988.

Malin, M.C., and M.F. Sheridan, Computer-assisted mapping of pyroclastic surges, *Science, 217*, 637-640, 1982.

Malone, S.D., Volcanic earthquakes: Examples from Mount St. Helens, in *Earthquakes, Theory, and Interpretation*, edited by H. Kanamori and E. Boschi, Soc. Itla. di Fisica, pp. 436-455, Bologna, Italy, 1983.

Markhinin, E.K., A.N. Sirin, K.M. Timerbaeva, and P.I. Tokarev, An attempt of volcano-geographical ranging of Kamchatka and Kurile Islands, *Volcanological Station Bulletin No. 32*, p. 52-70, 1962. (In Russian)

Matahelumual, J., G. Lokon-Empung, *Berita Berkala Vulkanologi, Edisi Khusus, no. 114*, 52 pp., map scale 1:50,000, Direktorat Vulkanologi (Volcanological Survey of Indonesia), 1986.

Matahelumual, J., G. Banda-Api, *Berita Berkala Vulkanologi, Edisi Khusus, no. 115*, 48 pp., map scale 1:26,000, Direktorat Vulkanologi (Volcanological Survey of Indonesia), 1988.

May, R.J., Thermoluminescence dating of Hawaiian basalt, *U.S. Geol. Surv. Prof. Paper, 1095*, 47 pp., 1979.

McKee, C.O., Recent eruptive history of the Rabaul Volcanoes, present volcanic conditions, and potential hazards from future eruptions, *Geol. Surv. Papua New Guinea Rep., 81/5* (unpublished), 16 pp, 1981.

McKee, C.O., Volcanic hazards at Uluwan volcano, *Geol. Surv. Papua New Guinea Report 83/13*, map scale 1:100,000. 1983.

McKee, C.O., and P.L. Lowenstein, Results of volcano monitoring programs at Rabaul, Papua New Guinea and potential hazards from future eruptions [abstract], *Abstracts 1981 IAVCEI Symposium--Arc Volcanism, Tokyo and Hakone, Japan, 28 August-9 September, 1981*, 226, 1981.

McKee, C. O., D.A. Wallace, R.A. Almond, and B. Talai, Fatal hydro-eruption of Karkar volcano in 1979: development of a maar-like crater, *in* Cooke-Ravian Volume of Volcanological Papers, edited by R.W. Johnson, *Geol Surv. Papua New Guinea, Mem., 10*, pp. 63-84, 1981.

McKee, C.O., P.L. Lowenstein, P. de St. Ours, B. Talai, I. Itikarai, and J.J. Mori, Seismic and ground deformation crises at Rabaul Caldera: Prelude to an eruption?, *Bull. Volcanol. 47-2*, 397-411, 1984.

McKee, C.O., R.W. Johnson, P.L. Lowenstein, S.J. Riley, R.J. Blong, P. de St. Ours, and B. Talai, Rabaul Caldera, Papua New Guinea: Volcanic hazards, surveillance, and eruption contingency plans, *J. Volcanol. Geotherm. Res., 23*, 195-237, 1985.

McNutt, S. R. and Harlow, D. H., Seismicity at Fuego, Pacaya, Izalco and San Crístobal volcanoes, Central America, 1973-1974, *Bull. Volcanol., 46*, 283-297, 1983.

McTaggart, K.C., The mobility of nuées ardentes, *Amer. J. Sci., 258*, 369-382, 1960.

Meade, B.K., Corrections for refraction index as applied to electro-optical distance measurements, *U.S. Dept. Commerce Environmental Sci. Services Admin., Coast and Geodetic Survey*, 1969.

Mehringer, P.J., Jr., Late-Quaternary pollen records from the interior Pacific Northwest and northern Great Basin of the United States, in *Pollen Records of Late-Quaternary North American Sediments*, edited by V.J. Bryant, Jr. and R.G. Holloway, pp. 167-189, Amer. Assoc. Stratigraphic Palynologists Foundation, 1985.

Mehringer, P.J., Jr., Eric Blinman, and K.L. Petersen, Pollen influx and volcanic ash, *Science, 198*, 257-261, 1977.

Melson, W.G., Monitoring the 1980-1982 eruptions of Mount St. Helens: Compositions and abundances of glass, *Science, 221*, 1387-1391, 1983.

Miller, C.D., Potential hazards from future eruptions in the vicinity of Mount Shasta volcano, northern California, *U.S. Geol. Surv. Bull. 1503*, 43 pp., 1980.

Miller, C.D., Potential volcanic hazards from future volcanic eruptions in California, *U.S. Geol. Surv. Bull., 1847*, 17 pp., in press.

Miller, C.D., D.R. Mullineaux, and M.L. Hall, M.L., Reconnaissance map of potential volcanic hazards from Cotopaxi volcano, Ecuador, *U.S. Geol. Surv. Miscell. Invest. Map I-1072*, 1978.

Miller, C.D., D.R. Mullineaux, and D.R. Crandell, Hazards assessments at Mount St. Helens, *in* The 1980 eruptions of Mount St. Helens, Washington, edited by P.W. Lipman and D.R. Mullineaux, *U.S. Geol. Surv. Prof. Paper, 1250*, pp. 789-802, 1981.

Miller, C.D., D.R. Mullineaux, D.R. Crandell, and R.A. Bailey, R.A., Potential hazards from future volcanic eruptions in the Long Valley-Mono Lake area, east-central California and southwest Nevada--a preliminary assessment, *U.S. Geol. Surv. Circular 877*, 10 pp., 1982.

Miller, T.P., and R.L. Smith, Spectacular mobility of ash flows around Aniakchak and Fisher calderas, Alaska, *Geology, 5*, 173-176, 1977.

Minakami, Takeshi, On the distribution of volcanic ejecta, Part I. The distributions of volcanic bombs ejected by the recent explosions of Asama, *Bull. Earthquake Res. Inst., Tokyo Imperial University, 20*, 65-92, 1942.

Minakami, T., Fundamental research for predicting volcanic eruptions, Part I, *Bull. Earthquake Res. Inst., 38*, 497-544, 1960.

Minakami, T., Seismology of volcanoes in Japan, in *Physical Volcanology*, edited by L. Civetta, P. Gasparini, G. Luongo, and A. Rapolla, Elsevier Scientific Publishing Company, pp. 1-27, Amsterdam, The Netherlands, 1974.

Minakami, T., T. Ishikawa, and K. Yagi, The 1944 eruption of Volcano Usu in Hokkaido, Japan, *Bull. Volcanol., 11*, 45-157, 1951.

Mizuyama, T., A. Yazawa, and K. Ido, Computer simulation of debris flow depositional processes, in Erosion and Sedimentation in the Pacific Rim, edited by R.L. Beschta, T. Blinn, G.E. Grant, G.G. Ice, and F.J. Swanson, *Inter. Assoc. Hydrological Sciences Publication No. 165*, pp. 179-190, 1987.

Moore, J.G., Base surge in recent volcanic eruptions, *Bull. Volcanol., 30*, 337-363, 1967.

Moore, J.G., Relationship between subsidence and volcanic load, Hawaii, *Bull. Volcanol., 34*, 562-576, 1970.

Moore, J.G., Subsidence of the Hawaiian Ridge, *in* Volcanism in Hawaii, edited by R. W. Decker, T.L. Wright, and P.H. Stauffer, *U.S. Geol. Surv. Prof. Paper, 1350*, pp. 85-100, 1987.

Moore, J.G., and Melson, W.G., Nuées ardentes of the 1968 eruption of Mayon volcano, Philippines, *Bull. Volcanol., 33*, 600-620, 1969.

Moore, J.G., and T.W. Sisson, Deposits and effects of the May 18 pyroclastic surge, *in* The 1980 eruptions of Mount St. Helens, Washington, edited by P.W. Lipman and D.R. Mullineaux, D.R., *U.S. Geol. Surv. Prof. Paper, 1250*, pp. 421-438, 1981.

Moore, J.G., and D. J. Fornari, Drowned reefs as indicators of the rate of subsidence of the Island of Hawaii, *J.. Geol., 92*, 752-759, 1984.

Moore, J.G., and G.W. Moore, Deposit from a giant wave on the island of Lanai, Hawaii, *Science, 226*, 1312-1315, 1984.

Moore, J.G., and C.J. Rice, Chronology and character of the May 18, 1980, explosive eruptions of Mount St. Helens, in *Explosive Volcanism: Inception, Evolution, and Hazards*, Washington, National Academy Press, pp. 133-142, 1984.

Moore, J.G., K. Nakamura, and A. Alcaraz, The 1965 eruption of Taal volcano, *Science, 151*, 955-960, 1966.

Moore, R.B., D.A. Clague, Meyer Rubin,and W.A. Bohrson, Hualalai volcano: A preliminary summary of geologic, petrologic, and geophysical data, *in* Volcanism in Hawaii, edited by R.W. Decker, T.L. Wright, and P.H. Stauffer, *U.S. Geol. Surv. Prof. Paper, 1350*, pp. 571-585, 1987.

Mori, Jim, and Chris McKee, Outward-dipping ring-fault structures at Rabaul Caldera as shown by earthquake locations, *Science, 235*, 193-195, 1987.

Mortensen, C.E., and D.G. Hopkins, Tiltmeter measurements in Long Valley caldera, California, *J. Geophys. Res., 92*, 13,767-13,776, 1987.

Moyer, T.C., and D.A. Swanson, D.A., Secondary hydroeruptions in pyroclastic-flow deposits: An example from Mount St. Helens, *J. Volcanol. Geotherm. Res., 32*, 299-319, 1987.

Mullineaux, D.R., Preliminary overview map of volcanic hazards in the 48 conterminous United States, *U.S. Geol. Surv. Miscell. Field Studies Map MF-786*, scale 1:7,500,000, 1976.

Mullineaux, D.R., Summary of pre-1980 tephra-fall deposits erupted from Mount St. Helens, Washington, U.S.A., *Bull. Volcanol., 48*, 17-26, 1986.

Mullineaux, D.R., and D.R. Crandell, D.R., Recent lahars from Mount St. Helens, Washington, *Geol. Soc. Amer. Bull., 73*, 855-870, 1962.

Mullineaux, D.R., D.W. Peterson, and D.R. Crandell, Volcanic hazards in the Hawaiian Islands, *in* Volcanism in Hawaii, edited by R.W. Decker, T.L. Wright, and P.H. Stauffer, *U.S. Geol. Surv. Prof. Paper, 1350*, pp. 599-621, 1987.

Nairn, I.A., Rotomahana-Waimangu eruption, 1886: Base surge and basaltic magma, *New Zealand J. Geol. Geophys., 22*, 363-378, 1979.

Nairn, I.A., and Stephen Self, Explosive eruptions and pyroclastic avalanches from Ngauruhoe in February 1975, *J. Volcanol. Geotherm. Res., 3*, 39-60, 1978.

Nakamura, Kazuaki, Volcano-stratigraphic study of Oshima volcano, *Earthquake Research Institute Bulletin, Tokyo University, 42*, 649-728, 1964.

Naranjo, J.A., and Peter Francis, High velocity debris avalanche at Lastarria volcano in the northern Chilean Andes, *Bull. Volcanol., 49*, 509-514, 1987.

Naranjo, J.L., H. Sigurdsson, S.N. Carey, and W.G. Fritz, Eruption of Nevado del Ruíz volcano, Colombia, 13 November 1985: Tephra fall and lahars, *Science, 233*, 961-963, 1986.

Nash, D.B., Morphologic dating and modeling degradation of fault scarps, in *Active Tectonics*, Washington, D.C., National Academy Press, pp. 181-194, 1986.

Neall, V.E., Lahars as major Geological hazards, *Inter. Assoc. Engineering Geology Bulletin, no. 14*, 233-240, 1976.

Neall, V.E., Volcanic hazard map of Mount Egmont, *New Zealand Department of Science and Industrial Research*, scale 1:100,000, 1982.

Newhall, C.G., A method for estimating intermediate- and long-term risks from volcanic activity, with an example from Mount St. Helens, Washington, *U.S. Geol. Surv. Open-File Report 82-396*, 59 pp., 1982.

Newhall, C.G., Short-term forecasting of volcanic hazards, in Proceedings, Geologic and Hydrologic Hazards Training Program, compiled by M.E. Williams and C. Kitzmiller, *U.S. Geol. Survey Open-File Report 84-760*, pp. 507-592, 1984.

Newhall, C.G., and D. Dzurisin, Historical unrest at large Quaternary calderas of the world, *U.S. Geol. Surv. Bull., 1855*, 1108 pp., 1988.

O'Keefe, P., and K.N. Westgate, Some definitions of disaster, *Disaster Research Unit, University of Bradford, Occasional Paper 4*, Bradford, England, 1976.

Okada, Hm., H. Watanabe, I. Yamashita, and I. Yokoyama, Seismological significance of the 1977-1978 eruptions and the magma intrusion process of Usu volcano, Hokkaido, *J. Volcanol. Geotherm. Res., 9*, 311-334, 1981.

Omori, F., The Usu-san eruption and the elevation phenomena. II. [Comparison of bench mark heights in the base district before and after the eruption.], *Bull. Imp. Earthquake Comm., 5*, 105-107, 1913.

Omori, F., The Sakura-jima eruptions and earthquakes, *Bull. Imp. Earthquake Invest. Comm., 8, No. 1-6*, 525 p., 1914.

Ostercamp, W.R., and C.R. Hupp, Dating and interpretation of debris flows by geologic and botanical methods at Whitney Creek gorge, Mount Shasta, California, *in* Debris flows/avalanches: Process, Recognition, and Mitigation, edited by J.E. Costa and G.F. Wieczorek, *Geol. Soc. Amer. Reviews in Engineering Geology, 7*, pp. 157-164, 1987.

Otway, P.M., Vertical deformation associated with the Taupo earthquake swarm, June 1983, *in* Recent Crustal Movements of the Pacific Region, edited by W.I. Reilly and B.E. Hartford, *Royal Soc. New Zealand Bull. 24*, 187-200, 1986.

Otway, P.M., G.W. Grindley, and A.G. Hull, Earthquakes, active fault displacement and associated vertical deformation near Lake Taupo, Taupo Volcanic Zone, *New Zealand Geol. Survey Report 110*, 73 pp., 1984.

Parascandola, A., *I fenomeni bradisismici del Serapeo di Pozzuoli*, Genovese, Napoli, Italy, 1947.

Pardyanto, L., L.D. Reksowirogo, F.X.S. Mitrohartono, S.H. Hardjowarsito, and K. Kusumadinata, Volcanic hazard map, Merapi volcano, central Java, *Indonesian Geological Survey*, scale 1: 100,000, 1978.

Parra, Eduardo, Hector Cepeda, and J.-C. Thouret, Mapa actualizado de amenaza volcánica potencial del Nevado del Ruíz, *INGEOMINAS, Bogotá, Colombia*, scale, 1:100,000, 1986.

Peña, Olympio, and C.G. Newhall, Philippines, in *Source-Book for Volcanic-Hazards Zonation: Natural Hazards 4*, edited by D.R. Crandell, B. Booth, K. Kusumadinata, D. Shimozuru, G.P.L. Walker, and D. Westercamp, pp. 65-67, UNESCO, Paris, 1984.

Perret, F.A., The eruption of Mt. Pelée 1929-1932, *Carnegie Institute of Washington, Publication 458*, 125 pp., 1937.

Perret, F.A., Volcanological observations, *Carnegie Institute of Washington Publication 458*, 162 pp., 1950.

Peters, D.C., and R.S. Crosson, Application and prediction analysis to hypocenter determination using a local array, *Bull. Seismol. Soc. Amer., 62*, 775-788, 1972.

Peterson, D.W., Volcanoes: Tectonic setting and impact on society, in *Active Tectonics*, Geophysics Study Committee, National Research Council, National Academy Press, Washington, D.C., pp. 231-246, 1986.

Peterson, D.W., Mount St. Helens and the science of volcanology: A five-year perspective, in *Mount St. Helens: Five Years Later*, edited by S.A.C. Keller, pp. 3-19, Eastern Washington University Press, Cheney, Washington, 1987.

Peterson, D.W., Volcanic hazards and public response, *J. Geophys. Res., 93, no. B5*, 4161-4170, 1988.

Pierce, K.L., Dating methods, in *Active Tectonics*, Washington, D.C., National Academy Press, pp. 195-214, 1986.

Pierson, T.C., Initiation and flow behavior of the 1980 Pine Creek and Muddy River lahars, Mount St. Helens, Washington, *Geol. Soc. Amer. Bull., 96*, 1056-1069, 1985.

Pierson, T.C., and K.M. Scott, Downstream dilution of a lahar: Transition from debris flow to hyperconcentrated streamflow, *Water Resources Research, 21, no. 10*, 1511-1524, 1985.

Podesta, Bruno and R.S. Olson, Science and the state in Latin America - Decision making in uncertainty, in *Managing Disasters, Strategies and Policy Perspectives*, edited by L.K. Comfort, pp. 296-311, Duke University Press, Durham and London, 1988.

Prescott, W.H., and J. Svarc, Precision of Global Positioning System measurements for crustal deformation studies:

Initial results, *Proc. 4th Inter. Geod. Symposium on Satellite Positioning, 2*, pp. 993-1002, Univ. Texas, Austin, 1986.

Press, Frank, and D. Harkrider, Air-sea waves from the explosion of Krakatoa, *Science, 154*, 35-136, 1966.

Rampino, M.R., and Stephen Self, Historic eruptions of Tambora (1815), Krakatau (1883), and Agung (1963), their stratospheric aerosols, and climatic impact, *Quaternary Research, 18, no. 2*, 127-143, 1982.

Rampino, M.R., and Stephen Self, The atmospheric effects of El Chichón, *Scientific American, 253*, 48-57, 1984.

Rampino, M.R., and R.B. Stothers, Flood basalt volcanism during the past 250 million years, *Science, 241*, 663-668, 1988.

Rees, J.D., 1979, Effects of the eruption of Parícutin volcano on landforms, vegetation, and human occupancy, in *Volcanic Activity and Human Ecology*, edited by P.D. Sheets and D.K. Grayson, pp. 249-292, Academic Press, New York, 1979.

Richter, C.F., *Elementary Seismology*, 768 pp., W.H. Freeman and Co., San Francisco, 1958.

Rittmann, Alfred, 1962, *Volcanoes and Their Activity*, 305 pp., John Wiley and Sons, New York, 1962.

Rose, W.I., Jr., Scavenging of volcanic aerosol by ash: Atmospheric and volcanological implications, *Geology, 5*, 621-624, 1977.

Rose, W.I., and Reinaldo Mercado, Reporte a UNDRO/OFDA misión al Volcán Tacaná, *Instituto Nacional de Sismología Vulcanalogía, Meteorología e Hidrología (INSIVUMEH, Guatemala)*, 40 pp., map scale 1:50,000, 1986.

Rose, W.I., Jr., T. Pearson, and S. Bonis, Nuée ardente eruption from the foot of a dacite lava flow, Santiaguito volcano, Guatemala, *Bull. Volcanol., 40*, 1-16, 1977.

Rose, W.I., Reinaldo Mercado, Otonil Atias, and Jorge Giron, Evaluación de Riesgo del domo de Santiaguito, Guatemala, informe preliminar, *Instituto Nacional de Sismología Vulcanología, Meteorología e Hidrología (INSIVUMEH, Guatemala)*, 19 pp., map scale 1:500,000, 1988.

Rosenbaum, J.G., and R.B. Waitt, Jr., Summary of eyewitness accounts of the May 18 eruption, *in* The 1980 eruptions of Mount St. Helens, Washington, edited by P.W. Lipman and D.R. Mullineaux, *U.S. Geol. Surv. Prof. Paper 1250*, pp. 53-67, 1981.

Rosi, M., and R. Santacroce, Volcanic hazard assessment in the Phlegraean Fields: A contribution based on stratigraphic and historical data, *Bull. Volcanol., 47, no. 2*, 359-370, 1984.

Ross, C.S., and R.L. Smith, Ash-flow tuffs, their origin, Geological relations and identification, *U.S. Geol. Surv. Prof. Paper, 366*, 77 pp., 1961.

Rowley, P.D., M.A. Kuntz, and N.S. MacLeod, Pyroclastic-flow deposits, *in* The 1980 eruptions of Mount St. Helens, Washington, edited by P.W. Lipman and D.R. Mullineaux, *U.S. Geol. Surv. Prof. Paper, 1250*, pp. 489-524, 1981.

Rubin, Meyer, L.K. Gargulinski, and, J.P. McGeehin, Hawaiian radiocarbon dates, *in* Volcanism in Hawaii, edited by R.W. Decker, T.L. Wright, and P.H. Stauffer, P.H., *U.S. Geol. Surv. Prof. Paper, 1350*, pp. 213-242, 1987.

Rueger, J.M., and F.K. Brunner, EDM-Height traversing versus Geodetic Leveling, *The Canadian Surveyor, 36*, 69-88, 1982.

Ruelo, H.B., Morphological and crater development of Mt. Tabaro eruption site, Taal Volcano, Philippines, *Phil. Jour. Volcanol., 1, no. 2*, 19-68, 1983.

Ryall, A., and F. Ryall, Spasmodic tremor and possible magma injection in the Long Valley caldera, eastern California, *Science, 219*, 1432-1433, 1983.

Salomons, J.B., Paleoecology of volcanic soils in the Colombian Central Cordillera, *Dissertationes Botanicae, 95, Berlin, J. Cramer* (Ph.D. dissertation, University of Amsterdam), 1986.

Sarna-Wojcicki, A.M., Susan Shipley, R.B. Waitt, Jr., D. Dzurisin, and S.H. Wood, Areal distribution, thickness, mass, volume, and grain size of air-fall ash from the six major eruptions of 1980, *in* The 1980 eruptions of Mount St. Helens, Washington, edited by P.W. Lipman and D.R. Mullineaux, *U.S. Geol. Surv. Prof. Paper, 1250*, pp. 577-600, 1981a.

Sarna-Wojcicki, A.M., R.B. Waitt, Jr., M.J. Woodward, Susan Shipley, and Jose Rivera, Premagmatic ash erupted from March 27 through May 14, 1980--extent, mass, volume, and composition, *in* The 1980 eruptions of Mount St. Helens, Washington, edited by P.W. Lipman and D.R. Mullineaux, *U.S. Geol. Surv. Prof. Paper, 1250*, pp. 569-576, 1981b.

Sarna-Wojcicki, A.M., D.E. Champion, and J.O. Davis, Holocene volcanism in the conterminous United States and the role of silicic volcanic ash layers in correlation of latest-Pleistocene and Holocene deposits, in *Late-Quaternary Environments of the United States, Volume 2, The Holocene*, edited by H.E. Wright, Jr., pp. 52-77, University of Minnesota Press, Minneapolis, 1983.

Sato, Y., and D. Skoko, Optimum distribution of seismic observation points (2), *Bull. Earthquake Res. Inst., Univ. Tokyo, 43*, 451-457, 1965.

Schick, R., Source mechanisms of volcanic earthquakes, *Bull. Volcanol., 44, no. 3*, 491-497, 1981.

Schuster, R.L., Effects of the eruptions on civil works and operations in the Pacific Northwest, *in* The 1980 eruptions of Mount St. Helens, Washington, edited by P.W. Lipman and D.R. Mullineaux, *U.S. Geol. Surv. Prof. Paper, 1250*, pp. 701-718, 1981.

Schuster, R.L., Engineering aspects of the 1980 Mount St. Helens eruptions, *Assoc. Engineering Geologists Bull., 20, no. 2*, 125-143, 1983.

Schuster, R.L., and D.R. Crandell, Catastrophic debris avalanches from volcanoes, *Proceedings of the IV International Symposium on Landslides, Toronto, 1*, 567-572, 1984.

Schutz, B.E., Satellite positioning, *Rev. Geophys., 25, no. 5,* 883-887, 1987.

Scott, K.M., Origins, behavior, and sedimentology of lahars and lahar-runout flows in the Toutle-Cowlitz river system, *U.S. Geol. Surv. Prof. Paper, 1447-A,* A1-A74, 1988.

Scott, K.M., Lahars and Lahar-runout flows in the Toutle-Cowlitz River system, Mount St. Helens, Washington-- magnitude and frequency, *U.S. Geol. Surv Prof.Paper, 1447-B,* in press.

Scott, W.E., Hazardous volcanic events and assessments of long-term volcanic hazards, *in* Proceedings of the Geologic and Hydrologic Hazards Training Program, compiled by M.E. Williams and C. Kitzmiller, *U.S. Geol. Surv. Open-File Report 84-760,* pp. 447-498, 1984.

SEAN, Mayon Volcano, *Scientific Event Alert Network (SEAN) Bull., 9, no. 8,* 2-3, 1984a.

SEAN, Mayon Volcano, *Scientific Event Alert Network (SEAN) Bull., 9, no. 9,* 3-4, 1984b.

SEAN, Ruíz Volcano, *Scientific Event Alert Network (SEAN) Bull., 10, no. 8,* 8, 1985a.

SEAN, Ruíz Volcano, *Scientific Event Alert Network (SEAN) Bull., 10, no. 9,* 2-3, 1985b.

SEAN, Ruíz Volcano, *Scientific Event Alert Network (SEAN) Bull., 10, no. 11,* 2-5, 1985c.

SEAN, Canlaon Volcano, *Scientific Event Alert Network (SEAN) Bull., 12, no. 4,* 11, 1987a.

SEAN, Canlaon Volcano, *Scientific Event Alert Network (SEAN) Bull., 12, no. 5,* 17-18, 1987b.

Searle, E.J., Volcanic risk in the Auckland metropolitan district, *New Zealand J. Geol. Geophys., 7,* 94-100, 1964.

Segerstrom, Kenneth, Erosion studies at Parícutin, State of Michoacán, Mexico, *U.S. Geol. Surv. Bull., 965-A,* 164 pp., 1950.

Sheridan, M.F., and M.C. Malin, Application of computer-assisted mapping to volcanic hazard evaluation of surge eruptions: Vulcano, Lipari, and Vesuvius, *J. Volcanol. Geotherm. Res., 17,* 187-202, 1983.

Sheridan, M.F., and K.H. Wohletz, Hydrovolcanism: Basic considerations and review, *J. Volcanol. Geotherm. Res., 17,* 1-29, 1983.

Sheridan, M.F., F. Barberi, M. Rosi, and R. Santacroce, A model for plinian eruptions of Vesuvius, *Nature, 289,* 282-285, 1981.

Shi Diguang, Tangshan earthquake and its damage to civil engineering, in *Proceedings of Expert Working Group Meeting cum Workshop on the Urban Geology of Coastal Areas (First Draft), Shanghai, China, Sept. 13-22, 1987,* 113-117, 1987.

Shimozuru, D., A seismological approach to the prediction of volcanic eruptions, in *The Surveillance and Prediction of Volcanic Activity,* pp. 19-45, UNESCO, Paris, 1972.

Shimozuru, D., reporter for the Working Group on Mitigation of Volcanic Disasters, IAVCEI, Compiled list of dangerous volcanoes and associated information *Bull. Volcanol., Supplement to volume 38,* 81 pp., 1975.

Shimozuru, D., Volcano surveillance in Japan: An intricate cooperative program, *Episodes, 1,* 23-27, 1981.

Shimozuru, Daisuke, Volcano hazard assessment of Mount Fuji, *Natural Disaster Science, 5, no. 2,* 15-31, 1983.

Shimozuru, D., T. Miyazaki, N. Gyoda, and J. Matahelumual, Volcanological survey of Indonesian volcanoes, Part 2. Seismic observation at Merapi Volcano, *Bull. Earthquake Res. Inst., 47,* 969-990, 1969.

Shipley, Susan, and A.M. Sarna-Wojcicki, Distribution, thickness, and mass of late Pleistocene and Holocene tephra from major volcanoes in the northwestern United States: A preliminary assessment of hazards from volcanic ejecta to nuclear reactors in the Pacific Northwest, *U.S. Geol. Surv. Miscell. Field Studies Map Mf-1435,* 1983.

Siebert, Lee, Large volcanic debris avalanches--characteristics of source areas, deposits, and associated eruptions, *J. Volcanol. Geotherm. Res., 22,* 163-197, 1984.

Siebert, Lee, Harry Glicken, and Tadahide Ui, Volcanic hazards from Bezymianny- and Bandai-type eruptions, *Bull. Volcanol., 49,* 435-459, 1987.

Sigurdsson, Haraldur, Volcanology, in *Encyclopedia of Physical Science and Technology, 14,* pp. 406-435, Academic Press, Inc., New York, 1987.

Sigurdsson, H., J.D. Devine, and A.N. Davis, The petrologic estimation of volcanic degassing aerosols, *Jökull, 35,* 1-8, 1985a.

Sigurdsson, Haraldur, Steven Carey, Winton Cornell and Tullio Pescatore, The eruption of Vesuvius in A.D. 79, *National Geographic Research, 1,* 332-387, 1985b.

Sigurdsson, Haraldur, S.N. Carey, and, R.V. Fisher, The 1982 eruptions of El Chichón volcano, Mexico (3): Physical properties of pyroclastic surges, *Bull. Volcanol., 49,* 467-488, 1987a.

Sigurdsson, Haraldur, J.D. Devine, F.M. Tchoua, T.S. Presser, M.K.W. Pringle, and W.C. Evans, Origin of the lethal gas burst from Lake Monoun, Cameroun, *J. Volcanol. Geotherm. Res., 31,* 1-16, 1987b.

Simkin, Tom, and K.A. Howard, Caldera collapse in the Galapagos Islands, 1968, *Science, 169,* 429-437, 1970.

Simkin, T., and R.S. Fiske, *Krakatau 1883: The volcanic eruption and its effects,* 464 pp., Smithsonian Institution Press, Washington, D.C., 1983.

Simkin, T., and L. Siebert, Explosive eruptions in space and time: Duration, intervals, and a comparison of the world's active volcanic belts, in *Explosive Volcanism: Inception, Evolution, and Hazards,* pp. 110-121, Geophysics Study Committee, National Research Council, National Academy Press, Washington, D.C., 1984.

Simkin, T., L. Siebert, L. McClelland, D. Bridge, C. Newhall, and J.H. Latter, *Volcanoes of the World: A Regional Directory, Gazetteer, and Chronology of Volcanism During the Last 10,000 Years,* 240 pp., Hutchinson & Ross, Stroudsburg, Pennsylvania, 1981.

Slater, L.E., and G.R. Huggett, A multiwavelength distance-measuring instrument for geophysical experiments, *J. Geophys. Res., 81*, 6299-6306, 1976.

Slingerland, R.L., and Barry Voight, Occurrences, properties, and predictive models of landslide-generated water waves, in *Rockslides and Avalanches, 2, Engineering Sites,* edited by Barry Voight, pp. 317-400, Elsevier, Amsterdam, 1979.

Smith, G.A., Coarse-grained nonmarine volcaniclastic sediment: Terminology and depositional process, *Geol. Soc. Amer. Bull., 97, no. 1*, 1-10, 1986.

Smith, R.L., Ash flows, *Geol. Soc. Amer. Bull., 71*, 795-842, 1960.

Soliven, M., Let's keep politics out of Taal Volcano tragedy, *Manila Times*, September 30, 1965a.

Soliven, M., Confusion, ineptitude, petty rivalry in Taal, *Manila Times*, October 5, 1965b.

Souther, J.G., R.I. Tilling, and R.S. Punongbayan, Forecasting eruptions in the circum-Pacific, *Episodes, 7, no. 4*, 10-18, 1984.

Sparks, R.S.J., Grain size variations in ignimbrites and implications for the transport of pyroclastic flows, *Sedimentology, 23*, 147-188, 1976.

Sparks, R.S.J., Gas release rates from pyroclastic flows: An assessment of the role of fluidisation in their emplacement, *Bull. Volcanol., 41, no. 1*, 1-9, 1978.

Sparks, R.S.J., The dimensions and dynamics of volcanic eruption columns, *Bull. Volcanol., 48*, 3-15, 1986.

Sparks, R.S.J., and Lionel Wilson, A model for the formation of ignimbrite by gravitational column collapse, *J. Geol. Soc. London, 132*, 441-452, 1976.

Sparks, R.S.J., Stephen Self, and G.P.L. Walker, Products of ignimbrite eruptions, *Geology, 1*, 115-118, 1973.

Sparks, R.S.J., H. Pinkerton, and G. Hulme, Classification and formation of lava levees on Mount Etna, Sicily, *Geology, 4, no. 5*, 269-271, 1976.

Sparks, R.S.J., Lionel Wilson, and G. Hulme, Theoretical modeling of the generation, movement, and emplacement of pyroclastic flows by column collapse, *J. Geophys. Res., 83*, 1727-1739, 1978.

Sparks, R.S.J., J.G. Moore, and C.J. Rice, The initial giant umbrella cloud of the May 18th, 1980, explosive eruption of Mount St. Helens, *J. Volcanol. Geotherm. Res., 28*, 257-274, 1986.

Spiess, F.N., Suboceanic geodetic measurements, *IEEE Trans. on Geoscience and Remote Sensing, GE-23(4)*, 502-510, 1985.

Spiess, F.N., J.A. Hildebrand, and D.E. Boegeman, New systems for seafloor studies [abstract], *Eos, Amer. Geophys. Union Trans., 68, no. 44*, 1335, 1987.

Stewart, G.A., Description of a volcanic eruption in the island of Sumbawa, *Trans. Literary Society of Bombay, 2*, 109-114, 1820.

Stothers, R.B., The great Tambora eruption in 1815 and its aftermath, *Science, 224*, 1191-1198, 1984.

Stuiver, Minze, and Renee Kra, editors, Calibration issue, *Radiocarbon, 28, no. 2B*, 805-1030, 1986.

Stuiver, Minze, and G.W. Pearson, High-precision calibration of the radiocarbon time scale, AD 1950-500 BC, *Radiocarbon, 28, no. 2B*, 805-839, 1986.

Sudradjat, Adjat, and R.I. Tilling, Volcanic hazards in Indonesia: The 1982-83 eruption of Galunggung, *Episodes, 7, no. 2*, 13-19, 1984.

Suryo, I., G. Semeru: *Berita Berkala Vulkanologi, Edisi Khusus, no. 111*, 52 pp., Direktorat Vulkanologi (Volcanological Survey of Indonesia), 1986.

Suryo, I., and M.C.G. Clarke, The occurrence and mitigation of volcanic hazards in Indonesia as exemplified at the Mount Merapi, Mount Kelut, and Mount Galunggung volcanoes, *J. Engineering Geol., 18*, 79-98, 1985.

Swanson, D.A., Pahoehoe flows from 1969-1971 Mauna Ulu eruption, Kilauea volcano, Hawaii, *Geol. Soc. Amer. Bull., 84, no. 2*, 615-626, 1973.

Swanson, D.A., T.L. Wright, and R.T. Helz, Linear vent systems and estimated rates of magma production and eruption for the Yakima Basalt on the Columbia Plateau, *Amer. J. Sci., 275, no. 8*, 877-905, 1975.

Swanson, D.A., W.A. Duffield, and R.S. Fiske, Displacement of the south flank of Kilauea volcano: The result of forceful intrusion of magma into the rift zones, *U.S. Geol. Surv. Prof. Paper, 963*, 39 pp., 1976

Swanson, D.A., P.W. Lipman, J.G. Moore, C.C. Heliker, and K.M. Yamashita, Geodetic monitoring after the May 18 eruption, *in* The 1980 eruptions of Mount St. Helens, Washington, edited by P.W. Lipman and D.R. Mullineaux, *U.S. Geol. Survey Prof. Paper, 1250*, 157-168, 1981.

Swanson, D.A., T.J. Casadevall, D. Dzurisin, S.D. Malone, C.G. Newhall, and C.S. Weaver, Predicting eruptions at Mount St Helens, June 1980 through December 1982, *Science, 221*, 1369-1376, 1983.

Swanson, D.A., T. J. Casadevall, D. Dzurisin, Holcomb, R.T., C.G. Newhall, S.D. Malone, and C.S. Weaver, Forecasts and predictions of eruptive activity at Mount St. Helens, USA: 1975-1984, *J. Geodynamics, 3, no. 3/4*, 397-423, 1985.

Swanson, D.A., D. Dzurisin, R.T. Holcomb, E.Y. Iwatsubo, W.W. Chadwick, Jr., T.J. Casadevall, J.W. Ewert, and C.C. Heliker, Growth of the lava dome at Mount St. Helens, Washington, (USA), 1981-1983, *in* The Emplacement of Silicic Domes and Lava Flows, edited by J.H. Fink, *Geol. Soc. Amer. Special Paper, 212*, 1-16, 1987.

Sylvester, A.G., Crustal tilt in Long Valley, California, *Annual Technical Report, Marine Science Institute and Dept. of Geol. Sciences, Univ. California, Santa Barbara*, 43 pp (plus two appendices), 1984.

Sylvester, A.G., Near-field tectonic geodesy, in *Active Tectonics*, pp. 164-179, Geophysics Study Committee, National Research Council, National Academy Press, Washington, D.C., 1986.

Symons, G.J., editor, *The Eruption of Krakatoa, and Subsequent Phenomena, Report of the Krakatoa Committee of the Royal Society of London*, 494 pp., Trübner and Co., London, 1888.

Talai, B., Volcanic hazards at Langila volcano, *Geol. Surv. Papua New Guinea Report 87/25*, map scale 1:100,000, 1987.

Tayag, J., and R.E. Rimando, Assessment of public awareness regarding geologic hazards, in *Geologic Hazards and Preparedness Systems*, Philippine Institute of Volcanology and Seismology, p. 102-128, 1987.

Tayag, J., R. Cola, and R. Natividad, Socio-economic impacts of the 1984 Mayon Volcano eruptions, *unpublished Final Report, Philippine Institute of Volcanology and Seismology*, 120 pp., 1984.

Taylor, G.A.M., The 1951 eruption of Mt. Lamington, Papua, *Bureau of Mineral Resources of Australia, Geology and Geophysics Bulletin 38*, 117 pp., 1958

Tazieff, Haroun, An exceptional eruption: Mt. Nyiragongo, Jan. 10th, 1977, *Bull. Volcanol.*, *40*, 189-200, 1977.

Tazieff, H., and J.-C. Sabroux, editors, *Forecasting Volcanic Events, Developments in Volcanology 1*, 635 pp., Elsevier Publishers, Amsterdam, The Netherlands, 1983.

Thorarinsson, Sigurdur, The eruption of Hekla 1947-1948. II, 3, The tephra fall from Hekla on March 29th, 1947, *Visindafelag Islendinga, Reykjavik, Leiftur*, 1954.

Thorarinsson, Sigurdur, The Lakagigar eruption of 1783, *Bull. Volcanol.*, *33, no. 3*, 910-929, 1969.

Thorarinsson, Sigurdur, On the damage caused by volcanic eruptions with special reference to tephra and gases, in *Volcanic Activity and Human Ecology*, edited by P.D. Sheets and D.K. Grayson, pp. 125-159, Academic Press, New York, 1979.

Thorarinsson, Sigurdur, The application of tephrochronology in Iceland, in *Tephra Studies*, edited by Stephen Self and R.S.J. Sparks, pp. 109-134, NATO Advanced Study Institutes Series, D. Reidel Publishing Company, Boston, 1981.

Tilling, R.I., Rockfall activity in pit craters, Kilauea Volcano, Hawaii, in *Proceedings, Andean and Antarctic Volcanology Problems Symposium*, edited by O. González-Ferrán , IAVCEI, Rome, Italy, pp. 518-528, 1976.

Tilling, R.I., Overview of Mount St. Helens volcano eruption, *Proc. Volume 278, Soc. Photo-Optical Instrumentation Engineers Technical Symposium '81, Annual Meeting, April 20-24, Washington, D.C.*, 3-10, 1981.

Tilling, R.I., reporter for Working Group of the World Organization of Volcano Observatories on "Adequate minimum volcano observatory," *J. Volcanol. Geotherm. Res.*, *12, nos. 1-2*, 183-184, 1982.

Tilling, R.I., Monitoring active volcanoes, *U.S. Geol. Surv. General-Interest Publication Series*, 13 pp., 1983.

Tilling, R.I., Eruptions of Mount St. Helens: Past, present and future, *U.S. Geol. Surv. General-Interest Publication Series*, 46 pp., 1984.

Tilling, R.I., Volcanology, in *Encyclopedia of Science and Technology, 19*, pp. 274-281, McGraw-Hill Publishing Company, New York, 1987.

Tilling, R.I., Volcanic hazards and their mitigation--Progress and problems, *Rev. Geophys.*, in press, 1989.

Tilling, R.I., and Bailey, R.A., Volcano Hazards Program in the United States, *J. Geodynamics, 3, no. 3/4*, 425-446, 1985.

Tilling, R.I., and Newhall, C.G., Volcanology, *Geotimes, 32, no. 2*, 59-61, 1987.

Tilling, R.I., R.Y. Koyanagi, P.W. Lipman, J.P. Lockwood, J.G. Moore and D.A. Swanson, Earthquakes and related catastrophic events, island of Hawaii, November 19, 1975: A preliminary report, *U.S. Geol. Surv. Circular 740*, 33 pp., 1976.

Tilling, R.I., Christina Heliker, and T.L. Wright, Eruptions of Hawaiian volcanoes: Past, present, and future, *U.S. Geol. Surv. General-Interest Publication Series*, 54 pp., 1987.

Tokarev, P.I., On a possibility of forecasting of Bezymianny Volcano eruptions according to seismic data, *Bull. Volcanol.*, *26*, 379-386, 1963.

Tokarev, P.I., Prediction and characteristics of the 1975 eruption of Tolbachik Volcano, Kamchatka, *Bull. Volcanol.*, *41, no. 3*, 251-258, 1978.

Tokarev, P.I., *Volcanic earthquakes of Kamchatka*, Izd. Nauka, 164 pp. Moscow, U.S.S.R., 1981.

Tomblin, John, UNDRO's role in responding to volcanic emergencies, *UNDRO News*, 7-10, March/April, 1988.

Tryggvason, E., Multiple magma reservoirs in a rift zone volcano: Ground deformation and magma transport during the September 1984 eruption of Krafla, Iceland, *J. Volcanol. Geotherm. Res.*, *28*, 1-44, 1986.

Tryggvason, E., Myvatn lake level observations 1984-1986 and ground deformation during a Krafla eruption, *J. Volcanol. Geotherm. Res.*, *31*, 131-138, 1987.

Tsuboi, C., The water surface of a lake as an indicator of crustal deformation, *Bull. Earthquake Res. Inst.*, *15*, 935-943, 1937.

Tsumura, K., Determination of earthquake magnitude from total duration of oscillation, *Bull. Earthquake Res. Inst.*, *45*, 7-18, 1967.

Tsuya, Hiromichi, Geological and petrological studies of Mt. Fuji, v. 5, on the 1707 eruption of volcano Fuji, *Bull. Earthquake Res. Inst., Tokyo University, 33, part 3*, 341-383, 1955.

U.S. Army Corps of Engineers, *Final Mount St. Helens, Washington, Feasibility Report and Environmental Impact Statement, Toutle, Cowlitz, and Columbia Rivers*, U.S. Army Corps of Engineers, Portland District (Oregon), 1984.

Uhrhammer, R.A., Analysis of small seismographic station networks, *Bull. Seismol. Soc. Amer.*, *70*, 1369-1380, 1980.

Ui, Tadahide, Volcanic dry avalanche deposits--identification and comparison with nonvolcanic debris stream deposits, *J. Volcanol. Geotherm. Res.*, *18*, 135-150, 1983.

Ui, Tadahide, Hiroshi Yamamoto, and Keiko Suzuki-Kamata, Characterization of debris avalanche deposits in Japan, *J. Volcanol. Geotherm. Res., 29*, 231-243, 1986.

Umbal, J.V., Recent lahars of Mayon Volcano, in *Geologic Hazards and Preparedness Systems*, Philippine Institute of Volcanology and Seismology, pp. 56-76, 1987.

UNDRO/UNESCO, *Volcanic Emergency Management*, 86 pp., Office of the United Nations Disaster Relief Co-ordinator (UNDRO), United Nations Educational, Scientific, and Cultural Organization (UNESCO), United Nations, New York, 1985.

UNESCO, *The Surveillance and Prediction of Volcanic Activity: A Review of Methods and Techniques*, 166 pp., United Nations Educational, Scientific, and Cultural Organization (UNESCO), Paris, France, 1972.

Valdes, C., *PCEQ User guide*, 19 pp., 1988.

Valencia, T.F., Government unprepared for national emergency, *Manila Times*, October 4, 1965.

Vallance, J.W., Postglacial lahars and potential volcanic hazards in the White Salmon drainage basin near Mount Adams volcano, southwestern Washington, *U.S. Geol. Surv. Bull.*, in press.

Verbeek, R.D.M., *Krakatau*, 495 pp., Imprimerie de l'Etat, Batavia, 1885.

Verosub, K.L., Geomagnetic secular variation and the dating of Quaternary sediments, *in* Dating Quaternary Sediments, edited by D.J. Easterbrook, *Geol. Soc. Amer. Special Paper 227*, pp. 123-138, 1988.

VL, *The Volcano Letter, 193*, Hawaiian Volcano Observatory, September 6, 1928, 1928.

VL., *The Volcano Letter, 390*, Hawaiian Volcano Observatory, August 1932, 1932.

Voight, B., Countdown to catastrophe, *Earth and Mineral Sciences, 57, no. 2*, 17-30, 1988.

Voight, Barry, Harry Glicken, R.J. Janda, and P.M. Douglas, Catastrophic rockslide avalanche of May 18, *in* The 1980 eruptions of Mount St. Helens, Washington, edited by P.W. Lipman and D.R. Mullineaux, *U.S. Geol. Surv. Prof. Paper, 1250*, pp. 347-377, 1981.

Voight, Barry, R.J. Janda, Harry Glicken, and P.M. Douglas, Nature and mechanism of the Mount St. Helens rockslide avalanche, *Geotechnique, 33*, 224-273, 1983.

Waitt, R.B., Devastating pyroclastic density flow and attendant airfall of May 18--stratigraphy and sedimentology of deposits, *in* The 1980 eruptions of Mount St. Helens, Washington, edited by P.W. Lipman and D.R. Mullineaux, *U.S. Geol. Surv. Prof. Paper, 1250*, pp. 439-458, 1981.

Waitt, R.B., Comment on Walker and McBroome, 1983, *Geology, 12*, 693, 1984.

Waldron, H.H., Debris flow and erosion control problems caused by the ash eruptions of Irazú volcano, Costa Rica, *U.S. Geol. Surv. Bull., 1241-I*, 37 pp., 1967.

Walker, G.P.L., Lengths of lava flows, *Phil. Trans. Royal Soc. London, 274*, 107-118, 1973.

Walker, G.P.L., A volcanic ash generated by explosions where ignimbrite entered the sea, *Nature, 281*, 642-646, 1979.

Walker, G.P.L., The Taupo pumice: Product of the most powerful known (ultraplinian) eruption?, *J. Volcanol. Geotherm. Res., 8*, 69-94, 1980.

Walker, G.P.L., Volcanic hazards, *Interdisciplinary Science Reviews, 7, no. 2*, 148-157, 1982.

Walker, G.P.L., Ignimbrite types and ignimbrite problems, *J. Volcanol. Geotherm. Res., 17*, 65-88, 1983.

Walker, G.P.L., Characteristics of dune-bedded pyroclastic surge bedsets, *J. Volcanol. Geotherm Res., 20*, 281-296, 1984.

Walker, G.P.L., and L.M. McBroome, Mount St. Helens 1980 and Mount Pelée 1902--flow or surge?, *Geology, 11*, 571-574, 1983.

Walker, G.P.L., and L.A. Morgan, Reply to Hoblitt and Miller (1984) and Waitt (1984), *Geology, 12*, 693-695, 1984.

Ward, P.L., and S. Gregerson, Comparison of earthquake locations determined from a network of stations and small tripartite arrays on Kilauea Volcano, Hawaii, *Bull. Seismol. Soc. Amer., 63*, 679-711, 1973.

Warrick, R.A., Volcanoes as hazard: An overview, in *Volcanic Activity and Human Ecology*, edited by P.D. Sheets and D.K. Grayson, pp. 161-194, Academic Press, New York, 1979.

Warrick, R.A., Four communities under ash after Mount St. Helens, *Program on Technology, Environment, and Man, Monograph 34*, Institute of Behavioral Science, University of Colorado, 143 pp., 1981.

Westercamp, Denis, Une methode d'evaluation et de zonation des risques volcaniques a la Soufrière de Guadeloupe, Antilles Francaises, *Bull. Volcanol., 43, no. 2*, 431-452, 1980.

Westercamp, Denis, Cartographie du risque a la Soufrière de Guadeloupe: Retrospective et tendance actuelle, *Inter. Assoc. Engineering Geology Bull., no. 23*, 25-32, 1981a.

Westercamp, Denis, Assessment of volcanic hazards at Soufrière de Guadeloupe, F.W.I., *Bureau de Recherches Geologiques et Minieres Bulletin, Section 4, no. 2*, 187-192, 1981b.

Westercamp, Denis, Appraisal and zonation of volcanic hazards in the French Lesser Antilles: Preliminary results, in *Forecasting Volcanic Events*, edited by Haroun Tazieff, and J.-C. Sabroux, pp. 111-130, Elsevier, Amsterdam, 1983.

Westercamp, Denis, French West Indies, in *Source-Book for Volcanic-Hazards Zonation: Unesco Natural Hazards 4*, edited by D.R. Crandell, Basil Booth, K. Kusumadinata, Daisuke Shimozuru, G.P.L. Walker, and Denis Westercamp, pp. 50-55, UNESCO, New York, 1984.

Westercamp, Denis, and H. Traineau, The past 5,000 years of volcanic activity at Mt. Pelée, Martinique (F.W.I.): Implications for assessment of volcanic hazards, *J. Volcanol. Geotherm. Res., 17*, 159-185, 1983.

Westphal, J.A., M.A. Carr, W.R. Miller, and D. Dzurisin, Expendable bubble tiltmeter for geophysical monitoring, *Rev. Scientific Instruments, 54, no. 4*, 415-418, 1983.

Whalen, C.T., Preliminary test results of Precise trig-leveling with the Wild T2000-DI5 system, *ACSM Bulletin*, December 1984.

Wharton, W.J.L., On the seismic sea waves caused by the eruption of Krakatoa August 26th and 27th, 1883, in *The Eruption of Krakatoa, and Subsequent Phenomena*, edited by G.J. Symons, pp. 89-151, Report of the Krakatoa Committee of the Royal Society, London, Trübner and Co., 1888.

White, G.F., and J.E. Haas, *Assessment of Research on Natural Hazards*, 487 pp., The MIT Press, Cambridge, Mass., 1975.

Wier, G.J., Kinematic wave theory for Ruapehu lahars, *New Zealand Journal of Science, 25*, 197-203, 1982.

Wijkman, Anders, and Lloyd Timberlake, *Natural disasters: Acts of God or acts of man?*, 145 pp., Earthscan, Washington, D.C., 1984.

Wilcox, R.E., Some effects of recent volcanic ash falls with special reference to Alaska, *U.S. Geol. Surv. Bull. 1028-N*, pp. 409-476, 1959.

Williams, Howel, and A.R. McBirney, *Volcanology*, 397 pp., Freeman, Cooper, & Co., San Francisco, California, 1979.

Williams, M.E., and C. Kitzmiller, compilers, Proceedings of the Geologic and Hydrologic Hazards Training Program, *U.S. Geol. Surv. Open-File Report 84-760*, 1112 pp. 1984.

Williams, R.S., and J.G. Moore, Iceland chills a lava flow, *Geotimes, 18, no. 8*, 14-17, 1973.

Williams, R.S., and J.G. Moore, Man against volcano: The eruption on Heimaey, Vestmannaeyjar, Iceland, *U.S. Geol. Surv. General Interest Publications Series*, 28 pp., 1983.

Williams, S.N., and Hansjuergen Meyer, A model of Nevado del Ruíz Volcano, Colombia, *Eos, Amer. Geophys. Union Trans., 69, no. 45*, 1554-1556, 1988.

Wilson, C.J.N., The role of fluidisation in the emplacement of pyroclastic flows: An experimental approach, *J. Volcanol. Geotherm. Res., 8*, 231-249, 1980.

Wilson, C.J.N., The role of fluidisation in the emplacement of pyroclastic flows, 2: Experimental results and their interpretation, *J. Volcanol. Geotherm. Res., 20*, 55-84, 1984.

Wilson, Lionel, R.S.J. Sparks, and G.P.L. Walker, Explosive volcanic eruptions--IV. The control of magma properties and conduit geometry on eruption column behaviour, *Geophys. J. Royal Astronom. Soc., 63*, 117-148, 1980.

Wintle, A.G., and D.J. Huntley, Thermoluminescence dating of sediments, *Quaternary Science Reviews, 1*, 31-53, 1982.

Wood, C.A., Morphometric analysis of cinder cone degradation, *J. Volcanol. Geotherm. Res., 8*, 137-160, 1980.

Wood, H. O., The seismic prelude to the 1914 eruption of Mauna Loa, *Bull. Seismol. Soc. Am., 5*, 39-50, 1915.

Wright, J.V., Stratigraphy and geology of the welded airfall tuffs of Pantelleria, Italy, *Geologische Rundschau, 69*, 263-291, 1980.

Wright, J.V., A.L. Smith, and S. Self, A working terminology of pyroclastic deposits, *J. Volcanol. Geotherm. Res., 8*, 315-336, 1980.

Wyatt, F., R. Bilham, J. Beavan, A.G. Sylvester, T. Owen, A. Harvey, C. Macdonald, D.D. Jackson, and D.C. Agnew, Comparing tiltmeters for crustal deformation measurement--A preliminary report, *Geophys. Res. Lett., 11, no. 10*, 963-966, 1984.

Yamaguchi, D.K., New tree-ring dates for recent eruptions of Mount St. Helens, *Quaternary Research, 20*, 246-250, 1983.

Yamaguchi, D.K., Tree-ring evidence for a two-year interval between recent prehistoric explosive eruptions of Mount St. Helens, *Geology, 13, no. 8*, 554-557, 1985.

Yamashita, K.M., Dry tilt: a ground deformation monitor as applied to the active volcanoes of Hawaii, *U.S. Geol. Surv. Open-File Report 81-523*, 21 pp., 1981.

Yamashita, K.M., El inclinometro seco: un vigilante de la deformación ligada al vulcanismo active en Hawaii, *Boletín de Vulcanología (Costa Rica), 12*, 11-17, 1982. [Spanish translation of Yamashita (1981) by R. Van der Laat V.].

Yamashita, K.M., and M.P. Doukas, Precise level lines at Crater Lake, Newberry Crater and South Sister, Oregon, *U.S. Geol. Surv. Open-File Report 87-293*, 31 pp, 1987.

Yokoyama, I., A model for the crustal deformation around volcanoes, *Jour. Phys. Earth, 19, no. 3*, 199-207, 1971.

Yokoyama, I., A geophysical interpretation of the 1883 Krakatau eruption, *J. Volcanol. Geotherm. Res., 9, no. 4*, 359-378, 1981.

Yokoyama, I., Volcanic processes revealed by geophysical observations of the 1977-1982 activity of Usu Volcano, Japan, *J. Geodynamics, 3*, 351-367, 1985.

Yokoyama, I., Seismic energy releases from volcanoes, *Bull. Volcanol., 50, no. 1*, 1-13, 1988.

Yokoyama, I., H. Yamashita, H. Watanabe, and H.M. Okada, Geophysical characteristics of dacite volcanism - The 1977-1978 eruptions of Usu Volcano, *J. Volcanol. Geotherm. Res., 9*, 335-358, 1981.

Yokoyama, I., R.I. Tilling, and R. Scarpa, *International Mobile Early-Warning Systems(s) for Volcanic Eruptions and Related Seismic Activities*, UNESCO (Paris), FP/2106-82-01(2286), 102 pp., 1984.

Zen, M.T., and Djajadi Hadikusumo, The future danger of Mt. Kelut (Eastern Java-Indonesia), *Bull. Volcanol., 28*, 275-282, 1965.

Zollinger, H., *Besteigung des Vulkanes Tambora auf der Insel Sumbawa und Schilderung der Erupzion desselben im Jahr 1815*, 1-20, Winterthur, Wurster, 1855.